"Noting the radical and revolution
century Reformations in the manifo.
authors of this inspiring volume poi.
tions that seek to address real-life issu.  ...on, the
..riptural interpreta-
..vis human experience. The expan-
sive and multiplying seeds of the Reformation theologies have spread through a
variety of sources, influences, and structures that have ordered Christian societies' realities and cultures. The story is not complete, however. The gift of the
reformed-yet-still-reforming theological orientations is in the theologically articulated promise to continue to shift power dynamics and to emancipate and feed
both the souls and bodies. Readers interested in the continued relevance of the
Protestant theological-spiritual-political traditions will find this book a gift!"
—Kirsi I. Stjerna, First Lutheran, Los Angeles/Southwest
California Synod Professor of Lutheran History
and Theology, Pacific Lutheran Theological Seminary

"The authors remind us that at a time in history—the late sixteenth century—
when 'religion' was not sequestered from other realms of human thought and
aspiration, the early Protestant reformers' theological creativity contributed to
new directions in art and music, in law and politics, and in the everyday arrangements of the home and of the public sphere. And at another time in history—
the early twenty-first century—when 'theology' is reclaiming its most expansive
connotations, *The Protestant Reformation of the Church and the World* offers a
primer in the promise as well as the dangers of theological engagement with the
economic and geopolitical challenges of our own times for those theologians
who aim to address them."
—Christine Helmer, Professor of German and Religious Studies,
Northwestern University, and author of *Theology and the End of Doctrine*

"This collection of essays presents thoughtful and often thought-provoking
reflections on both expected (e.g., justification) and less traditional topics (e.g.,
consumerism), weighing aspects of the Protestant Reformation in light of their
relevance for today's church and world. The editors have brought together a
constellation of German and North American voices in a fruitful conversation rich with perceptive comments and language (e.g., speaking of the 'Holy
Spirit, who effects faithful but unpredictable improvisations on a reconciliation
already achieved in Jesus Christ,' p. 87) and constructive criticism (e.g., '*sola
scriptura*, functioning as a lodestar for personal redemption, . . . has also acted
as an engine of self-assertion,' pp. 27–28) or useful distinction (between interest
and usury, p. 172)."
—Elsie McKee, Professor of Reformation Studies and the History
of Worship, Princeton Theological Seminary

"Anything as badly misunderstood and wildly misrepresented as Protestantism, needs all the help it can get! This book is helpful. Its authors represent a commendable cross section of what remains of principal Reformation theological and ethical emphases. They avoid the intellectual absurdities of ultra-orthodoxy without sacrificing the *skandalon* of the gospel; and they avoid the shallowness and exhibitionism of identity-and-cause theologies without sacrificing contextual pertinence. This is *responsible* Christian theology."

—Douglas John Hall, Professor Emeritus of Christian Theology,
McGill University, and author of *What Christianity Is Not*

"A thoughtful as well as highly competent collection of essays by a group of junior and senior scholars. The essays offer a panoramic view of current scholarly interests in Martin Luther and the Reformation, useful for both experts and novices."

—Hans Hillerbrand, Professor Emeritus
of Religious Studies, Duke University

"In 2017, we celebrated the quincentenary of Luther's Reformation. Though a triumph of a kind and a liberation of another kind, the still unending ripples of Luther's defiance are far from being an unqualified good. It has had second, third, fourth generations of unintended consequences that continue to dismantle insecure certainties. Luther torched certain 'clerical disabilities' (e. g., exclusion from marriage) and thereby opened an unresolved argument between forms of clergy power and state (lay) power. Appeal to conscience spawned identity politics. Faith-defined regimes bore fruit in the nation-state and ultimately in forms of populism. The rediscovered gospel both inspired and disappointed. The current crisis over Europe, migration, borders, and pooled resources cannot be understood without Luther. This well-chosen selection of probing essays gives us an overview of unparalleled breadth, and its editors are much to be commended."

—Iain R Torrance, President Emeritus,
Princeton Theological Seminary

The Protestant Reformation
of the Church and the World

The Protestant Reformation of the Church and the World

Edited by

JOHN WITTE JR. AND AMY WHEELER

Center for the Study of Law and Religion
Emory University

WESTMINSTER
JOHN KNOX PRESS
LOUISVILLE • KENTUCKY

First edition
Published by Westminster John Knox Press
Louisville, Kentucky

18 19 20 21 22 23 24 25 26 27—10 9 8 7 6 5 4 3 2

Book design by Sharon Adams
Cover design by Lisa Buckley Design
Cover illustration: *Reformation Day*, in *Der Christliche Lutheraner stellet vor die Kirchen-Historien vom Jahr 1370. und was von selbiger Zeit darinnen ergangen: Darbey Köngl. Majest. in Preussen und Churfürstl. Durchl. zu Brandenburg allergnädigste Verordnung, wie das jetzige Kirchen-Jubilæum den 31 Octob. 1717.* Courtesy of the Pitts Theology Library, Candler School of Theology, Emory University.

Library of Congress Cataloging-in-Publication Data

Names: Witte, John, 1959– editor.
Title: The Protestant Reformation of the church and the world / edited by John Witte, Jr. and Amy Wheeler, Center for the Study of Law and Religion, Emory University.
Description: First edition. | Louisville, Kentucky : Westminster John Knox Press, 2018. | Includes bibliographical references and index. | Description based on print version record and CIP data provided by publisher; resource not viewed.
Identifiers: LCCN 2018012531 (print) | LCCN 2018031224 (ebook) | ISBN 9781611647624 (ebk.) | ISBN 9780664264154 (pbk. : alk. paper)
Subjects: LCSH: Reformation—Influence.
Classification: LCC BR307 (ebook) | LCC BR307 .R4155 2018 (print) | DDC 270.6—dc23
LC record available at https://lccn.loc.gov/2018012531

For
Ambassador Alonzo L. McDonald
and the Members of the McDonald Agape Foundation

Contents

Preface and Acknowledgments

The sixteenth-century Protestant Reformation had a revolutionary impact on church, state, society, and culture. It transformed theology, worship, catechesis, and daily spiritual life. It revolutionized art, music, literature, architecture, and aesthetics. It transformed economics, trade, banking, colonization, and more. It unleashed radical new campaigns for freedom and equality, democracy and constitutional order, sometimes triggering violent political and military rejoinders. And the Reformation caused a massive shift of power, property, and prerogative from the church to the state, triggering major reforms to the laws of family, education, charity, and crime.

In this authoritative but accessible study, twelve leading scholars analyze the kaleidoscopic impact of the Lutheran, Anabaptist, Anglican, and Calvinist Reformations over the past five hundred years—for better or worse, for richer or poorer, for the West and increasingly for the world. Mark Noll, David Ford, and Jeremy Begbie focus on the reformation of biblical studies and theology, the power of the new printing industry, and the transformation of choral and instrumental music and corporate worship. Michael Welker, John Witte, and Carter Lindberg analyze the revolutions of church, state, family, education, and charity born of the new Protestant theology, along with the new legal and social institutions that emerged. Wolfgang Huber, Jonathan Walton, Graham Tomlin, and Margot Kässmann reflect on the enduring and mixed contributions of the Reformation to Western social, economic, and cultural life, leading to the challenges that now face modern Protestant churches and cultures especially in Europe and North America, but also into the global south. The introduction by Martin Marty frames these chapters and shows the enduring and surprising provenance and power of cardinal Protestant teachings that surface for repeated discussion throughout the volume: justification by faith alone; *sola scriptura*; freedom of conscience; law and gospel; the priesthood of all believers; the Christian vocation; the offices of prophet, priest, and king; the uses of the law; covenant community; Christian discipleship; separation of church and state; the warmed heart; and more. A postscript by Wesley Granberg-Michaelson celebrates the Reformation in all of its diversity yet also warns against Protestant triumphalism.

We express our appreciation to a number of colleagues who helped in the creation of this volume. We are deeply grateful for the support of our colleagues in the Center for the Study of Law and Religion at Emory University—particularly Professors Frank Alexander, Silas Allard, and Rafael Domingo, and Ms. Anita Mann and Ms. Patti Ghezzi—who helped us host a memorable public conference in March 2017 that featured presentation of most of these chapters. We are grateful that Deans Jan Love and Jonathan Strom and the faculty at the Candler School of Theology at Emory University kindly joined us in cosponsoring this conference. The lovely woodcut images that adorn each chapter of this volume come courtesy of Professor Patrick Graham, the director emeritus of the Pitts Theology Library, which houses a remarkable treasure trove of Reformation materials. We would be remiss in not expressing our deep appreciation to Dr. Gary Hauk for sharing his refined wordsmith skills so generously and doing such a marvelous job in copyediting the manuscript. And we give thanks to our friends at Westminster John Knox Press—Daniel Braden, Michele Blum, Shannon Brown, and Associate Publisher David Dobson—for sharing their fine publishing talents with us again.

This volume has been made possible by the generosity of the McDonald Agape Foundation, a private family foundation dedicated to sponsoring "distinguished Christian scholars at distinguished universities" such as Harvard, Yale, Chicago, Emory, Duke, Georgetown, Cambridge, and Oxford. The Foundation has graced our Center for the Study of Law and Religion with five major grants over the past two decades and generously supported John Witte as the McDonald Distinguished Professor at Emory University. Most of the chapters that appear herein were first presented as part of the McDonald Distinguished Christian Scholars Lecture series that has brought dozens of major scholars to distinguished lecterns at Emory, Oxford, and St. Mellitus. We wish to express our profound thanks to the founding director of the Foundation, Ambassador Alonzo L. McDonald, and his wife, Mrs. Suzie McDonald, as well as members of the Foundation who have been kind enough to participate in our Center's work over the years, notably President Peter McDonald, Dr. Robert Pool, Mrs. Jennifer Peters, and Mr. Mark Maurice. In expression of our appreciation for their generosity, we dedicate this volume to Ambassador McDonald and his colleagues at the McDonald Agape Foundation.

John Witte Jr. and Amy Wheeler
Center for the Study of Law and Religion
Emory University

Illustrations

Cover
Reformation Day. In *Der Christliche Lutheraner stellet vor die Kirchen-Historien vom Jahr 1370. und was von selbiger Zeit darinnen ergangen: Darbey Köngl. Majest. in Preussen und Churfürstl. Durchl. zu Brandenburg allergnädigste Verordnung, wie das jetzige Kirchen-Jubilæum den 31 Octob. 1717.* Courtesy of the Pitts Theology Library, Candler School of Theology, Emory University

Introduction
The Reformation Candle Cannot Be Extinguished, by John Shirley (fl. 1680–1702). Courtesy of the Pitts Theology Library, Candler School of Theology, Emory University

Chapter 1
Historiated Title-Page Border, in *Martin Luther's Complete Bible*. Low German Bible, translated by Martin Luther, 1533. Courtesy of the Richard C. Kessler Reformation Collection, Pitts Theology Library, Candler School of Theology, Emory University

Chapter 2
The Apostle John, in *Biblische Figuren des Alten vnd Newen Testaments: Gantz künstlich gerissen; durch den weitberhümpten Vergilium Solis zu Nürnberg*, by Virgil Solis. Courtesy of the Richard C. Kessler Reformation Collection, Pitts Theology Library, Candler School of Theology, Emory University

Chapter 3
Third stanza of the chant "A Mighty Fortress Is Our God," by Martin Luther, before 1529. Courtesy of United Archives / Carl Simon / Bridgeman Images

Chapter 4
Image title: *Pope Leo X vs. Martin Luther*, by unknown artist, in *Des Ehrwirdigen Herrn Doctoris Martini Lutheri, gottseligen, Triumph, und Verantwortung, wider die gottlosen Schmehschrifft, der newen Münch, der Jesuiter, welche sie vnter dem Titel, Anatomia Lutheri, ausgesprenget haben: Aus dem Latein in deudsche Vers durch den Poeten selbst verfasset*, by Martin Luther and Jesuits, 1568. Courtesy of the Richard C. Kessler Reformation Collection, Pitts Theology Library, Candler School of Theology, Emory University

Chapter 5
Historiated Title-Page Border, in *Der Stat Nurmberg verneute Reformation*, by Nuremberg (Germany), 1564. Courtesy of the Richard C. Kessler Reformation Collection, Pitts Theology Library, Candler School of Theology, Emory University

Chapter 6
Parable of the Great Banquet, in *Kercken Postilla, dat ys, Vthlegginge der Epistelen vnd Euangelien, an de Söndagen vnde vornemesten Festen*, by Doctor Martin Luther (1483–1546), 1563. Courtesy of the Richard C. Kessler Reformation Collection, Pitts Theology Library, Candler School of Theology, Emory University

Chapter 7
Contrast in Attitudes toward Money and Religion, in *Passional Christi und Antichristi*, by Lucas Cranach the Elder (1472–1553), 1521. Courtesy of the Richard C. Kessler Reformation Collection, Pitts Theology Library, Candler School of Theology, Emory University

Chapter 8
Business World, in *Ethica naturalis, seu Documenta moralia e variis rerum naturalium proprietatib[us] virtutum vitiorumq[ue] symbolicis imaginibus collecta, a Christophoro Weigelio*, by Christoph Weigel (1654–1725), ca. 1700. Courtesy of the Pitts Theology Library, Candler School of Theology, Emory University

Chapter 9
Contrast in Use of Power, in *Passional Christi und Antichristi*, by Lucas Cranach the Elder (1472–1553), 1521. Courtesy of the Richard C. Kessler Reformation Collection, Pitts Theology Library, Candler School of Theology, Emory University

Chapter 10
Vision of Four Beasts, in *Der Prophet Daniel Deudsch*, by Martin Luther, Wittenberg, 1530. Courtesy of the Richard C. Kessler Reformation Collection, Pitts Theology Library, Candler School of Theology, Emory University

Postscript
Witness of John the Baptist, by Virgil Solis (1514–62), in *Avßlegung der Epistelen vnd Euangelie[n]: Die nach brauch der Kirchen gelesen werden, durch den Advent, vnd dannenthin vom Christag biß auf den Sontag nach Epiphanie; Darin reichlich anzeygt vnd fürgebildet würt, was eim* [sic] *Christen menschen zuo*, by D. Martinus Luther, 1522. Courtesy of the Richard C. Kessler Reformation Collection, Pitts Theology Library, Candler School of Theology, Emory University

About the Contributors

Jeremy Begbie is Thomas A. Langford Research Professor of Theology at Duke Divinity School. He is also a Senior Member at Wolfson College, Cambridge, and an Affiliated Lecturer in the Faculty of Music at the University of Cambridge. He is Founding Director of Duke Initiatives in Theology and the Arts. A prolific author, Professor Begbie's books include *Theology, Music and Time* (Cambridge), *Beholding the Glory: Incarnation through the Arts* (Baker), *Resounding Truth: Christian Wisdom in the World of Music* (Baker), and *Music, Modernity, and God* (Oxford). He is an ordained minister of the Church of England and a professionally trained musician who has performed extensively as a pianist, oboist, and conductor.

David F. Ford, OBE, is Fellow of Selwyn College, Cambridge, and retired in 2015 as Regius Professor of Divinity at the University of Cambridge and Founding Director of the Cambridge Inter-faith Programme. He is also Co-Chair of Global Covenant Partners, Visiting Professor at St. Mellitus College, London, and has been theological adviser to three Archbishops of Canterbury (Runcie, Carey, and Welby). He was awarded the 2012 Coventry International Prize for Peace and Reconciliation. He is author of *Barth and God's Story* (Lang), *Self and Salvation* (Cambridge), *Christian Wisdom* (Cambridge), and *The Drama of Living* (Baker), among others. He has edited three editions of *The Modern Theologians* (Blackwell).

Wesley Granberg-Michaelson served as General Secretary of the Reformed Church in America 1994–2011 and as Legislative Assistant to

U.S. Senator Mark O. Hatfield, and Associate Editor and now Board Member of *Sojourners* magazine. He played a leading role in establishing Christian Churches Together in the USA, and he served as Director of Church and Society for the World Council of Churches. His numerous publications include *Future Faith: Ten Challenges Reshaping Christianity in the 21st Century* (Fortress), *From Times Square to Timbuktu: The Post Christian West Meets the Non-Western Church* (Eerdmans), *Leadership from Inside Out: Spirituality and Organizational Change* (Crossroad), and a memoir titled *Unexpected Destinations: An Evangelical Pilgrimage to World Christianity* (Eerdmans).

Wolfgang Huber taught theology and ethics at the Universities of Marburg and Heidelberg before serving as Bishop of the Evangelical Church in Berlin-Brandenburg from 1993 to 2009 and as member and chair of the national Council of the Evangelical Church in Germany (EKD). He continues to be the Dean of the Cathedral in Brandenburg/Havel and serves as an Extraordinary Professor at the University of Heidelberg, Humboldt University of Berlin, and Stellenbosch University. A world-renowned scholar of theological ethics, he has lectured throughout the world and has published more than sixty volumes, including recently *Glaubensfragen: Eine evangelische Orientierung* (Beck), *Gerechtigkeit und Recht* (3rd ed., Gütersloher Verlagshaus), *Christian Responsibility and Communicative Freedom* (LIT), *This I Trust: Basic Words of Christian Belief* (WCC), and *Ethics: The Fundamental Question of Our Lives* (Georgetown).

Margot Kässmann is a leading theologian and pastor who has served as Secretary General of the German Protestant Church Congress, Bishop of the Evangelical Lutheran Church of Hanover, and as Chairperson of the Evangelical Church in Germany (EKD). She has served in distinguished professorships at several universities, and has published several tomes, including *Overcoming Violence* (WCC), *With Hearts, Hands, and Voices: Spirituality for Everyday Life* (WCC), and *Perspectives 2017: Writings on the Reformation* (EKD). Since 2012, she has served as Special Envoy of the Evangelical Church in Germany for the Reformation Anniversary Celebration 2017.

Carter Lindberg is Professor Emeritus of Church History at Boston University School of Theology. A distinguished scholar of early modern history, his work has focused on the political implications of Reformation thought and the church's interaction with society at large. His many books include *Beyond Charity: Reformation Initiatives for the Poor* (Fortress), *Love: A Brief History through Western Christianity* (Blackwell), *The Pietist Theologians* (Wiley), *The Reformation Theologians* (Wiley), and *The European Reformations* (Wiley).

Martin E. Marty is Fairfax M. Cone Distinguished Service Professor Emeritus at the University of Chicago Divinity School. One of the world's greatest scholars of religion, Marty has published more than five thousand articles and sixty volumes, including *Righteous Empire* (Harper), *Modern American Religion* (3 vols., Chicago), *The One and the Many* (Harvard), *The Mystery of the Child* (Eerdmans), *Building Cultures of Trust* (Eerdmans), *The Christian World* (Modern Library), *Martin Luther* (Penguin), and *Dietrich Bonhoeffer's Letters and Papers from Prison: A Biography* (Princeton). Marty served for many decades as senior editor of *The Christian Century* and as editor of *Context*, and now he is weekly contributor to *Sightings*, an electronic editorial published by the Martin Marty Center at the University of Chicago. He is recipient of numerous honors, including the National Humanities Medal, the National Book Award, the Medal of the American Academy of Arts and Sciences, and eighty honorary doctorates.

Mark A. Noll is Francis A. McAnaney Professor of History Emeritus at the University of Notre Dame. A world-class church historian, he has published extensively on the Reformation and on American religious and intellectual history. His forty-plus volumes include *The Scandal of the Evangelical Mind* (Eerdmans), *America's God: From Jonathan Edwards to Abraham Lincoln* (Oxford), *In the Beginning Was the Word: The Bible in American Public Life, 1492–1783* (Oxford), *Protestantism: A Very Short Introduction* (Oxford), *Is the Reformation Over? An Evangelical Assessment of Contemporary Catholicism* (Baker), *Confessions and Catechisms of the Reformation* (Regent), and *Protestantism after 500 Years* (Oxford).

Graham Tomlin is Bishop of Kensington in the Diocese of London and Founding President of St Mellitus College. He has served as a curate in Exeter, Chaplain of Jesus College, Oxford, and Vice Principal at Wycliffe Hall, Oxford. He is the author of many articles and books, including *The Power of the Cross: Theology and the Death of Christ in Paul, Luther and Pascal* (Paternoster), *The Provocative Church* (4th ed., SPCK), *Looking through the Cross* (Bloomsbury), *The Widening Circle:*

Priesthood as God's Way of Blessing the World (SPCK), *Bound to Be Free: The Paradox of Freedom* (Bloomsbury), and *Luther's Gospel: Reimagining the World* (Bloomsbury).

Jonathan L. Walton is the Plummer Professor of Christian Morals at Harvard University and Pusey Minister in Harvard's Memorial Church. He is also Professor of Religion and Society at Harvard Divinity School. He has published and lectured widely on issues at the intersection of religion, politics, and media culture, including an award-winning title, *Watch This! The Ethics and Aesthetics of Black Televangelism* (NYU). Professor Walton's work and insights have been featured in several national and international news outlets, including the *New York Times*, CNN, and the BBC.

Michael Welker is Senior Professor at the University of Heidelberg, Director of the Research Center for International and Interdisciplinary Theology in Heidelberg, and Honorary Professor at Seoul Theological University. A world-class scholar of systematic theology and interdisciplinary religious studies, he has lectured and led research projects throughout the world. He has published 350 articles and 55 books, translated into a score of languages. Recent titles include *God the Spirit* (Fortress), *God the Revealed: Christology* (Eerdmans), *Creation and Reality* (Fortress), *What Happens in Holy Communion?* (Eerdmans), *The Theology and Science Dialogue* (Neukirchener Theologie), and *Europa Reformata: 48 Reformation Cities and Their Reformers* (Evangelische Verlagsanstalt).

Amy Wheeler is Associate Editor and Director's Associate in the Center for the Study of Law and Religion at Emory University. She is pursuing advanced studies at the Candler School of Theology with a focus on religion, music, and liturgy. She is coeditor of *The Equal Regard Family and Its Friendly Critics* (Eerdmans).

John Witte Jr. is Woodruff University Professor of Law, McDonald Distinguished Professor, and Director of the Center for the Study of Law and Religion at Emory University. He is also editor of the Cambridge Law and Christianity book series, *The Journal of Law and Religion*, and Emory University Studies in Law and Religion. A specialist in legal history, marriage law, religious liberty, and law and religion, he has published 250 articles, 17 journal symposia, and 31 books, including *Law and Protestantism* (Cambridge), *The Reformation of Rights*

(Cambridge), *Christianity and Law* (Cambridge), *The Sins of the Fathers* (Cambridge), *The Western Case for Monogamy over Polygamy* (Cambridge), *From Sacrament to Contract* (2nd ed., WJK), *Religion and the American Constitutional Experiment* (4th ed., Oxford), and *Church, State, and Family* (Cambridge).

The Reformation Candle Cannot Be Extinguished,
by John Shirley, fl. 1680–1702

Introduction: The Protestant (Re-)Reformations of the Church and the World

Martin E. Marty

Responsive and responsible people in the Protestant Reformation tradition affirm that the religious movement they observe and celebrate as "the Reformation" does not make up a completed event. A Latin phrase, *semper reformanda* (always reforming), summarizes their idea of continuing commitment to a reforming mission for the church.

When the editors of this book sent me the draft chapters in this volume, they included two complicating elements in their request for an introduction. One is their invitation to address the question "Why do we always need Reformations?" Who are the "we"? The answer to that will emerge in various contexts, but one cannot assume that secularists will see themselves in the company of those who assert the need for Christian-based reform of church, state, and society. The contributors to this collection manifestly have kept such secular readers in mind, but they also were aware that they do not share the theological and religious commitments of the authors.

Second, the editors added an "s" to render "Reformation" in the plural: "Reformations." This promotes a simple affirmation, common to all Protestants, not only that the church is always in need of reform, but also that the sixteenth-century Protestant movement was a series of quite variant reform movements from the start. The authors of the chapters that follow succeed in spelling out what this means in various circumstances, locales, and communities. They also share the assumption that certain documents spelled out or anticipated what reforms would or should mean for the community of committed readers of "Scripture alone." It is absurd to picture reforming the church on the basis of Cuban revolutionary documents or handbooks for national associations of manufacturers.

Instead, for Christian people an easily arrived-at base or starting point for reform is always the Bible.

In **chapter 1, Mark Noll** opens this book with a title, "The Gift of *Sola Scriptura* to the World," that comes as an unsurprising reminder that an appeal to the Bible recognizes that this singular sacred book comes to believers as a gift. The text of the Bible itself makes claims and sets forth clues about its gift-character. And whoever reads around in its pages does not need to ask, "Who is the donor of this gift?" The answer to that question is, again, obvious, so long as one keeps in mind the understanding that the biblical revelation is addressed by God to the church, for whose existence God is central. So far, so good.

More complicated is the addition of the last two words of Noll's title: the Bible is seen as intending to work the reform of "the world." While the church is *in* the world and works numberless effects in the world through its many particulars, we do not picture the world as such being as definable as the church. We know better than to suggest that the world, however defined, recognizes the character of this gift of Scripture as divine, or can determine how it fulfills its gift-giving intentions. Think of the people of the world with their energies and products worked in and through, for example, the United Nations, labor unions, Wall Street, the National Rifle Association, or the Olympics. Do these diverse entities and collectives give any evidence that the claim and notice of *sola scriptura*, Scripture alone, have any prominence among people who inhabit or support them?

On the other hand, not all who people these associations are necessarily opposed to Scripture. Still, we notice that those responsible for most human collectives do not regard themselves as being obliged to "reform" the world on the basis of or to carry out what the sacred Scriptures alone direct. It is true, they may tolerate and even welcome some of those believers who do add Scripture to the registers of many sacred and profane allures that bid for attention, but the Scriptures are not necessarily regarded as decisive, as they must be regarded in the biblically rooted community

I accent again: Noll's chapter title suggests to readers that they are bidden to see *sola scriptura* as a gift to them in the church *and* the world as they are seen *now*. The task of dealing with the text for the present and the future is, of course, complex. Noll speaks of *sola scriptura* as a "bane" and a "blessing," quoting a line from a hymn out of the past. A bane? Believers sing with the weight of the past predisposing them variously to be cautious, confused, indifferent, or weary.

It is also a blessing. This chapter is a call intelligently to confront whatever the future will bring. One element in any faithful strategy for doing so, suggests Noll, is to be mindful of the many elements in the scriptural legacy that impede efforts to respond to the call that believers find in it. Most of those in the scholarly company cited by Noll know well that many people have used the Bible not to promote blessings, but for activities that rely on the misuse of power, as in legitimations of slavery and war. They are likely to continue to misuse it, a fact that complicates positive encounters by believers with the world. As church, they need new and constant reformation.

Whoever is ready to use the chapters in this book as a nudge to help them effect changes is, in this chapter, reminded of problems that will confront them along the way. Right off, we read of "ambiguities" in the sacred text itself, and these must be taken into consideration and dealt with by readers. Are they basing their faith on *sola scriptura* to form their opinions and guide their actions? Because this readership involves people who offer varieties of interpretations, we begin to find reasons to enlarge the scope of our responses. For example, we are not to overlook the potential gifts of those who bring fresh readings to and uses of the text. Noll chooses to point, for example, to the rapidly expanding company of Pentecostal Christians.

Another hint in Noll's prescription is for the faithful not to reduce all varieties of interpretation until these become nothing but *argument*. Can the church be reformed through those who rely on arguments? Not likely, since argument is based on the suggestion that all participants in it have the answer to whatever comes up. It tends to evoke approaches that call on participants to be judgmental, abrupt, and dismissive. Readers of the Bible, as they work on responses and strategies, can do better, Noll contends, by employing instead the arts of *conversation*. This is so because the act of conversing bids all participants not to turn defensive but to stand ready to question and to learn. In certain cases argument can contribute to a lively future of the church, but it cannot be the sole strategy. Does and should the church then rely on conversation? On the conversational agenda there might well be fresh approaches to the text and to the world. These would include efforts to effect change through Bible-related arts, including music, which, Noll notes, plays a major part in the life of communities freshly confronted by biblical texts.

Those moved by Professor Noll's citing of moments in the past where *sola scriptura* served as a guard and a guide in interpreting Scriptures will find new motivations for meeting today's challenges. We can picture contemporary students telling stories and probing the meanings of these, especially as they suggest how and why, in our times, those who respond to the *sola scriptura* citation and its implicit call have effected change or can produce new results that contribute to the hoped-for re-Reformation, now of the world as well as of the church, which is "in the world."

In **chapter 2, by David F. Ford**, those who are ready to take part in the "re-reforming" of the church and the world, having appreciated with Mark Noll the gift of *sola scriptura*, are poised to set to their work with the aid of a concept found in Ford's chapter title: "surprise"! When we first encounter it, the word might seem out of context or largely decorative, a not deeply thought-out or engaged intrusion. Yet as one reads into the chapter, it becomes clear that the word signals a key element in Ford's argument; if he is right—as I believe he is—it can serve well, if *surprisingly*, to unlock a promising approach to theology in churchmanship and worldmanship that could advance reformative efforts.

Ford's bold-faced use of "surprise" is locked into the phrase at the head of the chapter: "a wisdom of surprise." Biblical scholars have a way of advancing their interpretations with such "of" phrases: We know of a "theology of hope," "the hermeneutics of suspicion," and many more. Reading further in Ford's chapter, we see that he uses the concept of "surprise" to guide the reader into some dimensions of thought from the sixteenth-century Reformation. Ford has no assignment to review all aspects of that version of the Reformation. He is interested in the basics of Christian faith and life. He has no authority to convoke a council and would no doubt be embarrassed if there were an expectation that, like Luther, he should post theses for debate and follow through.

Wait: I take some of that back as I reread his chapter. Modest as it is, there is something explosive in his assumptions and prescriptions. Let us play, for a moment, with his cherished terms. Everyone knows that what is "surprising" can come in forms that may be positive or negative in the lives of individuals and communities. "Surprise!" may be the summoning word at the start of a ceremonial party, at which relations can be discovered, developed, and fostered. In Christian contexts, we can connect the word to the concept of "promise," which in many Christian writings merges into the announcement of the gospel. On the negative side, "Surprise!" often comes with disturbing connotations and dispiriting announcements. "Surprise!" says the voice of the person who has dialed 9-1-1. "Come quickly, act fast, our child is having trouble breathing!" Or, "Surprise, you just got passed up for a job!"

The Gospel stories offer plenty of surprises—for example, in parables or stories about the coming of the Messiah ("Hail, Mary!") or of the arrival of the end times, after which there will be no more opportunities to heed God's call. Or a surprise may come with too many options, among which we are to choose the good or the bad. We can be bewildered in a pluralist and prosperous society by choices that distract from the one surprise that counts in the Gospel-centered reform of the church and the world. Open the singular gift as it is promised, and you will find many valuables. Always, however, there is only one pearl of great price, one seed that will bear fruit, one word that spells life and light in a world of shadows and darkness.

A reader of the Scriptures or of the record of ups and downs in Christian history learns that creative or saving reform comes not with armies and trumpets and thunderclaps. It arrives in the hearing of the poor and hitherto hopeless, through the still, small voice of informed conscience, or in the examples of people who make sacrifices for others. The church that is not open to the wisdom of "surprise!" will be closed to all that it offers for the future. Since one learns of all this from the word of the Scriptures, which arrives unadorned, uncomplicated, and with no strings attached, it is easy to see why any re-reform of the church must arrive in forms that do not distract. Alternatives in the forms of gimmicks will not serve.

The "wisdom of surprise" contains surprises-within-the-Surprise, and Professor Ford opens some of them, particularly in reference to Bible instances that often get classified as paradoxes. How surprising it is when one first hears that Jesus is fully God *and* fully human. Ford likes to discuss the paradox that best defined human nature and fate in the preaching and theology of the Reformation. It has to do with the human in action. Luther favored this formula: the individual who is joined with all others who share faith through *sola scriptura* and who experience grace, and grace alone, is at the same time (*simul*) justified and thus just (*iustus*), and yet sinner (*peccator*). This is not a philosophical contradiction; instead, as theologians remind us when they translate the Greek word *paradoxa*, it runs counter to opinion. For another example: what a surprise, the believer thinks, that the eternal God violates natural human opinion of how gods work or God works, by being born as a human infant. What a surprise, the believer thinks, that every individual in the church is regarded by God as acceptable when they are naturally unacceptable, and that God pronounces them justified. Ford likes to read of the surprising paradox in the Gospel of John: "and the Word was made flesh."

Ford introduces the concept of Scriptural Reasoning as an instrument for effecting change, to help us understand why, when the unexpected word of God comes, it strikes hearers in paradoxical and surprising ways.

Such has been the case through Christian history, and so it will be in the future, if it is regarded as a gift through *sola scriptura*.

Near the end of his chapter, Ford refers to music as an example of Scriptural Reasoning, or as expression that enhances or follows occasions when Scriptural Reasoning by itself gives out. This could happen when the questing human spirit is exhausted, or when ordinary speech does not reach deeply enough into the human spirit to satisfy. These moments occur when music in song goes from lover to lover, when children play, when grieving family members say good-bye to a dying parent, when armies or football players march, or when the words of the Gospels reappear in the choruses of great cantatas and masses. But the treatment of this phenomenon in this book cannot be confined to side references in various chapters. It demands attention on its own.

This it receives from **Jeremy Begbie** in **chapter 3**, "An Awkward Witness in a Worded World." Readers who know and worship in Anglican and Lutheran traditions may wonder from where Begbie snatched the concept of an "awkward" witness. Where is there awkwardness or unfittingness in Bach's *Mass in B Minor*, the chants in Westminster Abbey, or the lullaby-like songs of the Virgin Mary in many a folk-music context? Begbie answers this question by showing how other Reformation and post-Reformation musical examples do reflect some sense of awkwardness, for example, in Calvinist worship music. Professor Begbie demonstrates this as he spreads before us and then reflects on "awkward" forms or samples of music in some versions of Reformation worship or folk-music spiritual songs.

What one must ask, even before summoning examples from our "worded world," is this: given the varieties of music in Protestant churches, how can they all be traced back to anything that can be called Protestant? How can attention to music advance efforts to re-reform the church? Where has music carried the church forward? Where has it been neglected or scorned? What are the resources for attending to a proper place for this awkward element in church life? Why have some Protestants been suspicious of music in worship—and sometimes beyond worship?

Now and then in my wandering years, I was called upon to speak in campus chapels connected with church bodies where suspicion of music in worship is strong. I was disoriented to be in the company of students who blithely or vigorously sang hymns without accompaniment. The congregations' singers were as technically equipped and dynamically (loud and soft) varied as were we in what to me were "regular" styles of church life. But music, instrumentally backed, fit in at best awkwardly. One thinks of some versions of Churches of Christ. They first were founded in the backwoods or on the prairies. Their gospel songs and hymns first parallel, overlap with, or are often at home with traditional hymnody. Yet on the basis of their reading of *sola scriptura*, these churches silenced the organ, exiled the harpists, and muted the trumpets. They had special understandings, based on simple adages such as "Where the Scriptures speak, we speak, and where they are silent, we are silent!" Battles over the understandings of these "noninstrumental" churches were only one form of documenting the "awkwardness" that Professor Begbie amply and imaginatively addresses.

At the turn to the present century and in the years since, the Protestant churches in Euro-American cultures are suffering "worship wars," in which the advocates of competing styles of music are so intense that they cannot always coexist in the sanctuary. This is not the place to enter and wage the worship wars, but it is appropriate to notice that partisanship about music styles in worship and gatherings of believers has much to do with the future of Reformation-lined congregations, church bodies, and broadcasting. Those who favor what they call traditional styles are often put off by folk, rock, and not-yet-named schools and styles of music for worship. They consider the appeal of the new styles as threats to the future of authentic worship and descents into mere entertainment. Those in the other camp consider the traditionalists to be failing in the need to address their contemporaries and changing cultures. In cowardly fashion, I am reluctant to be a foot soldier on the many sides in these wars. My own preference for the traditional while being open to jazz, in particular, qualifies me well to deal with the subject in this chapter since I am confused and mixed-up, as are most bystanders and many partisans in the music zones.

Begbie leads off with an accounting of worship-war life. He follows with a helpful set of references to the suspicion many Protestants brought to music in worship. After this he provides what will strike many readers as an original framing of the issue by locating Luther's practices and concepts in his doctrine of creation. Here is where the concept of "giftedness," which appears again and again in this book, applies. We read that in Luther, "before anything else, music is to be seen not as an art or science but as an unconditional gift, *donum Dei*." As a bonus, we are told that Luther connects music to "the entire dynamic of donation," which "finds its supreme expression in the gospel itself, the gift of righteousness in Jesus Christ." Whoever knows Luther will find here the key to his celebration of music. Readers can find occasion to apply this observation to many dimensions of the music experience in choirs and congregations. But Begbie will not let his attention drift from his main subject: that *sola scriptura* is the source and norm for all that follows in the reformer's understandings of gospel and music.

In **chapter 4**, "The European Reformation: Advocacy of Education and Liberation," **Michael Welker** turns our attention to the ways the Protestant Reformers sought to spread and prolong their efforts. None of them seemed to think that if they tidied up things in their part of the empire or the church, their mission would be complete. They savored biblical words about "generations," "children," and "the world." Aware that the gospel had reached Germany and other sites of the Protestant Reformation because elders taught the young in their communities to devote themselves to *sola scriptura*, they responded to the quickening surprises offered by the gospel through enhancement of life and worship, thanks to music and other arts. But they needed more. Responsible reformers knew that they would have to devise agencies, institutions, and strategies to assure a future for the gifts they received and for their causes.

The natural instrument for effecting the change and longevity of the Reformation across generations was education. All histories of the Reformation stress the inventiveness of the Reformers as educators and entrepreneurs. If old institutions could not well serve them, they needed new ones. No longer could they rely on religious orders to set up schools or in other ways to advance learning. No longer could they expect civil authorities of the empire to put energies into training the youth among the reformers. No longer did they want to count on imperial armies and policing agencies to enforce discipline among the young and others. So they borrowed some traditional institutions, criticized what they saw as having gone wrong among them, and then devised new educational forms and norms.

The transition to the new practices could not in every circumstance be easy since many citizens, explicitly Christian or not, relied on habits or neglected responsibilities. The Reformers met heavy resistance among many Catholic authorities in local, regional, and empire-wide settings. Educating the young can sound very tame: the priest as teacher who paced among children was usually backed or fronted by a stick, since physical discipline was common (as it remained in Reformation circles). But the 1500s was not a time for serenity, quiet, and the privilege of being bored. The Reformers wanted change. Citizens of all ages, in the Reformers' vision and observation, were enslaved. Their oppressors were legalistic confessors and priestly rule makers and keepers. How could their ways of legalism coexist with the "freedom of the Christian" advocated by Luther and others?

Reform meant education and new measures of freedom, in the case of children being educated. The orientation to the gospel in education meant a linkage to the strongest impulse on the domestic level: to "re-form" ways of life. The records of the day reveal that the title of Welker's chapter is apt: "Education and liberation" were linked, often in imperfect ways but with consistent common intentions.

Liberation meant trampling on old norms, breaking the silence of the ignorant where there could be vital speech and action, as old ways were rejected. Together these records remind us that reform never is easy, that reformers never have a free ride, even among people who favor change. So to make sense of Welker's chapter and to plot ways of responding to it, those in the re-Reformation movements have to support and spread what Welker calls the "advocacy of education and liberation." He shows how the education and liberation efforts were necessarily linked, even where different institutions and agencies had to respond to their separate callings and assignments.

While the homily or sermon was a major instrument for educating the laity through the Christian centuries, if we may call them that, the well-educated Reformers never tired of pointing out that in practice, most preaching was routine, delivered by unlearned, incompetent, and not-always-alert friars and priests. The Reformation was a wake-up call for the Reformers, as congregations came expecting news about the Good News and new ways to replace corrupt and sluggish agents of peddled passivity. Such priests, now usually seen more as pastors than as authorities, used the new Bible translations, which abounded in ways that still stun chroniclers' accounts of the ubiquity of texts in the fairly new age of printing.

The Reformation churches had great opportunities to educate, and many of the new leaders produced texts, worked with publishers, and taught the newly literate teachers and their students. The Reformers had to come up with strategies for equipping families, founding nurseries, and tending to the substance of sermons and other messages. In the "priesthood of all believers," parents, civil authorities, and pastors took on responsibilities for educating. While their messages contributed to the risky struggles for liberation in an age marked by holy wars, they also led to experiences of freedom in confessional chambers, church pews, and public settings, where Christians of various callings beyond the priesthood were to be and often were agents of reform.

John Witte, author of **chapter 5**, "Faith in Law," has written at book length on the story of Protestantism and the law, so readers of his books and his contribution to this volume will find themselves on familiar terms with the main themes here. Still, the reader of Witte's earlier works will find new insights, because Witte is especially attentive to the impact of the Reformation on the theories and practice of law and legislation. His title also confirms what his readers have long observed: his is not a historical legal brief on its own terms. Note the first three words and then the rest of his headline: "Faith in Law: The Legal and Political Legacy of the Protestant Reformations." Witte remembers that most writers, dispensers, and adjudicators in the Christian lineage were keeping in mind the texts and impulses of Christian legal concerns. The keyword in their struggles is "faith," and Witte's account here demonstrates that accent clearly.

Almost slyly, his use of a form of another headlined word is a clue to his interests and approach. He is not writing about the singular Protestant Reformation but the plural and thus more accurately described as "Reformations." It is not that he does not find reason in some contexts to provide a coherent account of the turmoil of the sixteenth century as *the* Reformation. But with a constitutional lawyer and legal historian's eye, he sees that attempts to find what Reformers and the reformed have in common cannot be successfully comprehended and analyzed unless the topic is broken down, as it is here.

Five hundred years after Luther's Reformation of 1517, historians more than ever have to be frank about using the plural *Reformations*, a theme addressed afresh in this chapter. Reformations came in various national guises and contexts: Czech, English, Scottish, German, Swiss, and many more. By the way, each of these geographical versions brought distinctive accents to the fore, and only confusion will result if an author lumps everything together. Seldom is this more true than when the focus is on urgent subtopics such as law, which confronts the researcher and expositor in independent and conflicting ways. Lawyers, jurists, accusers, and the accused are particularized and not lump-summed if they want to be clear, honest, and of help.

Not that there are no elements in common between laws of this province or that, this nation or that. For instance, as Witte points out, law in the Christian tradition reflects some root in or tie to the sacred Scriptures. Recall from the first chapter how important *sola scriptura*, Scripture alone, was in many places on the map and remains so in history books and encyclopedias. Witte shows how the Decalogue plays its part wherever legal authorities in formally Christian jurisdictions have had to rely on and reflect concern by authorities and the people at large with the Bible. Some of the main themes of Christian theology, for instance, have developed among jurists who want to be faithful to the divine Trinity, to Jesus Christ as Savior and Lord, to the Holy Spirit seen as vivifying human law and keeping it from being merely legal.

When one reads compressed works like this chapter, there is always the potential for being challenged by a hint or an accent congenial to the searching interests of a particular legal historian. As one example, think of the generalization by author Witte, and then ponder whether it points to an important reality usually overlooked in books like this. I refer to Witte's concern with how the Reformation's lawyers and counselors, by downgrading or abandoning the attention to "vocations" for both men and women as observed in the monasteries, neglected all vocational interests of those unmarried in the new order. Here it is, in a reference to millions of Protestants in five centuries: "Ever since, adult Protestant singles have chafed in a sort of pastoral and theological limbo, objects of curiosity and pity, even suspicion and contempt." Changes in concepts of gender, sex, rights, and achievements have changed this reality drastically, but historical accounts show a lack of positive rationales for vocation in singlehood after vows of celibacy became irrelevant among Protestants.

Never again will or should those who have read Witte need to confuse the main interests and particularities in the four main cohorts of Protestants to whom he gives separate attention. The presence of Anabaptists in Witte's classification is the clearest way to understand this. When something of legal character affects or afflicts an Amish community, it quickly gets connected to the Amish version of Anabaptist faith and to faith in law. This happens in ways irrelevant to or not fully comprehensible among, for example, traditional Anglicans in their dealings with authority and law in church and state. Sometimes one is tempted to render in the plural some words in Witte's title: "faiths" in "laws" seem more appropriate because of the variety of Protestant Reformations and heritages. This chapter has served as a road map or a guide to family trees that endure in legal Protestantisms as they make up the whole of faithful Protestantism and its works in charities, theological exposition, and, yes, law.

A "paradigm shift" sounds like something only grammarians have to deal with, while the rest of the world passes it by. Yet the apparent innocence that the term connotes—even the word "shift" does not always suggest anything seismic—disguises drastic changes in human affairs. This is especially true when such a shift condenses the moves that occupy people for centuries, and in all dimensions of their lives. In **chapter 6, Carter Lindberg** examines how "Charity and Social Welfare" in the Reformation and, for our times, the re-Reformation imply a particular paradigm shift that suggests drastic changes in human lives and their arrangements. The first line of the title trades on and turns around a much-quoted biblical reference: "You always have the poor with you." Thanks to a new paradigm in the churches and the world affected by the Reformation, believers could envision a way of realizing some version or other of the change to be brought by the gospel and, of course, to the ways of life congruent with it and issuing from its new acceptance in society.

That line is code for all kinds of societal changes and the ways people experience them. While poverty was (and is) no doubt the most vivid social reality demanding attention in church and world, consequent and corollary issues appear in a new light when this kind of paradigm shift occurs. As is evident in Professor Lindberg's elaborations, this shift involves changed thought and action in church and world; biblical injunctions, prophecies, and dreams reveal how, in the divine world, preachers, disciples, and leaders of all sorts will receive new and different kinds of power as they treat human needs. The church's response can be coded as "social welfare" and often appears as such in rosters of church activity.

Thus as people are to be fed, so also must they be housed. They cannot live as God intended them to live—as sheltered, comfortable, safe individuals, families, or communities—without protection from the elements. If, for ages and in most cultures, shelter meant something that families or heads of families provided for those who lived together under one roof, this could not suffice as a mandate if it did not comprehend and account for the effects of war, migration, refugee status, crowding, social-class structures, and caring and curing in the face of physical pain, disease, and aging. Since education is the great enabler for people to have access to goods and opportunities, it should also be included under the rubric of social welfare. Luther's catechismal explanation of a petition in the Lord's Prayer points to the scope of the mandate. "Our daily bread" relates to everything that belongs to and supports the body. Modernity confronts all people with changes in ways of dealing with these needs. Although modernity does not mean repudiating or forgetting classical charity pointed to in the Bible, such as sharing the cup of cold water or handing coins to someone in need, it forces a new agenda on believers who want to be responsible and share the life of grace. For that, a paradigm shift was needed, and each generation and each locale will devise variations of the common approach.

Lindberg, like some other authors, associates the word "gift" with the Reformation changes. He writes: "The Reformation undercut the religious legitimation of poverty by displacing salvation as a human achievement with salvation as a divine gift." The consequence and corollary to this claim appear in Lindberg's next sentence: "The governing authorities of town councils and princes" were, thanks to the Reformation, "freed to engage in a new field of discourse regarding social issues. . . . With the new theology and active cooperation of Reformers . . . , they developed and passed new legislative structures for social welfare."

New inventions or drastic revisions of old ones followed; Lindberg dwells on the devising and promotion of "the common chest" in various locales and jurisdictions. These new approaches to welfare were developed alongside or in competition with novel forms of devotion to the profit motif in efforts to promote general welfare. Having sketched or summarized some of these elements in "the new paradigm," Lindberg begins to do what readers are henceforth asked to do: *think!* Are new paradigm shifts emerging? If so, how do they relate to existing forms? How does the gospel inform these? Changes in forms of government, definitions of the common good, and individual involvement will demand attention.

Increasing automation affects work and income, with constantly debated governmental adaptations and inventions, global interactions, and improvised and imposed involvements of government that will always be changing: in such an era being faithful to what are received as divine commands about "care of the other" will also be constantly changing. Those who consider the church of old and the ways of old to be the perfect solutions to problems of human need will be ill equipped to relate to the changes and new needs. That is why the church must be conceived as being "in process," or again, in Luther's own terms, a *becoming* more than a *being*. That can be a terrifying prospect unless it is grounded in faith in a loving God. In faith, it need not terrify. "We tremble not, we fear no ill," the Reformation congregations sang.

"Worldly Worship," the lead-in phrase to **Wolfgang Huber**'s title for **chapter 7**, like so many other references by the authors of this book, either tantalizes or misleads, depending on the expectations readers bring to it. "Worldly Worship" could suggest anything that goes on outside the sanctuary or other predictable worship sites and settings. Or it could do what many enterprising religious leaders do in our years, namely, play down the sacred and play up the profane, public, "far-out" experimental efforts to take worship out of stale and tired contexts and locate it in fresh, enlivening, and unexpected roles. Not quite. Huber instead connects "worldly worship" with "Reformation and Economic Ethics."

Economic ethics is something we would not ordinarily connect with worship. The chapter title seems to blur and mix two very independent, if not contradictory and distracting, themes. But we can forget about the "seems" in that sentence and take notice that Huber is very deliberate in his choice of words and is making a point congruent with and even reinforcing the main Reformation stress about worship. As always in this book, "Reformation" is associated with "gift," and here is a clear reaffirmation that worship is graced when it relates to the surrounding world, or that the surrounding world is graced if it touches on one or another or all of the worlds that God created but humans can and often do corrupt.

Bring up "economics" in the Reformation sphere, and almost instantly it will evoke the masterwork of the social-ethical thinker Max Weber. But here, as in other cases, while citing him is a tribute to his commanding influence, Weber's view of Protestantism elicits reservations, caution, revision, and partial abandonment. To Huber and others, Weber's Protestant ethic is not graced: it is bound up with the kind of zealous work that Reformation preachers of grace rejected.

Professor Huber and, in parallel ways, Kathryn Tanner, whom he introduces into the discussion, take up the world as described by Weber and others in his succession and then do something very daring—and thus something to be entertained and pursued by ethicists and others in the Reformation tradition(s). To get our attention and to inform in novel ways, Huber allows for a moment of entertainment by taking us to the German carnival in Cologne. In this scene the carnival-goers make fun of Weber's emphasis on labor and the suggestion that God favors with "the best seat near to God" those who work hard and earn a lot of the earth. Then he quotes memorable words from the refrain in the carnival act: "I am so happy that I'm not a Protestant, / they have nothing in mind but to work."

After this venture to Cologne, Huber takes us to China, where he was told that the Chinese approach to work was, among other things, Protestantism mixed with Confucianism. Not Luther or Calvin but Max Weber has influence in Chinese religion-and-economics. Huber again cites Kathryn Tanner in her Gifford Lectures for her challenge to Weber. Remarkably, but importantly for more arguments than one in this book, Tanner sets out to "demonstrate the capacity of Christian beliefs and practices to help people resist the dictates of capitalism in its present, finance-dominated configuration." If we are to project into the future some themes from these chapters, here might be an apparently topsy-turvy twist on Weber. Rather than use Protestant theology and ethics to promote capitalism, Christian beliefs and practices have the capacity to help people "resist the dictates of capitalism." The temptation here is strong to end that sentence with an exclamation point, for it encourages fresh thinking about dominant understandings and patterns of action.

In this context, Huber, agreeing with Tanner, proposes to look to another part of Reformation theology, the previously mentioned concept of *vocation*. It informs the work-life of human action valued with regard not to works but to grace. Luther chose to summarize the graced life in that concept of vocation, which "calls for unity of faith in God and of love to the neighbor as to oneself." To the point: "Work as vocation: that is the specific approach of the Reformation to economic ethics." Projecting into the future: can such a concept of vocation be recovered, understood, fostered, and applied in a work world where mere competition and self-regard and self-service are honored in most educational and other career-obsessed habits and recommendations?

Huber and the economic ethicists he favors do not only speak of vocation as if it were advancement of the self through economic effort and work. No, his approach strongly commits readers to "dealing with poverty." Here is another topsy-turvy item, familiar to those who studied "liberation theology," with its "preferential option for the poor." Do not give up, he virtually pleads, on the concept of vocation since it "would view human existence as active, creative, and productive life," as a source of "social recognition" and not mere "self-realization." One is tempted to say that for Reformation in the future, citizens should work zealously on such an approach. But this would work only if they revised the Weberian concepts of work and reenvisioned them, now, in the context of liberating "vocation."

In **chapter 8**, "The Protestant Ethic and the Spirit of Consumerism," **Jonathan Walton** brings accounting of Protestantism down to the present and leans into a vision of the future, as this introduction is supposed to do. A fair reader, in my estimation, would judge that none of the writers in this collection reveals an antiquarian impulse, lives with nostalgia, or, conversely, shows simple disdain for achievements by people in the past. These scholars are called to suggest how writers in the Bible and the Protestant Reformation of five centuries ago dwelt in or advocated a devotion to an earlier moment in history than our own. But Professor Walton is up to the minute, as of the year 2018 and those years immediately to follow, so he takes a necessary chance or risks enough faith in continuity to make his Protestantism-and-America of tomorrow something imaginable and relevant today.

For example, he immediately introduces and comments on a United States president of the moment and surrounds him with, for example, Protestant evangelists of today. Will they be remembered any more tomorrow than are celebrities of the 1920s, 1950s, or 1980s? This is no risk for Walton, since he immediately focuses on enduring issues, for which the figures crossing his stage at the moment represent ways of life that, added up, symbolize consumerism.

While the word "consumer" is at home in dictionaries, and has been for a long time, the addition of "ism" suggests bone-deep, long-term, highly visible attachments of consuming. In popular, colloquial, and slang dictionaries, "consumerism" is at home in many forms of discourse, where it bids for attention. Some references call it an addiction, and others name it a sin or attach elements of the Seven Deadly Sins (e.g., greed) to the "ism." Awareness of that usage helps us anticipate that the phenomenon will spread as it attaches itself to expanding desires, hungers, and impulses that are themselves reaching deeper and further.

Walton's celebrities may evoke a sense of pride in us. After all, *we* do not indulge in easy-to-caricature addictions. *They*, instead, are guilty of them. Yet it is not likely that Walton has bid for our attention by appealing to our sense of superiority. Some years ago, when social critics often were dubbed "prophets," I was put in my place when someone wrote that whoever has academic tenure is disqualified from prophethood. I could join fellow academics in civil rights marches, but most of us had little to lose, certainly nothing compared to what some would lose, such as dwellers in high-risk places from which they could not escape as we could, when our planes took off for safe landings and positive press coverage.

Here, as elsewhere, a contributor to this book finds Max Weber so distorting in his view of the Protestant ethic and its self-proclaimed adherents or highly visible case studies. Walton takes care of Weber early and moves on to more productive examples of pioneering delineators of the Protestant ethic. He defines them as ideologues. Rather than scorn Weber, Walton understands him and his projects and place as very much "one with his age." So were the liberal Protestant social ethicists and activists and many others not named here, given the word limits of a chapter in a book.

Take the Protestant ethic in Walton's view. As with other ideologues, those of the Protestant ethic "willfully obscure as much as they convey." For the present example, the Protestant ethic "as a cultural trope and political ideology has done much to encourage thrift, sobriety, and the disciplines essential for success," but "it has also willfully ignored how the promulgated ideal works to regulate and reify class hierarchies and distinctions based on cultural capital and tastes." To address this ambiguity, Walton will have readers notice what Pierre Bourdieu has noticed, that consumerism and consuming of goods were not the only problems: think of the role of preferences and tastes in determining status. His quote of Bourdieu is apt: "Taste classifies, and it classifies the classifier." Or had we not noticed that? If an implied suggestion of this whole book is appropriate and to the point, those [of us?] of various ideological bents will be creatively busy evaluating our "classification" of others, as if holding up a mirror to ourselves.

Graham Tomlin, in **chapter 9**, draws a convergence between past and future in observing that the five hundredth anniversary of the Reformation followed close on the heels of Brexit, raising the question "Whither Europe?" Writing from the vantage of the Anglican Church, Tomlin notes the pertinent debate whether the Reformation in England manifested an earlier "Brexit" moment of leaving Europe—in that case the pan-European Catholic Church—or instead was part of a broad European movement that transcended national boundaries. The question is not merely academic. It points, rather, to the imperative of vision for the future. Persuaded that the European Union has lost a vision that had sources in the postwar Christian Democratic movement, Tomlin reaches back to the Reformation as an exemplary period when Europe, breaking apart in the face of crises similar to those of today, found in the Gospels a new vision for union.

The case is compelling. In four particular ways, our day bears eerie similarity to the period leading to the Reformation. Both eras have witnessed the redefinition of the place of the individual in society; both have experienced deepening concerns about poverty and its impact on the migration of peoples; both have been riven by the revolt against elites; and both have pondered the rise of Islam in Europe.

Tomlin neatly traces the way early capitalism fostered the rise of a mercantile and banking class, leading to the medieval social order beginning to give way. Greater mobility offered freedom from traditional economic arrangements for peasants, artisans, and shopkeepers, yet for the first time presented the need for individuals to define their worth by forging a way through the puzzling new socioeconomic wilderness. At the same time, a medieval theology that offered salvation through myriad acts of penance and religious service weighed heavily on the conscience. Luther's insight that salvation comes through faith alone, by grace, lifted both of these burdens from the shoulders of individuals, offering worth to every vocation and value to every soul before a gracious God. W. H. Auden aptly captured the Reformers' solution in his poem "Luther" that the just who lived by faith "were glad" and never "trembled in their useful lives." Our day, too, with its consumerism and polycultural identities, challenges men and women to live useful lives in a world so easily given to disenchantment, alienation, and dread.

Like the sixteenth century, our own century is increasingly defined by huge disparities of wealth. And now, as then, these extremes lead to both new civic and church structures for helping the poor and new patterns of the poor helping themselves—by moving. As Reformation cities in Europe struggled to care for thousands dislodged by religious persecution or war, so Europe once again is wrestling with the influx of tens of thousands from war-torn parts of the Middle East and Africa, many of them religious refugees. In Tomlin's view, the European Union—and the United States, for that matter—might take a page from the playbook of the Reformers by bringing imagination and innovation to bear on these challenges.

Tomlin also notes that the fuel of populism powered the engine of the Reformation, as it appears to be driving so-called reform movements in our own time. Luther had nothing like Twitter at his fingertips, but he had something as new and impressive at his disposal: the printing press. In a way that suggests the power of cable news, social media, and other means of communication to bypass filters and reach directly into the attention of the masses, Luther "harnessed [new media] . . . as a genius at popular communication." For the elites accustomed to controlling access to knowledge—even knowledge of sacred Scriptures—the democratization of the word suddenly posed the possibility that knowledge in the minds of the masses might lead to power in their hands as well.

Perhaps most astonishing in Tomlin's chapter is the reminder that the contemporary presence of Islam in Europe—and Europe's perception of Islam as a threat—is but an echo of the very literal war between Islam and Europe that peaked with the unsuccessful siege of Vienna in 1529. Luther had both theological and practical things to say about the circumstances, but most interesting in our day may be his "grudging admiration," as Tomlin puts it, of the Islamic devotion to prayer, spiritual discipline, and study of the Quran. A "spiritually lax Europe" might learn much from such a religion.

Margot Kässmann concludes the chapters in this book with **chapter 10**, "The Challenges of Sixteenth-Century Europe and Our Global Challenges Today." Here she provides a clear, brisk, and sweeping summary of the historic period to which this collection is dedicated and an approach to "today." Yet the word "challenge" in her title and the challenge she accepts implies "tomorrow." Since this book deals with the Protestant Reformation of the church and the world, her chapter belongs to a category to which we have referred: "the re-Reformation." What use is it, one might fairly ask, to deal with the future by reference to an irretrievable past? What can "Reformation" Christians put to work for the future out of what they have been exploring in these chapters?

The answer by some historians comes to mind at once; it is evoked by recall to a historical figure, Abraham Lincoln. One of the most important and memorable sentences by the future president at the Republican Convention in June of 1858, just before the Civil War, merits pondering: "If we could first know where we are, and whither we are tending, we could then better judge what to do, and how to do it." The approach is very modest and, in its careful rhetoric, bids those who quote it now to be very modest in their claims and proposals. There was no claim *that* we know, only a suggestion, with the word "if," that exploration and contemplation are profitable and necessary. In short, Lincoln projected that it was worth looking around and assessing affairs. The future president did not define or document his "we," and that pronoun is a very portable designation: "we" Americans, "we" Northerners, "we" Republicans? Stated as it is, the quoted sentence has been of use to many citizens long after the Civil War, and it points to hoped-for political, military, and government relevance in many circumstances, such as those that confront us today.

Where were citizens then "tending"? Where did they locate themselves amid unfolding historical events? They were tending to war, the break-up of the Union, and the costs of war, especially in the death of many thousands. Still, Lincoln pushes on: "if" all that is in consideration, "then" they could "better judge." This did not mean that they would be assured of victory; they could not know, could not deal with all factors, but they, who had to judge, "might" better judge what to do. And with the gravity associated with eve-of-war leadership, the president posited that they might find instruments, tactics, and political sense; they might know "how to do it."

This little exercise of lingering with and pondering words of Lincoln serves in a way to provide a how-to approach to the re-Reformation. "We" do not have a Luther or Hus or Calvin or Knox, but who knows who individually and collectively might emerge and make a decisive contribution? The words in the quotation most applicable for those who would carry into the future what they might learn from our past are "where we are," which is what this book is about. Very few explicit predictions and not many more prophecies are here. Our writers leave such foolishness to others.

Almost a half century before I wrote these pages, I published *The Search for a Usable Future* (1969). I will do readers the favor of not revisiting at length that I-hope-dated book. I will only emphasize the title because it appears to me that the authors in this book, in the spirit of the Protestant Reformation, are searching for a usable future. No one in these pages does so more focally than Professor Kässmann, whose subtitles were reassuring to me, proposing concern with nationalism, ecumenism, dialogue of religions, justice and race, women, divisions, reconciliation, education, freedom, justification, and media. Events of the sixteenth century in Reformation Europe complement the topics of twenty-first-century re-Reformation global contexts and have provided tantalizing and provocative clues for those in the search for a usable future on some grounds that the Reformation era promises.

How do we begin to act? Try this: "I move that we study and then convene panels and conferences that will draw on the efforts of risk-taking but disciplined experts, such as the authors we have met on these pages, and then engage publics who may not yet know how potentially helpful their own ponderings and proposals might be." Is there a second to the motion?

Historiated Title-Page Border, in *Martin Luther's Complete Bible*,
Low German Bible, translated by Martin Luther, 1533

Chapter One

The Gift of *Sola Scriptura* to the World

Mark A. Noll

The Protestant principle of *sola scriptura*, like the Reformation itself, has been a great boon and a great bane to Western civilization. It has both abetted and retarded the development of secular modernity; it has both strengthened and undercut the cause of Christ. As the Reformation revived segments of the Western church, it also split that church. As it unleashed great Christian energy, it also unleashed other forces that disempowered Christianity. As it liberated individuals and communities from thralldom to the pope, it also delivered them into the control of kings, emperors, city councils, and a host of lesser earthly powers. And as it liberated the Scriptures to speak the words of God without fear or favor, it also trivialized those words through multiple iterations of what a sharp-eyed contemporary sociologist has called "pervasive interpretive pluralism."[1]

This chapter presupposes the tight intermingling of bane and blessing that has accompanied the Protestant exaltation of Scripture, especially in league with Protestant insistence on the interpretive authority of the individual conscience. It begins by reviewing definitive statements about the authority of the Bible from the earliest years of Protestantism, followed by a rapid survey to show that the ur-Protestant vision of a liberated Scripture leading to liberated selves has endured to the present. In the interest of interpretive balance, the chapter pauses to summarize weighty contemporary accounts of the damage, both unintended and deliberate, wrought by the notion of *sola scriptura*. It then sketches three moments in Protestant history when reliance on *sola scriptura* exposed admittedly large difficulties,

---

1. Christian Smith, *The Bible Made Impossible: Why Biblicism Is Not a Truly Evangelical Reading of Scripture* (Grand Rapids: Brazos, 2011).

but also produced beneficial results. The chapter closes by outlining some of the discriminating questions that should be asked to obtain a clearer understanding of how *sola scriptura* has actually functioned, leading finally to ecumenical reflections arising from an assessment of that history.

The Bible Alone

As is widely known, Martin Luther informed the Holy Roman Emperor at the imperial Diet of Worms in 1521 that he could not recant what he had published to condemn the sale of indulgences and other abuses he perceived in the late-medieval Catholic Church. The basis of his refusal was crystal clear. He told the emperor, "Unless I am convinced by the testimony of the scriptures or by clear reason (for I do not trust either in the pope or in councils alone, since it is well known that they have often erred and contradicted themselves), I am bound by the scriptures I have quoted, and my conscience is captive to the Word of God."[2] Within less than ten years, a host of other earnest seekers would follow Luther's reliance on Scripture and so receive divine grace, discover fresh motivation for godly living, or find the courage to stare death straight in the face. For some, it was nearly the same as for Luther, who, again famously, reported many years later that when his conscience became captive to the word of God, he experienced "the mercy of God" and "felt that I was altogether born again and had entered paradise itself through open gates."[3] In England, as a prime early example, Thomas Bilney, who was almost as scrupulous about his own need before God as Luther, reported that he had not "heard speak of Jesus" until he read Erasmus's Greek New Testament. But from that source, Bilney experienced "God's instruction and inward working" that first left him "wounded with the guilt of my sins," but then brought "a marvelous comfort and quietness, insomuch that my bruised bones leaped for joy."[4] Significantly, Thomas Bilney maintained this testimony even when it led to his execution as a lapsed heretic, taking him to the flames.

Others used different terms to describe the dramatic impact of personal encounter with the Scriptures. In Switzerland, the systematically minded Heinrich Bullinger, in David Steinmetz's summary, "read Luther and Melanchthon and concluded that their position was more in

2. "Luther at the Diet of Worms," in *Luther's Works* [*LW* hereafter in this book], trans. and ed. Jaroslav Pelikan et al., 55 vols. (Philadelphia: Fortress Press, 1955–68), 32:112.

3. "Preface to the Complete Edition of *Latin Writings* 1545," in *LW* 34:336–37.

4. Quoted in E. Gordon Rupp, *Studies in the Making of the English Protestant Tradition* (1949; Cambridge: Cambridge University Press, 1966), 22.

harmony with the teaching of the Bible and of the Fathers than was the doctrine of the Catholic church," which conclusion "led to his conversion in 1522."[5] In France, William (Guillaume) Farel published the first edition of his exposition of the Lord's Prayer in 1524, a work that would be reprinted fourteen times over the next twenty years. In it, as Carter Lindberg reports, Farel "emphasized the biblical basis for faith" with an exposition that "echoed Luther's emphasis on justification by faith by grace alone, faith as the free gift of God, complete human dependence on God, and the scriptural basis for these evangelical positions."[6] In 1527, Michael Sattler told the court in southwest Germany that would sentence him to death, "I am not aware that we have acted contrary to the gospel and the word of God. I appeal to the words of Christ."[7] Only a few years later, in the 1539 edition of *Institutes of the Christian Religion*, John Calvin identified "the godly" as those who "know the true rule of righteousness is to be sought from scripture alone."[8]

Sola scriptura, or the equivalent, was becoming a battle cry for Bilney, Bullinger, Farel, Sattler, Calvin, and many more because it had become a life-giving reality. The key was personal appropriation of the Bible, freed from what they considered (in the words of an early Anabaptist, Conrad Grebel) "the great and harmful error" of Catholic authorities.[9]

The conjunction of Scripture and spiritual liberation rapidly became mythic in Protestant self-definition, especially among Protestant evangelicals, as numberless individuals experienced that combination. In 1675, when Philipp Jakob Spener published *Pia Desideria*, a crucial work for sparking Pietism on the European continent, he appealed to "that true faith which is awakened through the word of God, by the illumination, witness, and sealing of the Holy Spirit." The first of Spener's six remedies for Germany's spiritual torpor demanded a return to Scripture, since the good news of the gospel and "the rules for good works" that pleased God could be found nowhere else.[10]

5. David Steinmetz, *Reformers in the Wings*, 2nd ed. (New York: Oxford University Press, 2001), 94.

6. Carter Lindberg, *The European Reformations* (Cambridge, MA: Blackwell, 1996), 279.

7. "The Trial of Michael Sattler," in *Spiritual and Anabaptist Writers*, ed. George Huntston Williams (Philadelphia: Westminster, 1957), 140.

8. John Calvin, *Institutes of the Christian Religion* 3.17.8; trans. F. L. Battles, ed. J. T. McNeil, 2 vols. (Philadelphia: Westminster, 1960), 1:811.

9. "Letter to Thomas Müntzer by Conrad Grebel and Friends," in *Spiritual and Anabaptist Writers*, 74.

10. Philipp Jakob Spener, *Pia Desideria*, trans. Theodore G. Tappert (Philadelphia: Fortress Press, 1964), 46, 87.

Even more famously, John Wesley, throughout the daylight hours of May 24, 1738, pondered 2 Peter 1:4 ("There are given unto us exceeding great and precious promises, even that ye shall be partakers of the divine nature" [cf. KJV]) and Psalm 130 ("Out of the depths have I called unto thee, O LORD. . . . For with the LORD there is mercy, and with him is plenteous redemption" [Ps. 130:1, 7 KJV]) before he attended a Moravian society meeting in Aldersgate Street. There, when someone read from Martin Luther's preface to Romans, "About a quarter before nine, while [the speaker] was describing the change which God works in the heart through faith in Christ, I felt my heart strangely warmed. I felt I did trust Christ, Christ alone for salvation, and an assurance was given me that he had taken away *my* sins, even *mine*, and saved *me* from the law of sin and death."[11]

All sorts of ordinary people out of the limelight underwent something similar. John Wesley's contemporary Susanna Anthony, of colonial Rhode Island, reported that she suffered from despair brought on by assaults of the devil until she was rescued by meditating on Hebrews 7 and Colossians 3: through them "the Spirit of God . . . [did] powerfully apply these truths to my soul."[12] Later in the eighteenth century, Olaudah Equiano organized the narrative describing his journey from chattel slavery to manumission around a parallel narrative of Bible-delivered spiritual liberation: "In the evening of the same day I was reading and meditating on the fourth chapter of Acts, twelfth verse, under the solemn apprehension of eternity. . . . In this deep consternation the Lord was pleased to break in upon my soul with his bright beams of heavenly light; and in an instant, as it were, removing the veil, and letting light into a dark place, Isa[iah] xxv.7."[13]

And so it has gone to this very day, but now with instances coming from far beyond Protestantism's original homelands. In China, the civil rights lawyer Gao Zhisheng has explained how his life was changed when, in 2004, he defended a fellow Chinese citizen against the charge of "illegal business practices." The illegal practices included possession of Bibles. In Zhisheng's own words, "While handling the legal defense of Pastor Cai Zhouhua . . . , I first read Scripture. At the time, it left me cold. My attitude changed when the Beijing authorities began to persecute me. In time,

11. *The Works of John Wesley*, vol. 18, *Journals and Diaries (1735–1738)*, ed. W. Reginald Ward and Richard P. Heitzenrater (Nashville: Abingdon, 1988), 249–50.

12. Samuel Hopkins, ed., *The Life and Character of Miss Susanna Anthony* (Worcester, MA: Hudson & Goodwin, 1799), 30–31.

13. Olaudah Equiano, *The Interesting Narrative and Other Writings*, ed. Vincent Caretta, 2nd ed. (New York: Penguin, 2013), 189–90.

I came to know God and join the brotherhood of Christians. Since then, God has given me great strength through difficult times. He has also given me visions, the first coming after I was abducted in August 2006."[14]

The way in which Protestant loyalty to Scripture has easily accommodated other spiritual resources is well illustrated in Gao Zhisheng's visions. Another variation appears in a report from Uganda by the president of Fuller Theological Seminary, Mark Labberton. When he visited a nighttime refuge for children in a region menaced by the Lord's Resistance Army, he met a middle-aged woman who supervised hundreds of children each night. To Labberton's question concerning why she performed this duty, she replied, "Well, I am what you call a Christian. I read the Bible every day, and every week I go to a church where we eat something called the Lord's Supper. I can't read the Bible every day and share in that meal and not come here at night."[15]

In Iran, a cab driver gave the artist Banafsheh Behzadian a copy of the New Testament in Farsi. She read it and soon afterward joined a church, which led to her dismissal as a professor at the University of Tehran. With her husband she then fled to Turkey and eventually emigrated to Canada, where she has recently painted *The Song of Salvation*, a series of portraits depicting women at various stages of life's journey, each accompanied by the biblical text that inspired the image.[16]

These latter-day testimonies to Scripture as the source of spiritual quickening sustain the tradition that the generation of Martin Luther did so much to propel. If the anti-Catholicism of historical Protestantism has fallen away from these contemporary witnesses, they nonetheless echo the liberating themes that have remained central throughout Protestant history. The Bible as an antidote to authoritarian oppression, tribal violence, and personal anomie remains a tonic almost as bracing in the twenty-first century as it was in the sixteenth.

Collateral Damage

Yet, as has been the case since Martin Luther's dramatic entrance onto the world stage, a personal elixir can easily become a social poison. As much as *sola scriptura*, functioning as a lodestar for personal redemption,

14. Gao Zhisheng, "Struggle against the Gods," *First Things* (April 2017): 22.

15. Mark Labberton, "The Plain Sense? Scripture May Be Clear, But It's Not Easy," *Christian Century*, April 12, 2017, 31.

16. Jenny de Groot, "Iranian Refugee's Paintings Displayed in British Columbia Church," *The Banner*, June 2017, 13.

has given hope to many individuals, it has also acted as an engine of self-assertion, leaving disorder in its wake. From the start, the foundational principle of *sola scriptura* that inspired the history of Protestantism ("My conscience is captive to the Word of God") also produced other effects. These effects included unprecedented controversy in biblical interpretation, unprecedented wrangling among personal consciences in conflict, and unprecedented strife over what it meant to follow the Word of God. Any attempt to highlight the benefits that have come from the Protestant reliance on *sola scriptura*—trusting the Bible as chief authority for individuals and the church—must also acknowledge the multiplied difficulties created by the same reliance.

To be sure, a focus today on the Protestant idea of *sola scriptura* takes place in a very different ecclesiastical context from when Martin Luther faced the emperor Charles V at Worms in 1521. It is also far from what such a consideration would have entailed in the mid-sixteenth century, when Catholic authorities issued a brief "Profession of Faith" that encapsulated the anti-Protestant conclusions of the Council of Trent. That Profession urged Catholics to "embrace the apostolic and ecclesiastical traditions, and all other observances and constitutions" of what the document called "the Holy Roman Church." Foremost in that guidance was a pledge directly repudiating *sola scriptura*: "I . . . accept Holy Scripture according to that sense which Holy Mother Church has held and does hold, to whom it belongs to judge of the true meaning and interpretation of the Sacred Scriptures; I shall never accept or interpret them otherwise than according to the unanimous consent of the fathers."[17]

Today, however, is not 1521 or 1564, when the Profession was issued. Beginning in the mid-twentieth century, Catholic proponents of a *nouvelle theologie* deployed Scripture and patristic biblical interpretation to modify traditional scholasticism. At the Second Vatican Council, the Dogmatic Constitution on Divine Revelation (*Dei Verbum*) reinterpreted tradition as standing alongside of, instead of in addition to, the revelation of Scripture. The Catholic Catechism of 1992 reaffirmed the value of tradition as guiding the interpretation of Scripture, but also defined the Bible, and its Christ-centered message, in terms at least partially reminiscent of early Protestant professions: "The divinely revealed realities, which are contained and preserved in the text of Sacred Scripture, have been written

17. "The Tridentine Profession of Faith, 1564," in *Creeds and Confessions of the Christian Tradition*, vol. 2, *Reformation Era*, ed. Jaroslav Pelikan and Valerie Hotchkiss (New Haven, CT: Yale University Press, 2003), 873.

down under the inspiration of the Holy Spirit. . . . The inspired book tells the truth." Moreover, Scripture as truth-telling is "not a written and mute word, but incarnate and living. If the Scriptures are not to remain a dead letter, Christ, the eternal Word of the living God, must, through the Holy Spirit, open our minds to understand the Scriptures."[18] Manifestly in the pontificates of John Paul II, Benedict XVI, and Francis I, a turn to direct scriptural authority has become a prime characteristic of contemporary official Catholicism. These emphases, while never equating to the Protestant claims of *sola scriptura*, have sparked a great renewal of attention to the Bible.

Over roughly the same period, a host of Protestants—including some thoroughly conservative voices—have publicly acknowledged significant Protestant abuses arising from the notion of *sola scriptura*. An example is the Anglican Reformed evangelical J. I. Packer, who finds it sad that "evangelical emphasis on the Bible has often led to the neglect of other important elements of Christian thought. It has meant evangelical isolation from the mainstream Christian heritage of Bible-based theology and wisdom over two millennia, which evangelicals should claim but which few seem to know or care about."[19]

Catholic deference to the irreplaceable life-giving authority of Scripture alongside chastened Protestant willingness to constrain excesses of Bible-infatuation have created a new climate for Christian ecumenicity. Still, even in an era moving beyond once commonplace Catholic-Protestant denunciations, no responsible effort to describe the positive results of *sola scriptura* can ignore the negative. The damage, as many responsible authors have pointed out, has already been done.

Of recent students of such problems, Brad Gregory, Vincent Wimbush, and R. S. Sugirtharajah have been among the most trenchant. To keep the gift of *sola scriptura* in perspective, it is important to register their complaints.

Brad Gregory's *The Unintended Reformation: How a Religious Revolution Secularized Society* offers a powerful account of modern Western debilities as arising in substantial part from the fact that "every anti-Roman, Reformation-era Christian truth claim based on scripture" led to "fissiparous disagreement among those who agreed that Christian truth

---

18. *Catechism of the Catholic Church*, English trans. (Liguori, MO: Liguori, 1994), 31 (paragraphs 105, 107, 108).

19. J. I. Packer, "The Bible in Use," in *Your Word Is Truth*, ed. Charles Colson and Richard John Neuhaus (Grand Rapids: Wm. B. Eerdmans Publishing Co., 2002), 59–78, at 76–77.

should be based solely on scripture."[20] Gregory does point out that the late-medieval church was falling woefully short of its own ideal, which he describes as a noncoercive Catholic regime of eucharistic charity. He also notes that these serious failures created some of the problems that Protestant Reformers tried to remedy by appealing to the Bible. Yet Gregory concentrates most on what he describes as the great crisis of authority that arose when Protestants, claiming to trust in a perspicuous self-interpreting Scripture, failed to unite theologically, ecclesiastically, politically, intellectually, or socially—and so failed to present a viable alternative to what they considered the fatally compromised medieval church.

Especially when the Protestant crisis of authority was compounded by the enforced conformity of Christendom's confessional states, the result was theological havoc and burgeoning governmental overreach as local states sought to replace the universal authority once exercised by the Western church. In turn, Gregory insists that the Protestant inability to operationalize a functioning program based on *sola scriptura* lay behind other slowly evolving maladies that have bestowed upon humanity the mass mayhem, the crass materialism, and the rootless anomie of the twenty-first century. In particular, Gregory depicts a long line of Western intellectual giants—Descartes, Hobbes, Spinoza, Locke, Hume, Rousseau, Kant, Schleiermacher, Nietzsche, and Heidegger—as trying but failing to provide answers to dilemmas created by the Protestant appeal to Scripture. In a word, Gregory's indictment is not unnuanced, but it is unbending: "the principle of *sola scriptura*," which Protestants advanced to resolve the difficulties of medieval Catholicism, "immediately became an unintended, enormous problem of its own. . . . Extrapolating from the fact of Protestant pluralism, by the end of the twentieth century, increasing numbers of people . . . had made either an atheistic inference that *no* religious truth claims are true, or drawn skeptical conclusion that it cannot be known."[21]

Gregory's account of the unintended consequences arising from the early Protestant turn to *sola scriptura* has a familiar ring. It reprises in sophisticated historical fashion the complaints that Roman Catholics once regularly made about the ordering of Protestant Christian faith. That complaint received a classic early formulation in the monumental polemic of a Jesuit, Cardinal Robert Bellarmine, published in several

20. Brad S. Gregory, *The Unintended Reformation* (Cambridge, MA: Belknap Press of Harvard University Press, 2012), 91.

21. Ibid., 109, 111.

parts during the 1580s as *Disputations on the Controversies over Christian Faith against the Heretics of the Day*. If, wrote Bellarmine, the Protestant "makes individual persons the judges in matters of faith, not only of the Fathers but also of the councils, he leaves almost nothing to the common judgment of the Church." In his view, this Protestant insistence doomed the Bible for captivity "to the spirit of individual persons."[22]

Contemporary critics schooled in the postmodern analysis of power have made an even more comprehensive indictment. To them, it is not just the concept of *sola scriptura* but also the whole Protestant deference to one authoritative text that has fueled the exploitation of the world's underclasses by its master races.

Vincent Wimbush, a pioneer in serious study of African Americans and the Bible, has recently published a provocative examination of how purported loyalty to Scripture facilitated the acceptance of slavery. Featuring Olaudah Equiano and his *Interesting Narrative*, which we have already referenced, Wimbush acknowledges that much of Equiano's memoir is taken up with his Christian conversion, his own deep immersion in Scripture, and his able use of the Bible to attack slavery. For Wimbush, however, Equiano's reliance on Scripture was ironic because he used it to subvert the exploitation carried out by the English-speaking Protestant master classes *with the Bible*. Wimbush's title is provocative: *White Men's Magic: Scripturalization as Slavery*. He summarizes his argument like this: "Insofar as Equiano understands that the dominant social and political structures in place are built around the Bible, drawing justification and power therefrom; so he proceeds to construct his life story in signifying/mimetic relationship to such arrangements. The black struggle for survival, freedom, and acquisition of power are understood by Equiano to turn around awareness of and response to the dominant culture's fetishizing of the book, the Bible."[23] For Wimbush, Protestant appeal to *sola scriptura* has been doubly problematic: that appeal masks the general abuse carried out by a supposedly advanced civilization on supposedly primitive people, and it hypocritically exploits the religious sanctions drawn from a sacred book to reinforce the systematic enslavement of a whole class of humanity.

Recent celebration of the four hundredth anniversary of the King James Bible prompted occasional application of liberationist ideology to

---

22. Robert Bellarmine, *Disputations*, as excerpted in appendix 3, in *Galileo, Bellarmine, and the Bible*, by Richard J. Blackwell (Notre Dame, IN: University of Notre Dame Press, 1991), 193.

23. Vincent Wimbush, *White Men's Magic: Scripturalization as Slavery* (New York: Oxford University Press, 2012), 18–19.

describe oppressive consequences of the Protestant principle of *sola scriptura*. R. S. Sugirtharajah made a particularly sharp statement in an essay titled "Postcolonial Notes on the King James Bible." To Sugirtharajah, it was significant that the translating committees for this version were called "companies," a word also used in the late sixteenth century for mercantile concerns like the Muscovy Company that, in Sugirtharajah's eyes, "are by nature competitive and even predatory."[24] More serious in his view, the King James translation promoted the English self-identification with the ancient Hebrews, which in turn worked toward "simultaneously denying and discrediting the agency of the 'other' and reifying and exaggerating the role of the master/colonizer."[25] More specifically, Sugirtharajah found England's championing of the King James Bible in its worldwide colonies, as well as the championing of Scripture by modern evangelical Americans, to be deeply implicated in imperialist aggression. Sugirtharajah's indictment links missionaries, colonizers, and the colonized in a vicious cycle of exploitation: "The eighteenth- and nineteenth-century British military and economic expansion was 'preceded and accompanied by missionary work based on the King James Bible.' . . . The KJB, with its accent on nation, national election, and establishment values, seemed to be the right text for the imperial occasion."[26] Wimbush and Sugirtharajah do not direct their claims directly against the doctrine of *sola scriptura*, but their criticism takes its force from the supposed malefactions of Protestants who had made *sola scriptura* a mainstay of the biblical religion they defined for themselves.

The bill of particulars that views *sola scriptura* as a distinctly Protestant curse is weighty. It includes doctrinal hyperpluralism, social disorder, unintended secularization, hegemonic dehumanization, and imperial aggression. To say the least, this is not the Bible that Protestants have been taught to honor as the Word of God, love as the doorway to salvation, and follow as the guide to holy living.

Instances

Examination of three historical moments can only hint at how well deserved such indictments are, but also how intimately both constructive

24. R. S. Sugirtharajah, "Postcolonial Notes on the King James Bible," in *The King James Bible after 400 Years: Literary, Linguistic, and Cultural Influences*, ed. Hannibal Hamlin and Norman W. Jones (New York: Cambridge University Press, 2010), 146–63, at 148.
25. Ibid., 150.
26. Ibid., 153, 154.

and destructive developments were intertwined. These three moments come from the seventeenth, nineteenth, and twenty-first centuries. Each includes a positive Protestant assertion about the Bible—an assertion that fuller historical context reveals as ironic, but not only ironic. The presence of overinflated claims about Scripture alongside circumstances undermining those claims—while also at least partially supporting them—makes these moments particularly revealing.

The first is a statement published in 1637 during the rising tide of political-religious strife that would soon issue in the English civil wars. In that year, William Chillingworth, a protégé of the Anglican Archbishop William Laud, was engaged in serious literary combat with a Jesuit who contended that England's official religion inevitably led to heresy. Chillingworth, who had himself briefly converted to Catholicism before returning to stout-hearted Anglican allegiance, begged to differ. And so he deployed a full range of his era's standard anti-Catholic polemics to defend the assertion of his book's title, *The Religion of Protestants: A Safe Way to Salvation*. Among his many arguments, Chillingworth's focus on Scripture was preeminent. He did concede that the religion of Protestants could not be defined by any one particular individual or confession; rather, it consisted in "that wherein they all agree, and which they all subscribe with a greater Harmony, as a perfect rule of their Faith and Actions." What was that perfect rule of faith and actions? "The BIBLE. The BIBLE, I say, THE BIBLE only is the Religion of Protestants!" Chillingworth then added several qualifications to his assertion while resolutely holding to his main contention: "Whatsoever else they believe besides it, and the plain, irrefragable, indubitable consequence of it, well may they hold it as a matter of Opinion, but as matter of Faith and Religion, neither can they with coherence to their own grounds believe it themselves, nor require the beliefe of it of others, without most high and most Schismaticall presumption."[27]

The ironies of Chillingworth's situation have been less often described than his famous words have been quoted. As a disciple of Archbishop William Laud, who used Scripture to define what he thought "the religion of Protestants" entailed, Chillingworth himself was mercilessly assailed by Presbyterians, Baptists, and other reforming Protestants who opposed the Laudians, including Chillingworth, as nothing better than crypto-Romanists. Although Chillingworth lived long enough to write against Scottish Presbyterians and to enlist for King Charles I in the

---

27. William Chillingworth, *The Religion of Protestants: A Safe Way to Salvation* (Lichfield, 1638; Short Title Catalogue, 1167:13), 375–76.

opening phases of the English Civil War, he died in 1644 and so did not witness the full hurricane of reform that Puritan understandings of Scripture unleashed in England during the next decade and a half. Nor could he witness the Restoration of 1660, when the return of monarchy and an Anglican established church forever ended efforts by the Puritans to convert what they considered a partially reformed England into a full-blown Bible commonwealth.

The Chillingworth example is poignant because it offers one of the historically most recognized definitions of Protestant religion as the doorway to salvation, with the frame of that doorway specified as "THE BIBLE only." But Chillingworth offered that definition at a particularly parlous moment. Puritan reformers in England and America, along with ardent Presbyterians in Scotland, were advancing audacious plans on the basis of scriptural truth. The thorough internalization of a biblical ideal of personal purification was generating a dynamic push for ecclesiastical and social purification. Yet at that very moment, the English Protestant world was tearing itself apart over what "the religion of Protestants" meant, how that religion should work to reform the church, and what it entailed for the body politic.[28] Chillingworth's formula—"THE BIBLE only is the Religion of Protestants"—seemed to produce the worst that Protestants were capable of.

And yet . . . the obsessive Puritan drive to construct all of life in accordance with the Word of God did produce marvels. As a striking instance, it is useful to remember that before Roger Williams migrated to the American colonies, he worked for the eminent Parliamentary jurist Sir Edward Coke. Williams's insistence on soul liberty and religious toleration, both extraordinarily rare in his age, grew directly out of his commitment to *sola scriptura*.[29] Those commitments, in turn, paralleled Coke's insistence on the rule of law. The biblicism of this radical Puritan, in other words, offered crucial support to one of the prime moral foundations of Western democratic civilization.

More generally, day-to-day life in Puritan Connecticut, Massachusetts Bay, and the Plymouth Colony witnessed a broader effort to employ *sola*

---

28. Essential background for the fractious effects of *sola scriptura* in the seventeenth century is found in Karl Gunther, *Reformation Unbound: Protestant Visions of Reform in England, 1525–1590* (New York: Cambridge University Press, 2014); one account of the result is Christopher Hill, *The English Bible and the Seventeenth-Century Revolution* (London: Allen Lane/Penguin, 1993).

29. For details concerning Williams's biblicism, see Mark A. Noll, *In the Beginning Was the Word: The Bible in American Public Life, 1492–1783* (New York: Oxford University Press, 2016), 134–36.

scriptura as a blueprint for organizing an entire society. That approach to Scripture certainly contributed to Puritan massacres of Native Americans, the witch trials at Salem Village, and a general suppression of human spontaneity. But it also contributed to what historians T. H. Breen and Stephen Foster once called "The Puritans' Greatest Achievement," which was to construct a society that for more than half a century enjoyed stronger social cohesion and more internal peace than anywhere else in the Western world of its day.[30] These New England Puritan societies offered a wider franchise than any European polity, their rates of literacy and longevity were the highest in the world, and their women enjoyed more rights than women almost anywhere else in the seventeenth century. In every case, *sola scriptura* was a driving force, which Alexis de Tocqueville recognized in the 1830s as he composed his landmark *Democracy in America*: "The founders of New England were at the same time ardent sectarians and impassioned innovators. Restrained by the tightest bonds of certain religious beliefs, they were free of all political prejudices. [Religion led them to enlightenment; the observance of divine laws brought them to liberty.]"[31]

The second illustration, coming two centuries later, is almost equally telling. Its author was Robert Baird, an American Presbyterian who published one of the first comprehensive histories of Christianity in the United States. In this work from 1844, aimed at the Europeans with whom Baird had lived for some time as an agent for the American Foreign Evangelical Society, he tried to explain why the "evangelical" denominations in the United States had been so successful in cooperating on so many fronts, with such great effect on the public life of the country. Baird first enumerated the great proliferation of church traditions that made up the American evangelical phalanx (Methodists, Congregationalists, Presbyterians, Baptists, Disciples, German and Dutch Reformed, "Christians," many Episcopalians, some Quakers, some Lutherans, and even a few conservative Unitarians). But then he also wanted Europeans to understand why these American Protestants, even though they represented many different denominations, had been able to unify their efforts so effectively. The key for Baird was voluntary, nonecclesial organizations

30. Timothy H. Breen and Stephen Foster, "The Puritans' Greatest Achievement: A Study of Social Cohesion in Seventeenth-Century Massachusetts," *William and Mary Quarterly* 60 (January 1973): 5–22.

31. Alexis de Tocqueville, *Democracy in America*, ed. Eduardo Nolla, trans. James T. Schleifer, 4 vols. (Indianapolis: Liberty Fund, 2010), 1:69. Brackets indicate wording that Tocqueville did not include in his published work.

that drew together Protestants of all sorts. In other words, Baird wanted his European audience to understand how the United States had become the most thoroughly evangelized, the most resolutely Bible-centered, and the most aggressively philanthropic country in the world—but *without* the formal ties between church and state that Europeans took for granted as indispensable for evangelization, Christian social ethics, and Christian philanthropy.

For Baird, loyalty to the Bible constructed the foundation for what today we would call a flourishing civil society. But Baird also went further to specify how American evangelicals used the Bible: they "hold the supremacy of the scriptures as a rule of faith, and that whatever doctrine can be proved from holy scripture *without tradition* is to be received unhesitatingly, and that nothing that cannot so be proved shall be deemed an *essential* point of Christian belief."[32] Unlike the Protestants of Chillingworth's England, a vast array of Protestants in Baird's United States were in fact uniting, rather than dividing, around "the Bible alone." In Baird's rendering, the ideal of "Scripture alone" was working, as it had not worked for Chillingworth's generation, because the American separation of church and state liberated the Bible from the crippling burdens of Christendom.

The irony of Baird's claim became manifest within two decades, when the United States fell apart in a Civil War that the nation's evangelical Protestants transformed into a holy war.[33] That transformation took place when a nearly universal belief in the God-given character of Scripture was joined to conflicting conclusions about biblical teaching on race and slavery. On both sides, combatants regarded their opponents not only as political enemies but also as infidels who willfully abused the Bible to support their unrighteous cause.

Of course, much else was involved in the American Civil War, but *sola scriptura* also played a large role. To many in the North as well as to almost all white Southerners, "the Bible alone" justified slavery as acceptable among Christians. How else could one possibly interpret the fact that the patriarch Abraham owned slaves, that the Levitical code regulated slavery, that Jesus never condemned the institution, and that the apostle Paul instructed the first Christians simply to live with the realities of

---

32. Robert Baird, *Religion in the United States of America* (Glasgow: Blackie & Son, 1844), 658, emphasis added.

33. On how conflicting scriptural interpretations contributed to that collapse, see Mark A. Noll, *The Civil War as a Theological Crisis* (Chapel Hill: University of North Carolina Press, 2006), 31–74.

Roman slavery? Just as ardently, abolitionists pointed to the New Testament's Golden Rule and to biblical teaching about the image of God in all humans as amounting to scriptural condemnation of slavery. A few careful students of Scripture—but only a few—pointed out that, whatever Scripture said about slavery in the abstract, it offered no justification for the kind of racially specific chattel slavery that prevailed in the United States. Yet disputing over what the Bible really taught went nowhere. Instead, the force of arms determined how Americans would read the Scriptures. The trust in the Bible without tradition that Robert Baird praised was working to destroy the very civilization that this trust had constructed.

And yet . . . focusing only on the American Protestant inability to overcome the evils of slavery by means of Protestantism's profession to follow the Bible alone unduly limits the focus. Between 1789 and 1861, it was by no means a perfect society that emerged on the North American continent.[34] But it was a society that promoted literacy in tandem with an ever-widening democratic surge, became the era's leader (after Britain) in Protestant missionary philanthropy, pioneered in humane prison reform, insisted on Sabbath observance as much to protect workers as to satisfy clergy, battled for temperance primarily to protect women and children, worked with mistaken zeal for African colonization, and witnessed expanding appeal to Scripture against slavery that nearly matched the even-more-powerful appeal to Scripture in favor of slavery. Once again, these mostly positive achievements, while not canceling out the negative, still owed much, directly or indirectly, to the principle of *sola scriptura*.

A third historical illustration brings us into the twenty-first century. It comes from Philip Jenkins's insightful book *The New Faces of Christianity*, about how non-Western believers have been reading the Bible. As one of his many illuminating instances, Jenkins documents a strikingly large number of settings where the familiar words of Psalm 23 have taken on fresh power in the newer Christian homelands.[35] For example, in Korea during its often-brutal occupation by Japan, the verse "though I walk through the valley of the shadow of death" (23:4 KJV) powerfully reassured many who faced prison, beatings, and family disruption for practicing their Christian faith. Among other "majority world" locations where this psalm resonates powerfully is Ghana, where the Pentecostal leader

34. For an outstanding general account of antebellum decades that is fully alert to both moral failures and moral achievements, see Daniel W. Howe, *What Hath God Wrought: The Transformation of America, 1815–1848* (New York: Oxford University Press, 2009).

35. Philip Jenkins, *The New Faces of Christianity* (New York: Oxford University Press, 2006), 147–48.

J. Kwabena Asamoah-Gyadu frequently brings healing services to a close by reciting, "Surely goodness and mercy shall follow me all the days of my life, and I will dwell in the house of the LORD forever" (23:5 KJV). During one exorcism of a woman possessed by a river goddess, Asamoah-Gyadu reports that along with hymns and prayer, a recitation of Psalm 23 became the means by which the pagan forces were calmed. In such a setting, *sola scriptura* worked as more than a metaphor, but as indeed a visibly active sword of the Spirit "against the spiritual hosts of wickedness in the heavenly places" (Eph. 6:12 RSV).

But there is also a backstory here that concerns the fuller ministry of the Rev. Asamoah-Gyadu. As it happens, he has cooperated with the Lausanne Continuing Movement to warn believers against the dangers of health-and-wealth gospels proclaimed in West Africa by new Pentecostal churches. Pastors in these churches often quote 3 John 2 (a passage about prayer for good health), Genesis 13:2 (about Abraham's wealth), and Galatians 3:14 (about the blessings of Abraham coming to the Gentiles) as biblical warrant for their popular message: trust God, bring offerings like Abraham's to the present-day manifestation of Melchizedek, and God will bless you with health and prosperity. Against this message, Asamoah-Gyadu, who is himself an advocate of Holy-Spirit religion, deploys other biblical passages, notably Psalm 23:4 ("Yea, though I walk through the valley of the shadow of death, I will fear no evil: for thou art with me; thy rod and thy staff they comfort me" KJV).[36] He wants believers to embrace a biblical picture that includes suffering with Christ as well as reigning with Christ. "The Bible only," in this majority-world cameo, is fully alive but seems to be moving at cross-purposes with itself.

Although many observers, including myself, have chronicled the wild and woolly career of Scripture in the contemporary majority world, it cannot be denied that the revolution in world Christianity that has occurred over the last century—and in no place more dramatically than in Gao Zhisheng's China or J. Kwabena Asamoah-Gyadu's Africa—owes a great deal to consciences, like Martin Luther's, becoming captive to the Word of God.

Thus, from the seventeenth, nineteenth, and twenty-first centuries, we see that *sola scriptura* has functioned powerfully, but also ambiguously. In England during the 1630s and 1640s, the tension lay between the Bible

---

36. J. Kwabena Asamoah-Gyadu, "Did Jesus Wear Designer Robes?," in *The Global Conversation for November 2009*, posted October 27, 2009, www.christianitytoday.com/globalconversation /november2009/.

as the pathway to purification and the Bible as inspiration for bloody warfare. In mid-nineteenth-century America, the tension lay between the Bible as a firm foundation for democratic civilization and a murky quicksand into which the democratic civilization of the United States nearly sank. In contemporary majority-world Christianity, the tension lies between the Bible as liberator and the Bible as a tool reoppressing those never liberated. Little wonder that those who question the coherence, wisdom, or even the possibility of *sola scriptura* have much to write about. But also little wonder that those who insist on a Protestant understanding of biblical authority are not left without historical evidence of their own.

Clarifying Questions

Historical clarification concerning the effects of *sola scriptura* is not the same as a theological apology. Clarification, in fact, must of necessity disappoint all who offer unequivocal condemnation or unequivocal commendation of the broad effects of Protestant exaltation of Scripture as supreme authority. If there is a credible historians' interpretation of *sola scriptura*, it will come in response to questions like the following:

1. Compared to what?
2. How does practice relate to theory?
3. What does it mean to follow the Bible alone?

Each of these questions leads to answers that, while not defending the concept as such, nonetheless open up historical contexts to remove at least some of the sting from indictments.

The first question is comparative. Even granting that much of the criticism of *sola scriptura* hits the mark, are there positive results of this Protestant commitment that compensate for the negative results? In particular, has the turn to *sola scriptura* created strengths in Protestant traditions that are less developed in other Christian traditions? The answer seems clearly affirmative. Protestant promotion of *sola scriptura*, along with Protestant convictions about the priesthood of all believers, has been associated with voluntaristic, democratic, antitraditional, entrepreneurial, and antiestablishmentarian culture. These traits do facilitate excesses and egregious blunders. Yet there are also positive results such as lay activism, lay ownership of Christian enterprises, great evangelistic energy, a considerable measure of lay-initiated social reform, vigorous participation in Christian worship, extraordinary opportunities for nonelites to receive theological training, skillful exploitation of popular media to communicate the Christian message, and, not least, widespread assimilation of biblical values in the lives of individual Bible readers.

To be sure, compared to Protestantism, Eastern Orthodoxy and Roman Catholicism are models of hermeneutical restraint. As defined by the official standards of these communions, Orthodoxy and Catholicism are clearly ahead of Protestants with doctrinal teaching that in principle is secure, authority that in principle is responsible, and Christian practices that are keyed directly to theological foundations.

On other matters, however, Protestants have been ahead. Compared to the Orthodox, Protestants have been far less beset by linguistic, nationalistic, and stultifying traditional constraints. Compared to both Orthodox and Catholics, Protestants in recent centuries have suffered much less from intramural struggles for political power, the abuse of clerical status and authority, lay passivity, religious nominalism defined by tribal loyalty, and the antinomian combination of ritual observance and personal dissipation.

Comparison with other lived realities, rather than hypothetical standards of perfection, is the key. While the Protestant idea of *sola scriptura* may have been scandalous in ways that other Christian traditions are not, in other dimensions of Christian existence those traditions compare poorly with Protestants.

The relation of *sola scriptura* to music and the visual arts deserves special mention, with comparison again important. On one hand, Ulrich Zwingli's Zurich banished instrumental music from church, and the entire Reformed tradition restricted hymn singing to versified psalms. Both of these are well-known instances where *sola scriptura* stifled artistic expression. Because these communities could not find explicit scriptural warrant for elaborated music in church, it was banned. Even more, the musical pabulum and crude pictorial imagery that have enthralled Protestant assemblies across the centuries and down to the present are not entirely the product of *sola scriptura*, but simple biblicism has contributed a great deal to wanton artistic deprivation.

On the other hand, *sola scriptura* of the strict Reformed sort produced some surprising results. Talented musicians, with Louis Bourgeois of Geneva in the lead, did not fret at the scanty plot of musical ground left to them by the mandate to sing only the psalms: they first produced affecting melodies and then exquisite harmonies to brighten what to others has seemed an artistic prison.

Even more dramatically, the narrow Reformed view of biblical authority that prevailed in the Netherlands into the seventeenth century and beyond nurtured the cultural soil from which extraordinary painting bloomed. The personal life of Rembrandt van Rijn (1606–69) could never be an advertisement for Calvinist propriety, but his art, steeped in the biblicism of the Dutch Reformation, has astounded the world. It is not just that roughly a third of his extraordinary output was inspired by scriptural narratives, but also that the resulting images communicated such deep humanity as well as such deep (though admittedly unorthodox) faith. Kenneth Clark has underscored the idiosyncratic elements of Rembrandt's biblicism: "In the end the Bible he illustrated was *his* Bible, that part of Holy Writ which supported his own convictions, those episodes that illustrated his own feelings about human life and . . . the Divine intervention on which he depended."[37] The result of absorbing the Bible fixation of his culture was a singular creative process. Rembrandt "began . . . with the biblical text," as one student has observed. "As he did so, he began entering the biblical world in ways that made that world a part of his experience. . . . His own world, as he worked, became entwined with the biblical world to such an extent that the gulf between the two often became blurred."[38] In short, works like *Belshazzar's Feast, Storm on the Sea of Galilee, The Prodigal Son*, or several depictions of the supper at Emmaus are unimaginable apart from a nurturing culture committed to *sola scriptura*.

Just as noteworthy were musical developments in Lutheran Europe, where a milder understanding of *sola scriptura* obtained. A summary by Felipe Fernández-Armesto and Derek Wilson includes Germany's great musical gift to England as well: "In the hands of such composers as Schütz, Bach, and Handel the full emotional impact of German and English Bible passages was driven home."[39] Where Calvinists tried to find in the Bible specific guidance for all of life, Lutherans understood *sola scriptura* to mean that nothing should be allowed that contradicted the Scriptures. With this latitude, music, beginning with Martin Luther himself, became an unusually effective means of community identity, personal encouragement, ecclesiastical survival, and artistic creativity. Luther's own hymns—ranging from loose biblical paraphrases ("A Mighty Fortress Is Our God") to translations of medieval standards ("All

37. Kenneth Clark, "Rembrandt and the Bible," in *An Introduction to Rembrandt*, by Kenneth Clark and Linda A. Stone-Ferrier (Norwalk, CT: Easton Press, 1978), 117, as quoted by John I. Durham, *The Biblical Rembrandt: Human Painter in a Landscape of Faith* (Macon, GA: Mercer University Press, 2004), 58.

38. Durham, *Biblical Rembrandt*, 84–85.

39. Felipe Fernández-Armesto and Derek Wilson, *Reformations: A Radical Interpretation of Christianity and the World, 1500–2000* (New York: Scribner, 1997), 44.

Praise to Thee, Eternal God") and meditations on themes of Christian redemption ("Christ Jesus Lay in Death's Strong Bonds")—inspired the generations that followed.

As Christopher Boyd Brown has suggested, Lutheran hymnody may have done more than any other single factor to preserve the tradition through decades of military defeat and political reversals.[40] The tradition consistently produced sturdy authors—with hymns particularly notable during the Thirty Years' War from the likes of Paul Gerhardt and Johann Hermann—and musicians of world historical importance like Johann Crüger, Hans Leo Hassler, and eventually Johann Sebastian Bach.

If Rembrandt represented singular mastery in his medium, Bach (1685–1750) became what Pablo Casals once called "The God of Music," owing considerably to a parallel immersion in the Scriptures.[41] Bach followed a Lutheran course as he brought an internalized biblical consciousness especially to his cantata and oratorio compositions. The result was breathtaking emotional range, yet all dependent on scriptural themes or even specific texts from the weekly lectionary. Week after week it proceeded, as can be illustrated randomly: John 3:16 (BWV 68, *Also hat Gott die Welt geliebt*), Psalm 19:1 (BWV 76, *Die Himmel erzählen die Ehre Gottes*), Psalm 84:11 (BWV 79, *Gott der Herr ist Sonn und Schild*), among many more others. Martin Geck once made this comparison of what he called the "huge" difference between Brahms's onetime compilation from Luther's Bible for his *Deutsches Requiem* and Bach's decades-long biblical engagement: "Bach did not use the words of the Bible just for a few oratorical works but Sunday after Sunday, year in, year out, [he] set to music its rhymed paraphrases with the utmost emphasis and unfailing energy: that was not craft or aestheticism but credo."[42]

That credo included a Lutheran embrace of *sola scriptura*. More generally, for questions about Protestants and the arts, it is not necessary to claim too much. Catholic, Orthodox, and secular motives have also inspired ever-memorable artistic developments. It is rather to point out the obvious: some of the monuments of Western culture owe a very great deal to Protestant exaltation of the Scriptures.

---

40. Christopher Boyd Brown, *Singing the Gospel: Lutheran Hymns and the Success of the Reformation* (Cambridge, MA: Harvard University Press, 2005).

41. Casals as heard on *The Joy of Bach*, narrated by Brian Blessed (Vision Video, 1978).

42. Martin Geck, *Johann Sebastian Bach: Life and Work*, trans. John Hargraves (2000; New York: Harcourt, 2006), 654. BWV = *Bach-Werke-Verzeichnis*, a thematic catalog of Bach's works, by Wolfgang Schmieder (Leipzig: Breitkopf & Härtel, 1950, and later editions).

A second question asks whether the individualistic fragmentation that critics see as arising from *sola scriptura* has been as bad in practice as the concept seems to suggest in theory. To be sure, Protestants have not enjoyed formal organizational unity that could discipline wild, woolly, and capricious uses of Scripture. Even without organizational unity, however, and even conceding much to those who have criticized *sola scriptura*, the history of Protestantism reveals a surprising amount of Bible-oriented cooperation, Bible-inspired harmony, Bible-derived agreement, and Bible-grounded solidarity.

Protestant convergence can be illustrated with many historical examples. Perhaps most impressive is the wide popularity of the best classic hymns, almost all of which are solidly grounded in Scripture either directly or indirectly and have attracted appreciative singers far beyond the denominational boundaries of their authors. As only one instance, in the eighteenth century Isaac Watts (a moderate Calvinist) and Charles Wesley (a not-so-moderate Arminian) may have embraced particularistic theologies that excluded other Protestants, but their hymns have worked powerfully in the opposite direction. Another example is the biblical effort and ability of individual Protestant preachers and authors to appeal to Christian audiences extending well beyond even Protestant boundaries: in only the English-speaking world, these include John Foxe, John Bunyan, George Herbert, Jonathan Edwards, Charles Finney, Harriet Beecher Stowe, D. L. Moody, Charles Haddon Spurgeon, Billy Graham, John Stott, and Marilynne Robinson. That contradictions are found among the work of such individuals may be less important than the overlapping circles of appreciation that have greeted their efforts. Still another example is the international events and organizations that, if they fall far short of neat organizational unity, nonetheless indicate a large measure of agreement at some significant level concerning what the Bible teaches. Instances include the nineteenth-century Evangelical Alliance, the 1910 Edinburgh World Missionary Conference, Faith and Order, the Oxford Movement, the World Council of Churches, and the Lausanne Congress on World Evangelization.

No one can deny that Protestants have been fragmented. It is also true, however, that this fragmentation may not have been as thorough as the individualistic implications of *sola scriptura* might suggest.

A third question about what it means to follow "the Bible only" requires attending to the actual experience of Protestants with the Scriptures. Here it is important to discriminate among at least four levels at which Protestants have put the Bible to use. Once these levels are distinguished, investigation becomes more complicated but also more useful. Following the lead of Vincent Wimbush, Olaudah Equiano's experience can usefully illustrate each level:

- *sola scriptura* as a message of hope, liberation, and salvation to groups or individuals: Equiano was born again and set on a path of purposeful living as a scriptural message of salvation reshaped the core of his being.
- *sola scriptura* as a guide for individuals and groups to define what it means to pursue godliness: Equiano followed his understanding of Scripture to live what he considered a holy life and to challenge what he saw as the abuse of Scripture to defend slavery.
- *sola scriptura* as a systematized blueprint for specific Protestant organizations: Equiano experienced difficulty finding support for his labors from most of the Protestant churches and denominations of his era who defined themes as following the Bible alone.
- *sola scriptura* as an enforced standard for confessional Protestant nations or entrenched social practices in Protestant parts of the world: Equiano, as Wimbush suggests, certainly suffered as an African because of how Scripture had been deployed to buttress coercive aspects of the eighteenth-century British Empire.

Picking apart the different levels at which *sola scriptura* has operated—as a message of redemption, a guide to life, an organizational blueprint, and a confessional standard—makes summary judgments about the concept much more difficult. Yet such discriminations are imperative to make nuanced interpretations for the historical career of *sola scriptura*. If we ask William Chillingworth, Olaudah Equiano, Robert Baird, or J. Kwabena Asamoah-Gyadu what that slogan means, we receive a host of answers.

In the welter of such answers lie fruitful prompts to interconfessional discussion and broader considerations of Western civilization as a whole. Yes, Protestant notions of *sola scriptura* have often run amok; they have often led to doctrinal strife and have exacerbated social disorder. But Protestant reliance on the Bible alone has also played a substantial role in the encouragement of oppressed peoples, the inspiration of world-class art and music, the stimulation of social reforms, and the deepening of lay Christian piety. A judgment of charity about *sola scriptura* does not require acceptance of the complete Protestant package. It does not mean that all Christians should be eager to follow where Martin Luther led. But it does mean recognizing that Luther blazed a trail along which God has often been honored and humankind in many places has flourished.

Judgments of charity are not the same as apologetic arguments. They do, however, deserve a prominent place at any contemporary table of inter-Christian, as well as interfaith, discussion. In the season of Protestant commemorations prompted by the five hundredth anniversary of the start of the Reformation, no Protestant principle deserves more searching scrutiny from Protestants—and more charity from non-Protestants and Protestants themselves—than the principle memorably articulated by Martin Luther when he affirmed "my conscience is captive to the Word of God."

IOAN. I.

Ioannes Euangelifta, Chrifti diuinitatis myfterium
fideliter tradens, aquilæ fpecie pingitur.

S. Joannes Euangelift / ift ins Adlers ge-
ftalt / befchreibt die heimligkeyt der Gottheyt
Chrifti.

The Apostle John, in *Biblische Figuren des Alten vnd Newen Testaments:
Gantz künstlich gerissen; Durch den weitberhümpten
Vergilium Solis zu Nürnberg,* by Virgil Solis

Chapter Two

Luther and the Gospel of John: A Wisdom of Surprise for Our Time

David F. Ford

John's Gospel is the one, fine, true, and chief gospel, and is far, far
to be preferred over the other three and placed high above them.
——Martin Luther

Introduction: A Fascinating Fruitfulness

I once spent some months working and sleeping in an utterly Lutheran
situation.[1] I was at the University of Tübingen, writing my doctorate on
Karl Barth and biblical narrative, and was attempting in a single semester
both to attend lectures and seminars and to consult all the relevant books
in that university's library that were not in the Cambridge University
Library. Early in my stay I met with Professor Eberhard Jüngel, and he
generously offered me a room in his home. It turned out to be not only
the room where he kept the whole Weimar edition of Luther's works, but
also directly beneath his study.

So there I was, surrounded by Luther as I worked and slept (from time to
time inspired by a bottle of good wine that Jüngel would occasionally hand
in to me when he visited the wine cellar next to my room), while above me
he worked on his writings and lectures. And that process was sometimes
audible. Especially on the nights before his lectures, I would often hear him
pacing up and down above me in his study as the lecture took shape into
the early hours of the morning. Then a few hours later I would turn up in
the Kupferbau, with about four or five hundred others, to hear the result: a

1. I am deeply grateful to Alan Ford, Micheal O'Siadhail, Miikka Ruokanen, Gregory Seach,
Giles Waller, and Simeon Zahl. I am also grateful to Micheal O'Siadhail for permission to quote
from his work *The Five Quintets* (Waco, TX: Baylor University Press, 2018).

virtuoso performance of high-octane Lutheran theology in eloquent German, delivered with passionate intellectual and spiritual intensity, often with touches of drama, plus humor with a strong dose of irony.

It was a strange experience, working there on Barth, who, although his Reformation sympathies were broad, yet always remained basically Calvinist. At Yale I had been introduced to Barth by Hans Frei, who had eventually become Anglican after a Quaker Sunday school in Berlin (sent there by his secular Jewish parents), a Quaker school in England, and some time in an American Protestant free church; I was being supervised for my doctorate by two other (very different) Anglicans, Stephen Sykes and Donald MacKinnon. I am an Irish Anglican, and my brother, Alan Ford, is a historian of the Reformation in Ireland. Yet in that Tübingen room's Luther-soaked atmosphere, I found myself immersed in a different stream of the Reformation, and through Jüngel a different interpretation of Barth. It was a Reformation tradition that had already gripped me through the works of Luther himself, Dietrich Bonhoeffer, Søren Kierkegaard, Paul Tillich, Rudolf Bultmann, and George Lindbeck. I had become fascinated by this tradition's richly diverse and often daring forms of theological creativity. Now Jüngel became a living example of it as he hospitably welcomed me into the small circle of his assistants that used to gather in his home.

More than four decades later, I remain fascinated and am continually amazed at the theological fruitfulness of Luther and of so many of those who have called themselves Lutheran or have been deeply influenced by him. Two activities in particular have increased my astonished appreciation.

One has been editing three editions of *The Modern Theologians*,[2] a textbook on Christian theology since 1918 from different traditions around the world. Engaging with that range of theologies (which has been one of the most educational experiences I have had as a theologian), and arriving, often very slowly, at my own discernments and judgments about them, I have repeatedly been struck by how many of those that I find most generative for the twenty-first century are Lutheran, including those already mentioned.

The other activity has been supervising doctoral work engaged with Luther and Lutherans. I have had the privilege of accompanying students, and myself being deeply affected by them, as they have been challenged, gripped, plunged into *Anfechtung*, reduced to despair, inspired, and opened up to new ways of being theologians by these texts.

---

2. The 3rd ed.: David F. Ford and Rachel Muers, *The Modern Theologians: An Introduction to Christian Theology since 1918* (Oxford: Blackwell, 2005).

Three of these students have grappled with Luther himself. One dealt with Luther on the Holy Spirit, following the controversial implications of Luther's way of relating Spirit and Word into the proto-charismatic theology of Christoph Friedrich Blumhardt ("the younger Blumhardt," 1842–1919) in the nineteenth and early twentieth centuries, on into the birth of the Pentecostal movement.[3] Another explored the relationship between Luther and tragedy, especially Greek and Shakespearean.[4] The third is still wrestling with Luther's polemical confrontation with Erasmus in *The Bondage of the Will*, and he is also currently engaged in an initiative in China that will figure later in this chapter.

Additionally, six students have focused on Bonhoeffer. This has unavoidably meant going back to Luther too and coming to terms with Bonhoeffer's great freedom with regard to Luther, a freedom both to improvise on him and to contradict him—both of which moves Luther helped to inspire in Bonhoeffer. That has proved to be an infectious freedom, encouraging students in their own thought and action to be as daring in free obedience as were Luther and Bonhoeffer.

At the five hundredth anniversary of the Reformation, the key question I want to address is the fascinating fruitfulness of Luther and of those who have been most deeply shaped by him, and how that fruitfulness might be renewed and continue to be generative in the twenty-first century. My approach to this topic, which is just one out of a great many that could be taken, will be probably the most obvious: through the fruitfulness and generativity of the Word of God. Within that vast topic, I will narrow down to Luther and the Gospel of John; and within that still very large topic, I will concentrate on a few chosen texts. Despite this narrow concentration, I will risk drawing some broad conclusions suitable for such an anniversary.

The Heidelberg Disputation: A Wisdom of Surprise and the Post-Johannine Paul

Let us start early, with the Heidelberg Disputation of April 26, 1518.[5] This captures well the initial thrust of Luther's reforming theology and,

---

3. See the published version, Simeon Zahl, *Pneumatology and Theology of the Cross in the Preaching of Christoph Friedrich Blumhardt: The Holy Spirit between Wittenberg and Azusa Street* (London: T&T Clark, 2010).

4. See the unpublished doctoral dissertation, Giles Waller, "Tragic Drama, Tragic Theory, and Martin Luther's *Theologia Crucis*" (Cambridge University, 2017).

5. All references to this text hereafter are from The Book of Concord, as available at bookofconcord.org/index.php.

as he says in his introduction to the Disputation's theses, the main biblical inspiration is the apostle Paul. Yet the Gospel of John is there too at crucial points.

I begin with three of the theses in relation to which Luther actually quotes from John. Thesis 13 declares, "Free will, after the fall, exists in name only, and as long as it does what it is able to do, it commits a mortal sin." On this Luther comments: "The first part is clear, for the will is captive and subject to sin. Not that it is nothing, but that it is not free except to do evil. According to John 8:34, 36, 'Everyone who commits sin is a slave to sin. . . . So if the Son makes you free, you will be free indeed.'"

Thesis 20 states, "He deserves to be called a theologian, however, who comprehends the visible and manifest things of God seen through suffering and the cross." After quoting Paul and Isaiah in support of this, Luther then says, "So, also, in John 14:8, where Philip spoke according to the theology of glory: 'Show us the Father.' Christ forthwith set aside his flighty thought about seeing God elsewhere and led Philip to himself, saying, 'Philip, he who has seen me has seen the Father' (John 14:9). For this reason true theology and recognition of God are in the crucified Christ, as it is also stated in John 14:6, 'No one comes to the Father, but by me.' 'I am the door' (John 10:9), and so forth."

Thesis 24 explains, "Yet that wisdom [the reference is to the wisdom discussed in previous theses, called in Thesis 22, 'That wisdom which sees the invisible things of God in works as perceived by man'] is not of itself evil, nor is the law to be evaded; but without the theology of the cross, man misuses the best in the worst manner."

Luther comments: "He, however, who has emptied himself (cf. Philippians 2:7) through suffering no longer does works but knows that God works and does all things in him. For this reason, whether God does works or not, it is all the same to him. He neither boasts if he does good works, nor is he disturbed if God does not do good works through him. He knows that it is sufficient if he suffers and is brought low by the cross in order to be annihilated all the more. It is this that Christ says in John 3:7, 'You must be born anew.' To be born anew, one must consequently first die and then be raised up with the Son of Man."

In these theses, three essential elements of Luther's position are explicitly connected with John: the complete incapacity of created human freedom to contribute to salvation; the centrality of the crucified Jesus Christ to salvation and knowledge of God, and therefore to theology; and the new life of faith as a pure gift, being born anew, being raised from death, together with the characteristically Lutheran reference to being "annihilated all the more." That set of realities, in interrelation with each other, runs through the rest of Luther's theology. They combine the logic of creation by God alone, ex nihilo, out of nothing—with the logic of resurrection, being raised from the dead by God alone, and with the logic of regeneration, new creation, new life, being born anew, freedom in Christ, received as a pure, utterly undeserved gift of God's grace alone, through faith alone, by those who are slaves of sin, dead in their sins, utterly impotent to help themselves.

Each of them—creation, resurrection, and regeneration through the crucified Jesus Christ received through faith—has the character of radical, divine surprise, of an ultimate newness, capable of being generated by God alone. Inseparable from this is the incapacity of human wisdom, human reason, and human imagination to comprehend it apart from a faith that accepts God's radical judgment on all the categories, frameworks, worldviews, theologies, and practices that do not take this set of surprises as good news, in the light of which everything else is to be rethought and reimagined.

It is no accident that Luther says in his introduction to the Heidelberg Disputation: "Distrusting completely our own wisdom, according to that counsel of the Holy Spirit, 'Do not rely on your own insight' (Proverbs 3:5), we humbly present to the judgment of all those who wish to be here these theological paradoxes, so that it may become clear whether they have been deduced well or poorly from St. Paul, the especially chosen vessel and instrument of Christ, and also from St. Augustine, his most trustworthy interpreter." That category of paradox, of inherent and intractable surprise that confounds our other categories and gives a fresh and repeatedly renewed beginning to thinking as well as living—surprise at God and God's creation, at the crucified and resurrected Jesus Christ, at grace received through faith (not just once but daily, minute by minute)—comes, I suspect, near to the heart of the astonishing generativity of Luther's own theology and the theology of those who have learned most from him. God does not cease to spring surprises in analogy with the surprises of creation, redemption, and regeneration.

One might say that for Luther the Reformation itself was such a surprise. Right to the end of his life he expresses amazement at what he has been part of. Wise faith is alert for such further surprises, acknowledging that we do not have a God's-eye view of reality, that we are not in control of it but are called to be open to its unfolding day by day, and that we must be humble enough to reread, rethink, reimagine, and wrestle with the mystery of new surprises: this God is *semper reformans*. Wise faith also

recognizes that the responses required in the present may be very different from those that seemed right in the past. One thinks of Bonhoeffer
learning from Catholic practices rejected by most of his fellow Lutherans, or deciding, in free responsibility before God and against most of his
fellow Lutherans and fellow Germans, to take on the guilt of conspiring
to kill Hitler.

I add some Johannine reflections on this Lutheran wisdom of surprise. First, Luther's Paul was always a post-Johannine Paul. His Paul
was also (explicitly in the Heidelberg Disputation) a post-Augustinian
Paul, but within the canon of Scripture for Luther the most important intertext with Paul was John. Augustine's Paul too was, of course,
post-Johannine. As Luther wrote later, "John's Gospel is the one, fine,
true, and chief gospel, and is far, far to be preferred over the other
three and placed high above them."[6] Luther is, as in the Heidelberg
Disputation, thoroughly intertextual in his engagement with Scripture
and is constantly inventive in how he brings texts into interplay. This
intertextuality is a vital source of fresh insight and improvisatory scriptural understanding. Within the New Testament, I suggest, there is
no more central or fruitful interplay in his theology than that between
the writings of Paul and John, and this is already evident in the Heidelberg Disputation. If one agrees that John is the single most influential
New Testament text in developing the doctrines of Christology and the
Trinity, then the significance of John for Luther increases still further.
Luther is also post-Nicene and post-Chalcedonian, and at the heart of
many of his theological paradoxes stands Jesus Christ as fully divine and
fully human.

Intertextuality, How to Read John, and the Lutheran *Simul*

So the contribution of Paul to Luther's theological ecology is inextricable from the contribution of John, and their interplay (itself inextricable from the almost infinitely rich interplay with all the rest of the Bible in

6. Preface to the New Testament, *LW* 35:363. The context of the quotation raises further
points: "If I had to do without one or the other—either the works or the preaching of Christ—I
would rather do without the works than without his preaching. For the works do not help me,
but his words give life, as he himself says [John 6:63]. Now John writes very little about the
works of Christ, but very much about his preaching, while the other evangelists write much
about his works and little about his preaching. Therefore John's Gospel is the one, fine, true,
and chief gospel, and is far, far to be preferred over the other three and placed high above them."

Luther's Scripture-soaked mind and imagination) is a model for reading and rereading Scripture in the Spirit. Both Paul and John are themselves richly intertextual, models for Luther of illuminating and often daring Scripture-led thinking.[7] In Johannine terms, this christologically shaped and Spirit-led intertextuality is one of the main ways through which Luther is "led into all the truth" (John 16:13). Down through the centuries Lutherans have, of course, been as prone as most of the rest of us to avoid the challenge of this intertextual improvisation; they have often been content to repeat what Luther said (frequently in formidably learned doctrinal tomes) rather than to imitate what Luther did.

Whether or not such fresh intertextual reading and rereading in the Spirit happens has become one of my basic criteria for discerning those who have learned best from him. But Luther would, I think, be the first to say that he is not the source of this generative practice, that he has learned it from Scripture, and above all from Paul and John. During recent years, while I have been writing a theological commentary on the Gospel of John, one of my main conclusions is that that Gospel tries to teach its readers how to read itself. The case, in brief, is as follows.

If (as a good many scholars have concluded) John (whoever the author[s] or editor[s] may have been) saw "himself" as writing Scripture, then in showing how he reads his own Scriptures, he is showing us how to read his Gospel. So how does he read his Scriptures?

First, he does repeat them through quotation from time to time, but far more frequently he alludes to them, showing that he is steeped in them; and often the allusions have resonances with more than one text, the products of an intertextual mind.[8]

Second, his main interpretative key is Jesus Christ and his life, death, and resurrection. John reads and rereads his Scriptures with Christ in view.

Third, he improvises in the Spirit, coming up with intertexts and interpretations that, so far as we know, no one had come up with before. In his own terms, he is being led by the Spirit into further truth. John's Prologue is a good example of this. It begins with the opening words of Genesis, "In the beginning," and then takes off into a midrashic improvisation centered on God and, inseparably, Jesus Christ. This improvisation

---

7. I once asked the New Testament scholar N. T. Wright how he thought the relationship between Paul and John might best be understood, and he said, "Through their ways of interpreting their shared Scriptures."

8. See David F. Ford, "Meeting Nicodemus: A Case Study in Daring Theological Interpretation," *Scottish Journal of Theology* 66, no. 1 (2013): 2–6.

includes such theological surprises as "the Word was God" and "the Word became flesh," and these are set in a dense web of intertextual echoes of Pentateuch, Prophets, Psalms, and Wisdom literature.

Fourth, how then does John expect his readers to read his text? The answer, I think, is to read intertextually, centered "in Christ" and as part of the Christian community with which John identifies in the "we" of the Prologue, and daring to improvise on John in the Spirit, free to come up with surprises not there in John.[9]

This, I suggest, is what Luther learns from John (as well as from other biblical authors). He does not just repeat what John said but does what John did, by thinking intertextually, christocentrically, and pneumatologically. His performance has inspired many others to do likewise.

Kierkegaard is a good student of Luther in this respect. His writings are full of biblical allusions, often not noticed by his commentators, and his distinctive thinking is deeply indebted to his Scripture-soaked imagination.

I think too of the remarkable close reading of Hegel's *Phenomenology of Spirit* by Nicholas Adams, which shows how unexpectedly steeped in Scripture, and especially in the Gospel of John, that Lutheran philosopher is, with implications for understanding the biblical resonances of German idealism far beyond Hegel.[10]

In our own time, there is Eberhard Jüngel's magnum opus, *God as the Mystery of the World*,[11] whose reception has been so disappointingly slow: perhaps, like Bach, Kierkegaard, and even Bonhoeffer, the challenge, depth, and originality are such that it can be received only after a lengthy breathing space, as if it requires a gathering of courage to attempt to do justice to it—or perhaps better, requiring the arrival of its opportune moment[12] or its prophetic interpreter,[13] when its worth can be grasped.

---

9. Cf. Richard Hays, *Echoes of Scripture in the Gospels* (Waco, TX: Baylor University Press, 2016), part 4; and on Hays, see David F. Ford, "Reading Backwards, Reading Forwards, and Abiding: Reading John in the Spirit Now," *Journal of Theological Interpretation* 11, no. 1 (Spring 2017): 69–84.

10. Nicholas Adams, *Eclipse of Grace: Divine and Human Action in Hegel* (Oxford: Wiley-Blackwell, 2013).

11. Eberhard Jüngel, *God as the Mystery of the World: On the Foundation of the Theology of the Crucified in the Dispute between Theism and Atheism* (Edinburgh: T&T Clark, 1983).

12. Think of the twentieth century's communist and fascist totalitarianisms, which were the occasion for the profundity of the mid-nineteenth-century Kierkegaard being recovered at an opportune time.

13. Think of the long labor of Eberhard Bethge to recover Bonhoeffer from a variety of far less thorough and profound interpreters.

Jüngel's work is intertextual in multiple ways and has rich, perceptive appropriations of both Luther and Lutherans, especially Hegel, Bonhoeffer, and Bultmann. But fundamental to it and pervading it is the sustained simultaneity in his thinking of the Johannine (signaled by his headline text from 1 John, "God is love") and the Pauline.

That simultaneity of Johannine and Pauline thought leads from intertextuality into a further Johannine consideration, about the distinctive role of the *simul* in Luther. The one he is most famous for is *simul justus et peccator*, "at the same time righteous and a sinner," but all his paradoxes depend on the simultaneous truth of two apparently incompatible elements. Among these is the simultaneous truth of Jesus being both God and a human being, and therefore the Johannine and Chalcedonian logic of Luther's theology is central. Regarding Luther's key affirmation of a theology of the cross and rejection of a theology of glory, arising from his cross-centered understanding of glory, it is arguable that John is even more insistent than Paul in identifying the crucifixion as the hour of glorification.

Rudolf Bultmann's theology of the Gospel of John can survive generations of scholarly critique, whether of his belief in Mandaean sources or of his complicated theories of redaction, because through his existentialist conceptuality (which is far from the language of Nicaea and Chalcedon) he has grasped something at the heart of both Paul and John. The very proportions of his *Theology of the New Testament*[14] enact Luther's own preference for John and Paul, who star as Bultmann's leading theologians, while the Synoptic Gospels almost vanish. Essential to this preference is a deep, existential appropriation of the Lutheran *simul*, both in the paradoxes of Pauline justification and living in faith, and in John's realized eschatology, his irony, and above all his Christology of "I am" ("Before Abraham was, I am," John 8:58), which indicates perhaps the basic Johannine temporal simultaneity, that of Jesus Christ both with God and with all reality and history—past, present, and future. Irony is a most tantalizing *simul*, with its simultaneity of what is said with what contradicts or radically modifies the overt meaning of what is said.

It should perhaps not be surprising that my favorite engagement with irony in the Gospel of John is by a Lutheran, the Norwegian Trond Dokka, in his essay "Irony and Sectarianism in the Gospel of

14. Rudolf Bultmann, *Theology of the New Testament*, 2 vols. (New York: Charles Scribner's Sons, 1951–55).

John."[15] He combines the historical, the literary, the philosophical, and the theological in a rich blend. His discussion of irony in the story of Nicodemus in John 3 is a nuanced tour de force that does not bear summary in the space available here. What I want to draw out of it now is its achievement of reenacting the disturbing, bewildering experience of Nicodemus in his encounter with Jesus so as to unsettle contemporary readers. Dokka perceptively identifies a paradox that in my experience (and that of many readers of John down the centuries) rings true: John is simultaneously both very accessible to beginners (simple Greek, widely resonant symbolism, well-crafted scenes, and so on) and also increasingly challenging to insiders: the more one lives with this Gospel, the more unsettlingly radical its message.[16] Dokka intensifies that challenge to insiders through his reading of the Nicodemus story. His basic conceptuality of irony, metaphor, and paradox helps reveal vitally important things about John, and in particular the ongoing challenging radicality of the cross.

I have wrestled with Dokka's text more than with any other piece of secondary literature on John and am still not clear what I think about it. The main reason for this is his Lutheran insistence on living with paradox and refusing to resolve it. Among his conclusions is this one:

> My guess is that the price to be paid for the openness of the text, for its ability to initiate outsiders, has been to destabilize and confuse every inner circle as soon as it is established. And I further believe that the linguistic fluctuations of this Gospel—from mother tongue to metaphor to mother tongue and so on endlessly—would have tended to subvert all linguistically fixed marks of identity, for the group as for individuals. In this sense I regard the Gospel of John as an almost self-destructive kind of writing.[17]

15. In Johannes Nissen and Sigfred Pedersen, eds., *New Readings in John* (London: T&T Clark International, 1999), 83–107.

16. "As open and understandable as the Gospel of John is to outsiders, so difficult is it often experienced to be by insiders. The tempting explanation is that while John teaches his language to the outsider, he de-teaches insiders and confuses their metaphorical competence by time and again fetching in the normal 'outside' meaning of his words." Trond Dokka, "Irony and Sectarianism in the Gospel of John," in *New Readings in John*, ed. Johannes Nissen and Sigfred Pedersen (London: T&T Clark International, 1999), 83–107, at 104. He says later, "The cognitive movement is not a one-way spiritual metaphorization. One cannot toy or toil long with any of them [the signs stories] before seeing their double effect of creating heavenly metaphors of normal human life—and of re-creating normal human life out of the heavenly metaphors." Ibid., 106.

17. Ibid., 106.

He goes on to interpret this linguistic subversion as John's version of the *theologia crucis*, with social relations that paradoxically involve "a distancing from the world verging on the absolute, *and* a deep unity with the world, also verging on the absolute. Securely above the world and defenselessly one with it. If a community ever *lived* this, it probably did not survive very long. Were this a truly *Johannine* community, the believers most likely expected its death—without really thinking of such an outcome as sad."[18] My Anglican sensibility, together with my understanding of the Johannine community, cry out against this, and I have argued with him about it in person.[19] But the unsettledness persists, and my Anglicanism, as well as my interpretation of John, are now irrevocably post-Dokka.

On Self-Security and Nicodemus

This experience of unsettledness recalls two related theses in the Heidelberg Disputation: the eighth, on "evil self-security," and the eleventh, on the arrogance of trusting in anything other than God and on avoiding even the inclination toward placing confidence in "creatures."[20] Luther's

---

18. Ibid., 107.

19. In critique, I returned to an earlier insight from Dokka: "There appears in the Johannine universe to be a surplus of meaning, meaning which is not lexicalized in any earthly language. And this, on Johannine terms, is to be regarded as constitutive. Without it there can be no gospel and no church." Ibid., 103. Dokka's insight that John both draws in new readers and continually challenges rereaders can be less paradoxically explained by that surplus of meaning, above all represented by the Spirit that is "given without measure." If the writing is self-destructive, it is so mainly in the sense that it never lets readers rest in the position they have reached: there is always more, so that closed, secure positions are overwhelmed. That believers might have expected that the cost of being true to the gospel would be the death of their community is not, I think, very likely. John's Gospel is concerned more than any other with succession and the future flourishing of the community, however much this vine might need pruning. The Farewell Discourses talk of it being better that Jesus goes away, because then the Spirit will be given, and Jesus promises that his followers will "do greater works" than he.

20. Thesis 8: "By so much more are the works of man mortal sins when they are done without fear and in unadulterated, evil self-security.

"The inevitable deduction from the preceding thesis is clear. For where there is no fear there is no humility. Where there is no humility there is pride, and where there is pride there are the wrath and judgment of God, 'for God opposes the haughty.' Indeed, if pride would cease there would be no sin anywhere."

Thesis 11: "Arrogance cannot be avoided or true hope be present unless the judgment of condemnation is feared in every work.

"This is clear from Thesis 4. For it is impossible to trust in God unless one has despaired in all creatures and knows that nothing can profit one without God. Since there is no person who

wrestling with the question of self-security is, I think, one of his most salutary contributions to theology. He was acutely aware of the constant temptation of Christian communities and especially their theologians, including himself, to find a security that is not the paradoxical security of being so utterly without security that one cries out to God and then is granted the security of the crucified Jesus Christ.

Luther's own reading of the Nicodemus story sees him as a distinguished Jewish leader and teacher who has his security radically challenged by Jesus's demand that he be born anew. In 1538, twenty years after the Heidelberg Disputation, when Luther preaches on John 3:1–21,[21] what he says exemplifies many of the points that I have made already by using the Heidelberg Disputation as a starting point. Above all, there is still sustained amazement at the God of grace, the crucified Jesus, and the life of faith through grace. In my terms these sermons might be understood as a matured theology of divine surprise.[22]

A Nasty Surprise, and Two Responses to It: Polemics against Papists, Jews, and Turks, and a Tale of Two Lutherans

Those Nicodemus sermons are also typical of something my students over several years, when asked to read Luther on John, unfailingly noted with some shock: Luther's vehement polemics. He uses the strongest and most offensive language, led by frequent reference to the devil, to consign to literal damnation those who, in his judgment, are enemies of the cross of Jesus Christ and of the gospel of salvation by faith through grace alone. The main targets are papists (that is, Roman Catholics), Jews, and Turks (that is, Muslims), though there are others too, especially heretics, schismatics, and enthusiasts.

This is a very serious and disturbing aspect of Luther, just as the Gospel of John's polemics against "the Jews"—as in chapter 8, where Jesus calls the Jews children of the devil—are serious and disturbing, and both have

---

has this pure hope, as we said above, and since we still place some confidence in the creature, it is clear that we must, because of impurity in all things, fear the judgment of God. Thus arrogance must be avoided, not only in the work, but in the inclination also, that is, it must displease us still to have confidence in the creature."

21. The 1538 *Sermons on the Gospel of St John Chapters 1–4* are in *LW* 22. Other sermons on John are in *LW* 25 and 69.

22. Perhaps the most intense exploration of the theme of security is in Luther's *Operationes in Psalmos*, also exemplary for its rich intertextuality, not least with both Paul and John. On this see Giles Waller, "Tragic Drama, Tragic Theory, and Martin Luther's *Theologia Crucis*" (PhD diss., Cambridge University, 2017), chap 5.

been part of an often-tragic history of reception that has included much anti-Semitism. This is one of several aspects of the Reformation that cry out for a theological response that has learned from the wisdom and para-doxes of tragedy, as well as from Paul, John, Augustine, Luther, and many others regarding the radicality and pervasiveness of sin and evil.

For now, I want to leap to recent years and tell a tale of two Lutherans who have contributed to attempts to heal parts of the tragic history with papists, Jews, and Turks (and also with others—Buddhists, Confucians, and Daoists—whom, had they been around in his time, Luther would probably also have consigned to hell).

George Lindbeck—Roman Catholics and Jews

The first Lutheran tale is of George Lindbeck, one of my own teach-ers. I think back to the mind-opening experience of taking his course on comparative dogmatics at Yale Divinity School—for example, exploring the parallels between Aquinas and Luther on hope and faith, seeing how what one said about faith often related better to what the other said about hope rather than faith, and so on. Lindbeck was immersed in the ecumeni-cal movement, was a Lutheran observer at the Second Vatican Council (1962–65), and later played an important role in writing the 1999 Joint Lutheran-Roman Catholic Declaration on Justification. As such, he con-tributed constructively to two great (and interrelated) Christian surprises of the twentieth century, ecumenism and Vatican II, both involving "papists." Both demonstrate, I think, a paradox that Lutherans should above all appreciate: while contradicting the letter of things that Luther said in his context, these two movements draw (at their best) on the resources of the Word of God to spring healing and creative surprises in later contexts.

This capacity of the Bible, to be invoked both to generate and continue a pathology and to serve as a resource in healing that same pathology, was also demonstrated by Lindbeck in his relationship with Jews and Judaism. He argued, above all from Paul, for a nonsupersessionist understanding of Christianity that contradicts much that Luther says or implies.

I was present in 1997 when Lindbeck addressed a conference of nearly a hundred Jewish text scholars, philosophers, theologians, and other academics at Drew University (including three Christians—Lindbeck, Daniel W. Hardy, and myself). We were gathered under the auspices of a group called Textual Reasoning, which had been meeting as a fringe event at the American Academy of Religion since the early 1990s. Tex-tual reasoners, who came from a range of traditions within Judaism, had developed an intertextual practice, inspired by Jewish rabbinic *chavruta* study, of intensive discussion around texts from Scripture, Talmud, and modern philosophy in interplay with each other. The embracing concern was to rethink Judaism in the aftermath of the Holocaust, the foundation of the State of Israel, and other religious and political developments. What Lindbeck pointed out was that Textual Reasoning had quite independently developed a Jewish approach analogous to Vatican II, combining three elements: intensive rereading of classic sources, critical and constructive responses to modernity and the contemporary situation, and openness to engagement across deep differences.

Lindbeck also said that he thought the Roman Catholic Church at that time (in the late 1990s) needed to examine the practice of Textual Reasoning and relearn what, from his experience in Rome as a participant, he identified as the secret at the heart of how traditional sources, contemporary realities, and conversation across differences came together to produce the remarkable documents of Vatican II. This was the process that the bishops and their scholarly and theological advisers developed, involving continual study and conversation around texts in larger and smaller groups, learning together "skills of interpretation, argument, deliberation, and application; combining historical-critical study and 'spiritual reading'; and, through all this, building a community within which bishops could become convinced of conclusions they would not have imagined coming to in advance"[23]—in other words, the surprising conclusions of the Second Vatican Council. But, he said,

> With the disbandment of the Council, there were no environments in which its reading practices could propagate. . . . Those skills were present in abundance, but their existence as identifiable, rule-governed, and deliberately transmissible behaviour was unknown. Not even an apprentice system was envisioned, and the spontaneous growth of textual reasoning in our society such as occurred at Vatican II is even more unthinkable now than forty years ago. It is only efforts such as those that convened the conference at Drew that give hope for the future. The results of these efforts are so far quantitatively unimpressive, but the qualitative progress has been

---

23. David F. Ford and Frances Clemson, eds., *Interreligious Reading after Vatican II: Scriptural Reasoning, Comparative Theology and Receptive Ecumenism* (Oxford: Wiley Blackwell, 2013), 95–96; a fuller account of Vatican II, Textual Reasoning, and their relationship to Scriptural Reasoning is given there.

immense . . . [in helping to] retrieve and improve the tradition-and-community restoring and reforming habits of thought and discourse that our society and religious bodies badly need.[24]

Even as Lindbeck voiced his pessimistic view of the future of this generative reading practice, some of the Textual Reasoners had joined with some Christians (including myself), and with Muslims, to form Scriptural Reasoning, in which this *chavruta*-inspired activity takes place around texts (and sometimes commentary on texts) from the Tanakh, the Bible, and the Qur'an.[25]

24. George Lindbeck, "Progress in Textual Reasoning: From Vatican II to the Conference at Drew," in *Textual Reasonings: Jewish Philosophy and Text Study at the End of the Twentieth Century*, ed. Peter Ochs and Nancy Levene (London: SCM, 2002), 252–58, at 257–58.

25. Some of us had sat in on Textual Reasoning sessions held on the fringe of the American Academy of Religion and had been fascinated and gripped by the multiple intensities we witnessed—of scholarship, and of textual, philosophical, theological, religious, and even ad hominem argument—to the point where I used to wonder whether the participants' relationships could stand it; but also appreciate the hilarious humor. Scriptural Reasoning takes further the potential of Textual Reasoning for conversation across differences, while continuing its wisdom-seeking rereading of classic texts and its engagement with modernity and contemporary issues. In David F. Ford, "Scriptural Reasoning and the Legacy of Vatican II: Their Mutual Engagement and Significance," in *Interreligious Reading after Vatican II: Scriptural Reasoning, Comparative Theology and Receptive Ecumenism*, ed. David F. Ford and Frances Clemson (Oxford: Wiley Blackwell, 2013), 93–119, I give an account of some other Scriptural Reasoning-related events besides the Drew conference, including the Princeton Center of Theological Inquiry 2003–6 project on Scriptural Reasoning involving Jewish, Muslim, and Christian scholars, philosophers, and theologians, who produced the book edited by Peter Ochs and William Stacy Johnson, *Crisis, Call, and Leadership in the Abrahamic Traditions* (New York: Palgrave Macmillan, 2009); the 2009 conference of the European Society for Intercultural Theology and Interreligious Studies at the University of Salzburg, Austria, on the theme of interreligious hermeneutics in a pluralistic Europe, which brought together Scriptural Reasoning and comparative theology (see esp. Nicholas Adams, "Scriptural Reasoning and Interfaith Hermeneutics," in *Interreligious Hermeneutics in Pluralistic Europe: Between Texts and People*, ed. David Cheetham, Ulrich Winkler, Oddbjørn Leirvik, and Judith Gruber [Amsterdam: Rodopi, 2011], 59–78); and the development of six-text Scriptural Reasoning in China through the Institute of Comparative Scripture and Interreligious Dialogue in Minzu University, Beijing. There have been many other developments in Scriptural Reasoning, including the online *Journal of Scriptural Reasoning*; incorporation into the program of the American Academy of Religion (AAR); the first graduate programs in Scriptural Reasoning at the University of Virginia; the introduction of Scriptural Reasoning to other academic institutions on four continents; the spread of Scriptural Reasoning to settings beyond the academy, including schools and prisons in the UK, hospitals in Israel and the Palestinian territories, and local synagogues, churches, and mosques in many countries; civil society initiatives; applications in leadership training and peacebuilding; and Rose Castle in Cumbria, under the Rose Castle Foundation, becoming the UK hub and the home of the www.scripturalreasoning.org Web site.

I have written a good deal about Scriptural Reasoning,[26] but for now I want simply to sum up my experience of it as a practice that among diverse faith traditions can enable the sort of surprising, transformative engagements that Vatican II exemplifies. At its best, Scriptural Reasoning can be a catalyst for multiple deepenings with accompanying surprises: deeper engagement both with one's own texts and with those of the other participants; deeper, joint commitment to the richer understanding and common good of our shared world; deeper appreciation of both agreements and disagreements—and in particular, in a context of unavoidable long-term disagreement on fundamental matters among religious people, improving the quality of our disagreements (in other words, disagreements without Luther-like polemics or worse); and finally, deepening the unusual sort of community shaped by coming together with those who are open to the other deepenings.

Miikka Ruokanen—Muslims, Buddhists, Confucians, and Daoists

The second Lutheran tale is about Scriptural Reasoning now in China. Miikka Ruokanen, professor of systematic theology at the University of Helsinki, is helping to lead a Scriptural Reasoning initiative involving Chinese universities and seminaries, while using some of his time in writing a Cambridge University doctoral dissertation (his second) on Luther's *The Bondage of the Will*. This is Scriptural Reasoning Chinese-style, with six texts on the table, from Judaism, Christianity, Islam, Buddhism, Confucianism, and Daoism. Several aspects of this are surprising.

First, there is the practice of sustained, intensive, and probably unprecedented intertextuality among those six traditions. Second, since there is relatively little interfaith engagement in China, the very fact that it happens is remarkable, especially as it involves state-funded universities and even the foundation of the state-funded Institute for Comparative Scripture and Interreligious Dialogue at Minzu University, Beijing. In addition, that institute's terms of reference make clear that it goes beyond the usual Chinese constriction of the university study of religion to "religious

26. Especially chap. 8 in Ford and Clemson, *Interreligious Reading after Vatican II*; David F. Ford, *Christian Wisdom: Desiring God and Learning in Love* (Cambridge: Cambridge University Press, 2007), chap. 8; Ford, "An Inter-Faith Wisdom: Scriptural Reasoning between Jews, Christians and Muslims," *Modern Theology* 22, no. 3 (July 2006): 345–66; and Ford, *The Future of Christian Theology* (Oxford: Wiley-Blackwell, 2011), chap. 7 on "Inter-Faith Blessing."

studies." In Scriptural Reasoning, students and academics can be explicitly committed participants in the religious communities whose texts are being studied. And there is much else remarkable about this development. But the leading question for now is this: why might a Lutheran theologian find so congenial this constructive, nonpolemical engagement with the modern successors of Luther's "Turks" as well as with others who would have been likely to suffer his polemical condemnation if they had figured within his horizon?

Guided by Professor Ruokanen, I would say that, besides the utterly crucial openness to divine surprise, key elements that resonate especially deeply with Luther and Lutherans include the following:

- the intensive intertextuality, in which multiple scriptures are simultaneously in interplay
- the freedom to follow conscience and the imperatives of love, even when these lead into surprising practices,[27] and an associated emphasis on the importance of experience
- the close association between Word and Spirit—as Professor Ruokanen says, "In Luther's theology, John 6:63 is crucially important: 'The words which I have spoken to you are Spirit and are life'"
- a trust in the clarity[28] as well as the generativity of the Word of God

27. Professor Ruokanen writes: "Moreover, another reason for the generativity [of Lutheran theology] could be Luther's emphasis on natural moral law in ethical issues. When the Calvinists look to Scripture for detailed instructions for Christian behaviour and general ethics, Lutherans trust in the God-given conscience where the Creator has engraved the principles of his law: Golden Rule, 'Love your neighbor. . . .' So there is more free consideration and choice in ethical decisions, morality is more flexible than in other brands of Protestantism." Personal communication, March 2017.

28. Professor Ruokanen writes:

Luther fully trusts the "external clarity" (*claritas externa*) of Scripture. The texts are clear and simple enough that the principal content of the text and the main intention of the writers can be easily comprehended by ordinary readers. Moreover, Luther also sticks to the "internal clarity" (*claritas interna*) of Scriptural texts: God's Holy Spirit assures the reader of the divine truth of the Gospel—"the divinely inspired doctrine"—which through the Holy Spirit was given to and transmitted through the prophetic and apostolic authors of Scripture. In Scripture, the "prophetic and apostolic doctrine, inspired by the Holy Spirit," can be understood as [meaning that] the same Holy Spirit who gave the message to the original writers will also enlighten the minds of its readers at any time. (Personal communication, March 2017)

Professor Ruokanen sums up the affinity:

> If we follow Luther's extremely keen attachment to Scripture as God's word and as Christological and pneumatological means of grace, Scriptural Reasoning becomes a very serious matter for us. If we believe in the clarity, *autopistia*, efficacy, and even the sacramental nature of God's word, we can assume that sharing biblical texts with representatives of other faith traditions will challenge them in a powerful way. Although Scriptural Reasoning is not a method of mission or evangelism, it does not leave the participants neutral in matters of truth claims. This, of course, is our Christian stance, but perhaps the followers of other faiths might have their own somewhat similar views.
>
> According to our experiences in China, participation in Scriptural Reasoning helps the participants both more clearly to articulate their own faith and to better understand the faith of the others. . . . In this sense, Scriptural Reasoning serves the *sola scriptura* principle and the principle of *claritas scripturae* for all participating faith traditions. Scriptures of all traditions become clarified and empowered as means of dialogue on truth. . . . Luther was through and through a man and a theologian of Scripture. Surely, he would have appreciated and promoted Scriptural Reasoning![29]

I suggest that one practical way of celebrating the five-hundredth anniversary of the Reformation is to continue to heal relations with victims of its polemics, moving on from Roman Catholics and Jews to Muslims, and further on into nonpolemical relations with other religious traditions, including those of China and India. I dare to hope that something analogous to the twentieth-century intra-Christian surprise of the ecumenical movement might be possible between religions in the twenty-first century. In historical terms, this is to hope that the lessons of the ecumenical

---

29. Personal communication, March 2017. Complementing this interfaith focus, the Chinese Scriptural Reasoning project is also concerned with the shaping of Chinese civil society, in line with my next section's concern for healthily plural civilization. Professor Ruokanen writes:

> We all know that civil society is almost nonexistent in China. As the moral credibility of Communism is declining, the ethical resources of the religions are becoming more and more relevant, they are rising up. Scriptural Reasoning would be the method of coming together and knowing and respecting each other. That could lead into concrete cooperation in social engagement, charities, etc. Civil society is a potential concept among Chinese scholars now.

movement might help different religions avoid the kind of intergroup experiences analogous to the devastating bloodletting between Catholics and Protestants that followed the Reformation. I think it is no accident that Miikka Ruokanen is a Lutheran whose writings include important work on ecumenism.

Beyond the Religions: Universities and Hope for a Healthily Plural Religious and Secular World

Professor Ruokanen's work, however, is about religions. What about the many nonreligious or even antireligious elements in our world? If our complexly plural global civilization of the twenty-first century—at once multireligious, multisecular, and with many hybrids—is to flourish, then there need to be spaces where those diverse elements engage with each other in peace.

Perhaps Luther could contribute here, too. More helpful than Luther the polemicist is Luther the teacher. He was a professor of biblical studies at the University of Wittenberg from 1511 until his death in 1546. In the centuries that followed, there was a blossoming of Reformation-inspired universities, as well as Counter-Reformation–inspired universities and secular universities.

It is no accident that Scriptural Reasoning began in universities and has now spread to many other spheres. Universities now constitute a remarkable global network of institutions that have multiplied and become increasingly important during the past century. They play a leading role in our civilization, educating most of those in positions of power and influence, and are essential to the knowledge economy, the learning society, and the information age. They engage with most contemporary discourses, disciplines, technologies, industries, professions, institutions, and spheres of life. Also, within these universities are people of all faiths and none, and as institutions some are explicitly religious, some secular, some complexly both multireligious and multisecular. They therefore have the potential to be catalysts for the sort of healthily plural civilization that our world needs.

Since the Reformation began in a university, might our universities become catalysts for a comparably transformative movement, but one that learns from the tragedies of post-Reformation conflicts and tries to model a more healthily plural, multifaith, and multisecular world? That might be an appropriate twenty-first-century challenge to those who wish to learn both positively and negatively from the Reformation.

Two Final Reflections: Passive Righteousness
and Abiding; Celebrating Bach

Zahl on Luther, Paul, and John. I have two final reflections. The first brings me back to my opening focus on Paul and John. Simeon Zahl, in his essay "What Has the 'Lutheran' Paul to Do with John? Passive Righteousness and Abiding in the Vine," writes: "My thesis is simple: that there is a surprising and generative degree of thematic and theological correlation between Luther's soteriological concept of 'passive righteousness,' which in his *magnum opus* on Galatians he describes as the key to Paul, and the concept of 'abiding'—*menein*—'in the vine' in John's Gospel." Zahl's aim is, he says, "to draw constructive theological attention to an under-recognized, biblically-grounded point of contact between the two broad soteriological approaches [of John and Paul]. In doing this, I hope to help soften in some small way the academic and theological divide between participatory and forensic approaches to salvation, creating further space for constructive dialogue on these at times bitterly contested issues."[30]

"Passive righteousness" (*iustitia passiva*) in Luther might be seen as a key concept that presupposes all three of the points I noted as specifically supported by quotations from John in the Heidelberg Disputation: the impotence of human freedom in relation to salvation; salvation through the crucified and resurrected Jesus Christ; and the salvific need to be born anew, by grace alone, through faith. Zahl confirms the main thrust of my argument that Luther is thoroughly and simultaneously both Pauline and Johannine, but he also does more than that.

In a nuanced analysis, Zahl both differentiates the Pauline and Johannine strands in Luther and shows how they are "overlapping, complementary, and mutually-reinforcing."[31] They converge in what he calls "an existence

---

30. Simeon Zahl, "What Has the 'Lutheran' Paul to Do with John? Passive Righteousness and Abiding in the Vine," in *The Vocation of Theology Today: A Festschrift for David Ford*, ed. Tom Greggs, Rachel Muers, and Simeon Zahl (Eugene, OR: Cascade Books, 2013), 61–76, at 61–63.
    31. Ibid., 72. Cf. the following:

> Part of what the vine image does is to take the "passive" element already present in *menein* and amplify it in two major ways. First, and most obviously, there is Jesus' own gloss on the image as emphasizing God's agency over and against human agency, when he interprets it as meaning that "apart from me you can do nothing," and, later in chapter 15, when he explains that "You did not choose me but I chose you. And I appointed you to go and bear fruit" (15:16). . . . The image fits beautifully with language of "participation" in God, and with the many other discussions of being "in" Christ as Christ is "in" the Father in John's Gospel. But equally, the

pregnant with creative possibility through the Spirit," one that "*simultane-ously* conveys fecundity, dynamism, and life, *and* uncompromised depen-dence on God."[32] It is an existence whose generative secret is the God who, as the Irish poet Patrick Kavanagh says, "must be allowed to surprise us." And when Zahl leaps to the creative contribution of this retrieval of Luther's post-Johannine Paul to our time, one of his points is that it enables "a certain kind of divinely-grounded freedom in relation to the world." Such freedom is, I have argued, seen in theological and philosophical forms in Kierkeg-aard, Bonhoeffer, Bultmann, Hegel, Jüngel, Dokka, Lindbeck, Ruokanen, and Zahl himself; this freedom is a sign of hope both for the twenty-first century of Christianity and for our global and plural civilization.

O'Siadhail on Bach. The concluding reflection is about how the five hundredth anniversary of the start of the Reformation can lead us to celebrate the fundamental importance of the Gospel of John for both the Lutheran Reformation and its broader implications, not least within twenty-first-century civilization. One suggestion is simply to listen to one of the great creative achievements of the post-Reformation era, Bach's *St John Passion*.[33]

Alternatively, one might celebrate the cultural impact of the Gospel of John through an appreciation of Bach in poetry that resonates with many of my points. The poetry is from the magnum opus of Micheal O'Siadhail, being published by Baylor University Press. *The Five Quintets* are five long poems on five topics—"Making" (on the arts), "Dealing" (on economics), "Steering" (on politics), "Finding" (on the sciences), and "Meaning" (on philosophy and theology). Each quintet moves from the Middle Ages through modernity and into our century. In the fifth canto of the first quintet, Bach appears in conversation with the poet. The form is a set of four sonnets with four *haiku*.

image deliberately and without qualification intensifies connotations of passivity and dependence relative to divine agency. . . . We might summarize this by saying that "abiding in the vine" describes a passive participation, while *iustitia passiva*, as a mode of living, is understood most accurately not robotically or "simply" forensically, but as implicating the whole person into a living relationship of dependence upon the agency of the Spirit, in all its creativity and fecundity. . . . Both descriptions leave the implicated person (the believer) in a state of freedom and creative expectation in relation to the world, waiting upon the activity of the Spirit. (Ibid., 69–70)

32. Ibid., 67, emphasis added.
33. I am most grateful to Professor Jeremy Begbie for the hours spent with him listening, score in front of us, to Bach's *St John Passion*, with him interpreting the music and theology of that work. See further chap. 3 below, by Jeremy Begbie.

I want to identify how this poem enhances our celebration of the Lutheran strand in the Reformation. In the first sonnet, there is appreciation of how the celebration of the generativity of the Word of God in chorales can be intensified through the creativity and freedom of music:

> Five generations so deep-rooted in
> A love of German Lutheran chorale,
> Your contrapuntal God can underpin
> With joy—"Nun freut euch, Gottes Kinder all' . . ."
> Such joy in what freewheels and intertwines;
> Incarnate heaven held between the lines.

The third sonnet celebrates how Bach both improvised on the traditions he inherited and helped to inspire much later music, such as the Romantics and jazz, in a creativity traced back to the "bursting" abundance of God:

> Motifs that flower in tunes turned inside-out,
> Traditions you transpose beyond their terms.
> Such flourishing is where all musics meet
> As in perfection futures spring alive—
> Romantics cry in moody cello suites,
> And jazz feeds Brandenburg concerto five.
> Is God's precision bursting at the seams
> In music ripe with tautly ravelled themes?

The final sonnet notes the strange neglect of Bach's music after his death: "Two centuries before my work's re-found."

But for my theme it is the second sonnet that resonates most strongly, as O'Siadhail testifies to Bach's gift for improvisation, for the paradoxical union of apparent opposites, for surprising "cascades of colour," and soaring "point and counterpoint":

> Long practice finds impromptu forms of prayer,
> As prayer in turn is processed by its form;
> A carelessness attained by years of care,
> Serenity that takes the ear by storm.
> To rid my favourite hymns of rust-like spores,
> Cascades of colour suddenly astound

In point and counterpoint as I unpod
A seed of dormant melody that soars
In ruffled blooms to coruscate around
The *cantus firmus* of capacious God.

As we enter the second half-millennium of the Reformation legacy, what further surprises might the Word of that capacious, gracious God have for us?

Third stanza of the chant "A Mighty Fortress Is Our God," by Martin Luther, before 1529. United Archives / Carl Simon / Bridgeman Images

Chapter Three

An Awkward Witness in a Worded World: Music and the Reformation

Jeremy Begbie

As far as the arts are concerned, the reputation of the Reformation is decidedly mixed. Indeed, for many it could hardly be worse.

> Protestantism—the adroit castrator
> Of art; the bitter negation
> Of song and dance and the heart's innocent joy—
> You have botched our flesh and left us only the soul's
> Terrible impotence in a warm world.[1]

It is not difficult to find evidence for R. S. Thomas's withering assessment. Few today need to be reminded of the negative intensity directed toward the arts in the sixteenth- and seventeenth-century reformations in Europe—the wholesale banishment of music from worship in many churches, the shattering of sculptures, the erasure of lavish colors in paint and glass. Fortunately, by now a growing number of writers tell a much more subtle and complex story than the kind of account many have been served up in school textbooks. These scholars point out that the opposition was rarely directed to the arts wholesale, but to the misuse of particular artistic objects and practices in the late-medieval church. They remind us of the obvious artistic wonders emerging from the Reformation

A version of this paper was delivered at the Institute for Theology, Imagination, and the Arts at the University of St Andrews in October 2017. I am very grateful for feedback and discussion on that occasion.

1. R. S. Thomas, from "The Minister," in his *Collected Poems, 1945–1990* (London: Phoenix, 1995), 54.

impulse—J. S. Bach, Rembrandt, hymn writers, woodcarvers, portrait and landscape painters, not to mention a host of literary giants.[2]

But we need to say rather more if we are to avoid painting the artistic culture of Protestantism merely as "a dark and forbidding sky" against which "occasional artistic meteors" cross.[3] As far as the arts are concerned, I am inclined to think that the most important contribution of the Reformation was the way it threw into relief the pivotal issues entailed in coming to terms with the arts theologically. This is especially evident in the case of music. The seismic upheavals beginning in the sixteenth century forced musicians and music theorists to struggle in fresh ways with theological matters of weighty and perennial importance, including the nature of the physical world as God's creation and our vocation within it. At the same time, church theologians were compelled to ask how the tumultuous eruptions on the ecclesiastical and social landscape might change the way we think about and go about the business of hearing and making music.

I turn the spotlight on one critical matter being wrestled with during this period: it concerns what happens when we, as creatures of language, encounter phenomena that are undoubtedly meaningful—coherent and intelligible—yet seem in quite fundamental ways to resist translation into language. Music is a supreme test case in this respect: here is an art form that most will agree possesses sense and communicative power, yet this sense and power do not seem to depend on the immediate presence of language, nor on many of language's most characteristic modi operandi.

This stubborn distinctiveness of music vis-à-vis language has often made it an awkward customer. Indeed, an uneasy tension between music and language has been one of the major shapers of music history in the modern West, and that tension has found its way into the church in many forms. We need only think of the anxiety that pastors often have about musicians, amounting sometimes to barely concealed jealousy. The preacher stands in the pulpit, painfully conscious of the chronically awkward choir director or worship leader below who has never read a word

---

2. See, e.g., Paul Corby Finney, ed., *Seeing beyond the Word: Visual Arts and the Calvinist Tradition* (Grand Rapids: Wm. B. Eerdmans Publishing Co., 1999); Christopher R. Joby, *Calvinism and the Arts: A Re-Assessment* (Leuven: Peeters, 2007); Arjun Gupta, *Lucas Cranach the Elder, Martin Luther, and the Art of the Reformation* (Calgary: Bayeux Arts, 2017). See the excellent and balanced treatment of many of the salient issues in Trevor A. Hart, "Protestantism and the Arts," in *The Blackwell Companion to Protestantism*, ed. Alister E. McGrath and Darren C. Marks (Oxford: Blackwell, 2006), 268–86.

3. Hart, "Protestantism and the Arts," 281.

of serious theology but who has just transported a congregation into an ecstasy of wonder, love, and praise, whereas all the preacher has is the plodding, clumsy currency of words.

The Protestant movement was of course marked by a passionate concern to recover a sense of God's direct investment in human language, supremely in the incarnation and, as a consequence of that, in the normativity of a particular collection of writings—Scripture, read and preached. Music was bound to be a troublesome presence in this worded environment, especially in worship; indeed, it was a giant fly in the liturgical ointment, since everyone knew it could speak with singular power, yet without speaking. The crucial theological questions this distinctiveness of music provoked (and still provokes), I suggest, are these: (1) Is it possible to have a theology of creation generous enough to do justice *both* to the immense capacities of language to engage fruitfully with the (human and nonhuman) world that we inhabit, *and* to the fact that this same world possesses types of order that language struggles to engage but which music seems to be able to articulate with ease? (2) Is such a theology possible while taking seriously a Reformational stress on God's appropriation of human language and on the normative role of Scripture? I explore these questions with particular reference to the writings of Martin Luther and the music of Johann Sebastian Bach.

Luther: *Musica Naturalis* and the Wordedness of the Gospel

Martin Luther (1483–1546) is well known for his musical prowess, for his passion that music be integral to the school curriculum, and perhaps most of all for his conviction that hymns and songs could and should be prime carriers of evangelical truth. Luther believed that when music is joined with a scriptural or scripturally based text for the proclamation of the gospel, it has extraordinary power to move the heart with respect to that text.[4] Luther's

---

4. Miikka E. Anttila, *Luther's Theology of Music: Spiritual Beauty and Pleasure* (Berlin: W. de Gruyter, 2013), 127–37; Christopher Boyd Brown, "Devotional Life in Hymns, Liturgy, Music, and Prayer," in *Lutheran Ecclesiastical Culture, 1550–1675*, ed. Robert Kolb (Leiden: Brill, 2008), 205–58, at 214. There has been much discussion of the extent to which Luther believed music itself could be regarded as a form of preaching. See Joyce L. Irwin, "'So Faith Comes from What Is Heard': The Relationship between Music and God's Word in the First Two Centuries of German Lutheranism," in *Resonant Witness: Essays in Theology and Music*, ed. Jeremy S. Begbie and Steven R. Guthrie (Grand Rapids: Wm. B. Eerdmans Publishing Co., 2011), 65–82; Robin A. Leaver, *Luther's Liturgical Music: Principles and Implications* (Grand Rapids: Wm. B. Eerdmans Publishing Co., 2007), 282–88.

practical commitment to music making, especially in worship, was never in doubt.[5]

Less well known are Luther's theological reflections on music. Admittedly, they come largely in brief references, scattered in multiple sources. Moreover, Luther was not a systematic thinker, in the sense of one who instinctively traces comprehensive patterns and connections in disparate data. This means we need to be careful not to project onto him inappropriate conceptual schemes. Nevertheless, when he speaks of music, some prominent accents are easily discernible. One of them gives Luther a quite distinctive flavor compared to the other Magisterial Reformers: namely, the way he appears to understand music first and foremost against the background of a doctrine of creation.[6] The background here is the venerable ancient and medieval tradition that viewed human-made music, and musical harmony in particular, as engaging with and making audible the God-given order of the cosmos (an order that embraces both human and nonhuman spheres). This tradition is rooted preeminently in the figure of Pythagoras, enters Western literature through book 10 of Plato's *Republic*, and passes into Christian music theory above all through Augustine and, later, Boethius.[7]

This vision is essentially mathematical or numerical. Being one of the "liberal arts" of the late-medieval university, music (*musica*) was usually situated in the quadrivium, as one of the four mathematical arts (the

5. The scholarly literature on Luther's approach to music is by now substantial. In addition to Anttila, *Luther's Theology of Music*, studies include Paul Nettl, *Luther and Music*, trans. Frida Best and Ralph Wood (New York: Russell & Russell, 1967); Patrice Veit, *Das Kirchenlied in der Reformation Martin Luthers: Eine thematische und semantische Untersuchung* (Stuttgart: Franz Steiner Verlag, 1986); Gracia Grindal, "Luther and the Arts: A Study in Convention," *Word and World* 3 (1983): 373–81; Carl Schalk, *Luther on Music: Paradigms of Praise* (St. Louis: Concordia Publishing House, 1988); John Barber, "Luther and Calvin on Music and Worship," *Reformed Perspective Magazine* 8, no. 26 (June 25 to July 1, 2006): 1–16; Hans Schwarz, "Martin Luther and Music," *Lutheran Theological Journal* 39, nos. 2–3 (August–December 2005): 210–17; and Dietrich Bartel, *Musica Poetica: Musical-Rhetorical Figures in German Baroque Music* (Lincoln: University of Nebraska Press, 1997), 3–9.

6. See Paul Helmer, "The Catholic Luther and Worship Music," in *The Global Luther: A Theologian for Modern Times*, ed. Christine Helmer (Minneapolis: Fortress Press, 2009), 151–72.

7. For a concise survey of this tradition from Plato to Boethius, see Wayne D. Bowman, *Philosophical Perspectives on Music* (New York: Oxford University Press, 1998), 19–68. For its appropriation in the Middle Ages, see Calvin M. Bower, "The Transmission of Ancient Music Theory into the Middle Ages," in *The Cambridge History of Western Music Theory*, ed. Thomas Christensen (Cambridge: Cambridge University Press, 2002), 136–67. See also Andrew J. Hicks, *Composing the World: Harmony in the Medieval Platonic Cosmos* (New York: Oxford University Press, 2017).

others being arithmetic, geometry, and astronomy). These were pursued alongside the trivium (grammar, rhetoric, and dialectic or logic).[8] *Musica*, strictly speaking, was a mathematical discipline that studied proportional relationships. At its best, the music we hear, sing, or play accesses and turns into sound the numerical order of the world at large. And this order in turn participates in, and in some manner grants access to, the eternal order of God the Creator.

Luther would have been familiar with this venerable stream of thought,[9] including its strongly theological versions. In his most extended essay on music, the *Preface to the Symphoniae Iucundae* (1538),[10] he unmistakably recalls it. *Musica artificialis*—composed music, of which the supreme instrument is the human voice—is to be understood in the light of *musica naturalis*: natural music, the music of the cosmos.[11] "From the beginning of the world," he says, music "has been instilled and implanted in all creatures, individually and collectively. For nothing is without sound or harmony [*numero sonoro*; sounding number]."[12] The difference between human music and birdsong, for example, is that the former has the ability to move the human heart; it has considerable affective or, more particularly, emotional power.[13]

Music making thus engages, derives from, and participates in a God-given musical matrix embedded in the created world, a world of which we as bodily creatures are part. Although this entails no denigration of language per se, Luther is clear that music does not derive from speech; he sees music as more primordial, with its own manner of operating by virtue of its embeddedness in the physical world at large.

By no means is this the only strand in Luther's theology of music, and its significance can certainly be overplayed,[14] but it does make sense of

8. For a detailed treatment, see Joseph Dyer, "The Place of Musica in Medieval Classifications of Knowledge," *Journal of Musicology* 24, no. 1 (Winter 2007): 3–71.

9. J. Andreas Loewe (Melbourne College of Divinity), "'Musica est Optimum': Martin Luther's Theory of Music," *Music and Letters* 94, no. 4 (2013): 573–605 = 1–51 online, mcd.academia.edu/loewe/Papers/1074845/Musica_est_optimum_Martin_Luthers_Theory_of_Music. See also Rebecca Wagner Oettinger, *Music as Propaganda in the German Reformation* (Aldershot: Ashgate, 2001), 41–44. Loewe argues that Luther was especially dependent on the works of the French theorist Johannes de Muris (ca. 1290–ca. 1355), as well as the late-medieval writings of Adam von Fulda, Nicolaus Wollick, and Matthäus Herbenus. Loewe, "'Musica est Optimum,'" 15–16 online.

10. Martin Luther, *Liturgy and Hymns, LW* 53:321–24.

11. Ibid., 324.

12. Ibid., 322.

13. Anttila, *Luther's Theology of Music*, 106–27.

14. Ibid., 85–86.

many of Luther's characteristic remarks on music. For example, especially prominent in Luther is a stress on music's giftedness. Before anything else, music is to be seen not as an art or science but as an unconditional gift, *donum Dei*, a capacity that God has given humans for their pleasure and delight, to enrich human life. This is Luther's commonest affirmation about music, and it is securely rooted in his doctrine of creation and in his belief in the Creator as giver. Just as the created world and its musical order are sheer gift, created wholly out of nothing as an expression of divine generosity, so the same applies to the human facility to fashion music from that order. For Luther, this entire dynamic of donation finds its supreme expression in the gospel itself, the gift of righteousness in Jesus Christ.[15]

The cosmic dimension also coheres well with Luther's conviction that music can keep disorder at bay, hold back the forces of sin and chaos. Insofar as it is grounded in the fundamental stability God has graciously given to the world, music can offer a haven of order amid a sea of confusion, playing out for us an ecology of peace that quells the unruly threat of evil.[16]

Of a piece with this is Luther's attitude to polyphony, which he sees as a sounding parable of the gospel, irrespective of the words being sung. In polyphony many voices sing simultaneously, in some versions around a central melody (the "tenor," or *cantus firmus*). John Calvin disallowed polyphony in worship because of the way it prevents a clear hearing and understanding of the text. By contrast, Luther can say: "It is most remarkable that one single voice continues to sing the tenor, while at the same time many other voices play around it, exulting and adorning it in exuberant strains and, as it were, leading it forth in a divine roundelay, so that those who are the least bit moved know nothing more amazing in this world."[17]

---

15. Mark C. Mattes, *Martin Luther's Theology of Beauty: A Reappraisal* (Grand Rapids: Baker Academic, 2017), 114–15. On music as gift, see Anttila, *Luther's Theology of Music*, 70–106. In lectures Luther delivered on Genesis, commenting on Gen. 4:21, "[Jabal's] brother's name was Jubal; he was the ancestor of all those who play the lyre and pipe," he is completely silent on the second part of the verse. Unlike many previous commentators, he does not trace music's origin to Jubal. See Leaver, *Luther's Liturgical Music*, 67–70, who explains (70): "The question of the origin of music cannot be answered simply in terms of history, chronology, or human progenitors; indeed, the question cannot be understood, let alone answered, without recourse to theology, since music per se was not invented by humans but rather created by God."

16. Leaver, *Luther's Liturgical Music*, 95–97. On this, see the illuminating article by Brian Horne, "A Civitas of Sound: On Luther and Music," *Theology* 88 (1985): 21–28.

17. Luther, *LW* 53:324.

But such music is not only a source of delight. According to Mark Mattes, in the dance of multiple voices around the *cantus firmus*, Luther sees a musical enactment of the freedom one has in Christ. While the gospel *cantus firmus* holds steady, the voices around it are surprising, unpredictable, creative: the surrounding parts are not liberated *from* the *cantus firmus*, but *by* it. Such is Christian freedom.[18]

Luther's approach to instruments in worship is also worth noting here. Given his belief that musical sound has its own integrity, even when combined with words, it is not surprising to find him much less nervous about instruments than some of those who followed him. Instruments are welcome in corporate worship. Indeed, the more the merrier: "Christian musicians should let their singing and playing to the praise of the Father of all grace sound forth with joy from their organs, symphonias, virginals, regals, and whatever other beloved instruments there are."[19]

However—and this takes us back to our main theme—it would be a mistake to read any of this as working against Luther's commitment to the normativity of Scripture or to the centrality of biblically based proclamation—in other words, to the theological priority of certain privileged uses of language.[20] The ability to perceive music as a good gift of creation, and to engage with it appropriately as embodied creatures, presupposes the faith that comes through hearing the life-changing *kerygma* of the gospel. And language, clearly, is intrinsic to that coming to faith.

This point has recently been drawn out tellingly in a study of Luther's theology of beauty by Mark Mattes.[21] He shows that in Luther's mature works, his thought on beauty is driven from first to last by a Christ-oriented soteriology, specifically by the dynamic of justification by faith, God's transforming grace, made known supremely in the verbally mediated *kerygma* of the gospel. Accordingly, God's beauty reaches its apogee in the saving mercy that God has enacted in Jesus Christ crucified. Christ's beauty is on display supremely in his compassion for the lost, his solidarity with the outcast, the miserable, and despicable. This divinely rooted beauty will not be patent to all. Far from it. It is hidden under its opposite (*sub contraria species*) and requires new eyes to see and fresh ears to hear. Christ appears ugly to those without faith—not merely in the sense that the crucified Christ is visually unattractive, but in that he is an

18. Mattes, *Luther's Theology of Beauty*, 127–28.
19. As quoted in Leaver, *Luther's Liturgical Music*, 70.
20. This has been a matter of lively discussion among Luther scholars; see Anttila, *Luther's Theology of Music*, 9–12.
21. Mattes, *Luther's Theology of Beauty*.

affront to human self-righteousness, to the fond belief that we have no need of saving, to our tendency to see ourselves as beautiful and on that basis attempt to secure some kind of standing with God. To those who insist on turning in on themselves, Christ will always be an offense, for he exposes our true ugliness.[22]

By contrast, Christ will be perceived as beautiful to those who, transformed by the gospel, see in this crucified figure none other than God meeting them in their ugliness, an overture of grace they can neither earn nor deserve. "Our beauty," Luther writes, "does not consist in our own virtues, not even the gifts we have received from God. . . . It consists in this, that if we apprehend Christ and believe in him, we are truly lovely [*vere formosi*], and Christ looks to that beauty [*decorum*] alone and at nothing besides."[23] Luther's overriding concern here, according to Mattes, is to undercut any kind of self-justification, whereby we attribute beauty as intrinsic to fallen humans, independently of Christ, and on that basis imagine we can in some way recognize and share in God's beauty.

Clearly, this conception of beauty sits uneasily alongside the more traditional medieval accounts of beauty that circle, typically, around the qualities of proportion, brightness, perfection, and eliciting pleasure on contemplation. These categories tend to recede when Luther is speaking of human beauty before God after the fall. For, as Mattes paraphrases Luther, "Christ associates with the disproportionate, the dark, and the imperfect, and he himself becomes all this ugliness."[24]

What then of human beauty before the fall and the beauty of creation at large? In this context, Luther does draw more readily on the medieval categories of proportion, brightness, and so forth.[25] But even here he appears cautious about what we read into them. Luther does not deny the intuition of beauties in creation at large, but he is anxious lest humans use these as a way of insulating themselves from the need for God's grace, to procure some standing before God apart from Christ. The hearing of the gospel confirms our intuition of creation's beauty, certainly, but more importantly witnesses to the primordial and free giving that lies behind not only the current beauty of the world but also its very coming into being. It is to this giftedness of creation that we

22. Ibid., 93–99.
23. As quoted in ibid., 98.
24. Ibid., 96.
25. Ibid., 105–11.

must be attuned before anything else. The gospel liberates us to perceive the created order as freely given and never as a mere tool for our
self-interested desire for salvation. "It is the gospel that allows sinners
to drop their guards and appreciate the wonder, mystery, and dignity of
creation *as a gift from God.*"[26]

The central point for us to carry forward here is this: although Luther
does indeed set music in a cosmological context, this never seems to
stand against, or even in tension with, his commitment to the positive
powers of human language, nor does his appreciation for the gift of
music diminish the centrality of language to the redeeming purposes
of God, to the gospel of Christ that exposes our self-righteousness and
reestablishes our standing with God. There is no retreat from Scripture and preaching. For our perception of the created world as divinely
bestowed, and our fruitful engagement with it, will ultimately depend
on hearing and being transformed by this scriptural, verbally mediated
good news. In short, for Luther it would make no sense to downplay
language in order to exalt music.

Shifts and Antagonisms

Among music theorists, the majestic cosmic vision had been pervasive for
centuries, but from the sixteenth century onward, we witness a gradual
loss of confidence in its claims, so that by the early eighteenth century it
was largely abandoned except as a literary trope. The factors at work were
many and various. Among them was the advent of the empirical study of
sound in the nascent natural sciences, which demonstrated that sounding
bodies do not wholly align with the numerical patterns believed to govern
the universe. Another factor was the growth of instrumental music and
new instruments such as the harpsichord and the modern violin. With
these developments, new types of music emerged—the violin concerto,
the keyboard solo, the concerto grosso—and these new forms proved
extremely popular. The trouble was that to play this music, the instruments had to be tuned outside the revered systems of "perfect" number.
This created a challenge for music theorists who wanted to show that
music was semantically respectable, that it could still be "meaningful"

---

26. Mattes, *Luther's Theology of Beauty*, 111, emphasis added. For Luther, "aesthetic experience
[the appreciation of beauty] takes place a posteriori to one's faith." Anttila, *Luther's Theology of
Music*, 171. Arguably, the concepts of proportion, clarity, perfection, and so forth are not so much
violated or rejected by Luther but begin to be radically reshaped by his Christ-formed soteriology.

when the older cosmic mathematics could no longer underwrite music in the way it once did. By far the commonest strategy here was to subsume music in some manner under the order of spoken and written language. Even when not tied to a text, music could be shown to operate in language-like ways, and typically this meant according to the rationality and patterns of representative language—where musical motifs and phrases are viewed as corresponding to, for example, particular affects or emotional states.[27]

In short, in the discourses surrounding music in the two centuries after Luther, a shift is discernible from a primarily *theological-cosmological* justification of music to an *anthropological* one, with an increasingly strong appeal to verbal language to ground music's power and significance. In this light, the contrast between Luther and Calvin is telling. Calvin, coming a generation after Luther, makes no reference to the cosmological tradition. The notion that music in some manner "sounds" the order of the cosmos is conspicuous by its absence. Even though Calvin would have been familiar with the literature of this stream of thought, music's power for him is accounted for solely in human terms and needs to be held in check by language: for Calvin, music in worship needed be tied directly to texts (the Psalms). In this respect, Calvin is more of an early modern than a late medieval theologian.[28]

As we might imagine, the various attempts to show that music operates in the manner of verbal language by no means satisfied everyone. And this led to all sorts of antagonisms, splits, and rivalries in the treatises of the time: between instrumental and vocal music, secular and sacred, Italian instrumental and French vocal, and so forth. The church, needless to say, was deeply implicated in these debates. In the Lutheran churches, heated and polarized disputes emerged concerning the relation of music to the cosmos, music to words, music to the passions, instrumental to vocal music, the judgment of theory to the judgment of the ear—disputes that in many ways strikingly prefigure the "worship wars" of the

---

27. The story is complex, but for a classic treatment, see John Neubauer, *The Emancipation of Music from Language: Departure from Mimesis in Eighteenth-Century Aesthetics* (New Haven, CT: Yale University Press, 1986). See also Downing A. Thomas, *Music and the Origins of Language: Theories from the French Enlightenment* (Cambridge: Cambridge University Press, 1995), chap. 1 and p. 174: "The verbal paradigm is central to eighteenth-century conceptions of music as a semiotic form."

28. For a full discussion of Calvin in this respect, see Jeremy Begbie, *Music, Modernity, and God: Essays in Listening* (Oxford: Oxford University Press, 2013), chap. 2.

contemporary church.[29] I suggest that these disputes would in many ways have puzzled Luther and, perhaps even more, J. S. Bach.

Bach's Theological Witness

There is no doubt among scholars that the composer J. S. Bach (1685–1750) stood firmly in the Lutheran tradition. His education was in Lutheran settings, a huge amount of his music was written for the Lutheran liturgies of his time, he gave formal assent to the doctrines of the Lutheran Book of Concord (1580), and he owned two sets of Luther's complete works, along with many volumes by Lutheran theologians.

My contention here will not be that Bach's theological mind and practice were in every respect confined or determined by Luther or Lutheranism: he pushed most of the envelopes of his time. Nonetheless, I will submit that much of his musical output bears witness to an imagination of music's relation to language, set within a generous vision of the created world under God, that resonates strongly with what we have discerned, albeit in a fragmentary way, in Luther.

As a point of entry, we could hardly do better than to glance at the opening movement of his Cantata 78, "Jesu, der du meine Seele," of 1724. The chorus reflects on the death of Jesus and the comfort that recalling it can bring in the midst of suffering. The sheer variety of musical styles compressed into this one piece is breathtaking:

> It is virtually impossible to imagine a grander, more comprehensive, more "universal" synthesis of historical and national styles than Bach has achieved in this movement—incorporating as it does elements of the secular as well as the sacred, the instrumental as well as the vocal; a movement whose frame of reference embraces both the Roman Catholic motet of the sixteenth century and the Lutheran chorale and whose procedures are indebted to the medieval cantus-firmus setting, the variation technique of the seventeenth-century passacaglia, and on to the modern Italian concerto and the French dance suite.[30]

29. See Joyce L. Irwin, *Neither Voice nor Heart Alone: German Lutheran Theology of Music in the Age of the Baroque* (New York: Peter Lang, 1993); Joseph Herl, *Worship Wars in Early Lutheranism* (Oxford: Oxford University Press, 2004).

30. Robert L. Marshall, *The Music of Johann Sebastian Bach: The Sources, the Style, the Significance* (New York: Schirmer, 1989), 79.

There appears to be no concern on Bach's part about exalting one style or type of music over another. And this comprehensiveness could hardly be more appropriate for the subject at hand: Christ's death extends to all times, all people, and all places. I want to suggest that this music—along with hundreds of other works—invites us to imagine a theological economy not ruled by the kind of tensions, splits, and antagonisms in early modernity of the sort we have just sketched.

To probe this a little further: what of that anthropological strand of early modernity, with its stress on music in the service of texts or, at the very least, operating in language-like ways? Is there evidence Bach thought in these terms?

In fact, Bach often employs what were then widely believed to be quasi-linguistic musical ploys. Thus in Cantata 78, for example, he uses a repeated descending bass line (the so-called *passus duriusculus*),[31] and this was stock-in-trade at the time as a symbol of lament, in the context of pain and suffering. (The text reads: "Jesus, by whom my soul, / Through your bitter death / From the devil's dark cave / And heavy affliction of the soul, / Has been forcibly torn out.")[32] Here, then, not only is music being used directly in the service of a text; it was also likely being thought of as operating in ways that suggest representative language, particular musical devices corresponding to particular affective states.

And yet alongside this anthropological aspect, or rather undergirding it, there seems to be a rather wider and indeed cosmological sensibility, one moreover that is theologically charged. There is no sign in Bach's musical practice, let alone in any of his (very few) writings, that he regarded instrumental music, music without texts, as unable to honor God in its own way, irrespective of its language-like features. In fact, just the opposite. To be sure, Bach seems to have had little time for the more arcane metaphysical and mathematical speculations of some of his musical colleagues. But there is substantial evidence that he was well acquainted with the musico-cosmological current that was still very much alive in some quarters of Lutheranism of the time, and everything suggests that he regarded music as able to glorify God without the direct mediation of words, by virtue of its distinctive *modi operandi* embedded in the God-given created order at large.[33]

---

31. The phrase translates as "a somewhat hard passage."

32. Just the same device underlies the "Crucifixus" of his *Mass in B Minor*.

33. See, e.g., John Butt, *Music Education and the Art of Performance in the German Baroque* (Cambridge: Cambridge University Press, 1994), 39–41; Christoph Wolff, *Johann Sebastian Bach:*

To press the point, we can ask: what kind of vision of the physical world at large does Bach's instrumental music invite us to conceive? Is there anything to support David Bentley Hart's extravagant (hyperbolic?) claim that "Bach's is the ultimate Christian music; it reflects as no other human artefact ever has or could the Christian vision of creation"?[34]

To begin with, we can turn the spotlight on something that Laurence Dreyfus has argued was central to Bach's art, namely, *inventio*, translated roughly as "invention."[35] The word *inventio* derives from classical rhetoric and in Bach's time was widely used as a metaphor for the basic unit of music that formed the subject matter of a piece. It could also denote the process of discovering that basic unit. The key for Bach, according to Dreyfus, was to find a generative invention, one that was capable of being developed richly, and in due course propagate an entire musical work. The business of discovering an invention was thus inextricable from thinking about its elaboration—*elaboratio*, to use the technical term. Take, for example, the fifth prelude from the first book of the forty-eight preludes and fugues, titled *Das Wohltemperirte Clavier*.

The piece begins with four notes

The Learned Musician (New York: W. W. Norton & Co., 2000), 1–11; Ruth Tatlow, *Bach's Numbers: Compositional Proportion and Significance* (Cambridge: Cambridge University Press, 2015).

34. David Bentley Hart, *The Beauty of the Infinite: The Aesthetics of Christian Truth* (Grand Rapids: Wm. B. Eerdmans Publishing Co., 2003), 283.

35. Laurence Dreyfus, *Bach and the Patterns of Invention* (Cambridge, MA: Harvard University Press, 2004).

which, it soon becomes clear, form the *invention* of the piece as a whole. If we take those four notes and flip them upside down, kicking the last note up an octave, the result is this:

If we bring these two together, the first eight notes of the piece appear:

Through processes such as these, an astonishing, continuous stream of sixteenth-notes emerges, lasting about three minutes in total—a virtuosic *elaboratio*. Bach displays an almost superhuman eye for how relatively simple sets of notes would combine and behave in various groupings in ways that would generate a sense of ever-fresh delight. It seems that Bach's contemporaries viewed *elaboratio* as among the duller tasks of composing. Not for him. "One might even be tempted to say that in Bach's works both invention and elaboration are marked by an almost equally intense mental activity. . . . In no other composer of the period does one find such a fanatical zeal directed so often toward what others considered the least interesting parts of a composition."[36]

Three comments can be made about this compositional process with a view to its theological resonances, and its resonances with a Christian doctrine of creation in particular. First, it is governed not by an external, pregiven logic but first and foremost by the musical material itself. Dreyfus demonstrates that, whatever the particular order in which Bach composed a piece, he did not typically operate with a fixed, precise, and unalterable large-scale form or mold that he then proceeded to fill in with music. Rather, he apparently searched for inventions with rich potential and accordingly found an appropriate form. A fugue, for example, was more like a texture with conventions than a PowerPoint template. Writing of the first movement of the third Brandenburg Concerto, Bettina Varwig observes: "It is . . . the kaleidoscopic display of continually

36. Ibid., 22, 24.

reformulated, ever-changing phrase segments and their myriad fragmentations and expansions that seems to govern the design of the movement, in which the instantaneous creation and fulfilment (or subversion) of expectations determine a trajectory . . . without necessarily being devised or heard against a pre-formulated template."[37]

If we allow this feature of Bach's music to provoke an imagination of the created world, it is one in which, as I have written elsewhere,

> creation is not, so to speak, a text that hides a more basic group of meanings. Rather than theological schemes in which forms are given an eternal status in God's mind, or schemes in which God initially creates ideas or forms and then subsequently creates the world, or schemes in which matter is created first and then shaped into forms, is it not more true to the biblical affirmation of the goodness and integrity of creation to affirm that it is created directly out of nothing, such that *it has its own appropriate forms*, forms that God honors and enables to flourish as intrinsic to the matter itself? . . . Creation's forms are beautiful as the forms *of its matter*.[38]

Second, we are provoked to hear, in a way that has perhaps never been surpassed, the simultaneous presence of extreme unity and extreme complexity. It is a music "both one and dense."[39] (*Elaboratio*, we recall, is no less important than the invention.) Even the resolutions in his music rarely cancel or undermine the richness that precedes them.[40] Likewise, the diverse particulars of God's creation are not merely an expansion or development of some more profound, more basic, uniform simplicity, any more than the threefoldness of God is the expression of a more fundamental singularity. And this diversity of particulars-in-unity will surely not be negated in the eschaton, but there find its full and ultimate

37. Bettina Varwig, "One More Time: J. S. Bach and Seventeenth-Century Traditions of Rhetoric," *Eighteenth-Century Music* 5, no. 2 (2008): 191.

38. Jeremy S. Begbie, "Created Beauty: The Witness of J. S. Bach," in *Resonant Witness: Conversations between Music and Theology*, ed. Jeremy S. Begbie and Steven R. Guthrie (Grand Rapids: Wm. B. Eerdmans Publishing Co., 2011), 83–108, at 100–101.

39. I owe the phrase to the poet Micheal O'Siadhail, *The Five Quintets* (Waco, TX: Baylor University Press, 2018), 46.

40. Indeed, Bach helps us perceive rich complexity in the apparently simple. In the *Goldberg Variations*, thirty variations spin out of a lyrical and stately saraband. At the very end, he asks for the opening saraband to be played again, note for note. Now we cannot hear it apart from the memory of all the variations in which it has been imagined: we hear the simple as replete with diversity.

splendor: the beauty of the new creation is not that of one note, or an endlessly repeated hymn tune (God forbid!), but an eternally proliferating counterpoint, whose elaborations are never a return to something more primal than the music itself.

Third, we are provoked to hear a combination of radical contingency and radical consistency. With almost any piece of Bach—although this is evident most of all in the solo instrumental works—the music will sound astonishingly free of necessity. (Not even a half bar of the D-major Prelude above is repeated exactly.) There is a subtle interplay of the predictable and the unpredictable, yielding a musical environment that is at once utterly convincing and delectably unforeseeable. Not only does Bach constantly adapt and reshape the forms and styles he inherits; even within the constraints he sets for himself for a piece, there is a remarkable contingency; Peter Williams even uses the word "caprice" of this aspect of the *Goldberg Variations*.[41] Tempting as it might be to say that the elaborations "organically" emerge from the inventions like plants from seeds, there is in fact rarely anything organic about Bach's music in the sense of a quasi-inevitable, smooth unfolding or expansion of an idea or motif.

Put differently, much of Bach's music sounds improvised. This was one of the dimensions of Bach that so intrigued the nineteenth-century composer and pianist Franz Liszt (1811–86), who himself transcribed and arranged many of Bach's works.[42] It also accounts for the attractiveness of Bach to many jazz musicians. (It is no accident that Bach was a famed improviser.)

The most distinguished Bach scholar in the United Kingdom, John Butt, with arias and choruses from the Bach's Passions in mind, writes, "Bach's pursuit of the idea that each invention should imply a piece of unified substance brings consequences that could not have been predicted, so that *what seems to be an enclosed world of predetermined connections can in fact imply an infinitude of possibilities.*"[43] Later he reflects: "There is something utterly radical in the way that Bach's uncompromising exploration of musical possibility opens up potentials that seem to multiply as soon as the music begins. By the joining up of the links in a seemingly closed universe of musical mechanism, a sense of infinity seems unwit-

---

41. Peter F. Williams, *Bach: The Goldberg Variations* (Cambridge: Cambridge University Press, 2001), 46.

42. Martin Zenck, "Reinterpreting Bach in the Nineteenth and Twentieth Centuries," in *The Cambridge Companion to Bach*, ed. John Butt (Cambridge: Cambridge University Press, 1997), 228.

43. John Butt, *Bach's Dialogue with Modernity: Perspectives on the Passions* (Cambridge: Cambridge University Press, 2010), 280, emphasis added.

tingly to be evoked."[44] And perhaps most significantly for our purposes, in one place Butt suggests that Bach evokes "a creative figure far more nuanced than the self-satisfied God who can sit back once the best possible of all machines has been set in temporal motion."[45]

It is surely no great stretch to correlate this perceived absence of determinism (whether mechanistic or organic) with theological accounts of the created order that take *both* God's ordering *and* God's free interaction with it seriously. So we might say, for instance, that the world's "contingent order"[46] is being "perfected" by the particularizing, proliferating ministry of the Holy Spirit, who effects faithful but unpredictable improvisations on a reconciliation already achieved in Jesus Christ. The resonances between this and what we observed in Luther's doctrine of creation are not hard to see: we recall Luther's stress on creation out of nothing, his love of the dense complexity of polyphony, and polyphony's interplay of consistency and contingency. And of course, in Bach the cruciform strand in Luther's theology of beauty comes into its own in a different but intense way through his extraordinary use of dissonance, not only in the vocal works such as the *St. Matthew Passion* (where we might expect it), but in numerous instrumental pieces as well.

My main concern here is not simply to register a series of correspondences between Luther and Bach, but to suggest that Bach conjures up a sonic imagination of the created order of the sort that is generous enough to take account *both* of the enormous powers of language to interact fruitfully with the (human and nonhuman) world that we inhabit, *and* of the fact that the created world possesses types of order not readily accessible to language yet capable of being rendered by music with singular potency. (It ought to be stressed that none of the forms of order we have just highlighted in Bach are natural to the way language operates.) Moreover, Bach does this without any sense that it needs to compromise a commitment to God's own investment in human language, of the normative role of scriptural texts. Indeed, one could argue that the imagination of the created order that emerges from this music is highly consonant with just those texts. If Bach is to be celebrated as *the* musical theologian of the Reformation, it would be highly misleading to suggest that this achievement comes at the expense of *sola scriptura*.

44. Ibid., 292.
45. Ibid., 243: here Butt has G. W. Leibniz (1646–1716) in mind.
46. Thomas F. Torrance, *Divine and Contingent Order* (Oxford: Oxford University Press, 1981).

Image title: *Pope Leo X vs. Martin Luther*, by unknown artist,
in *Des Ehrwirdigen Herrn Doctoris Martini Lutheri, gottseligen, Triumph,
und Verantwortung, wider die gottlosen Schmehschrifft, der newen Münch,
der Jesuiter, welche sie vnter dem Titel, Anatomia Lutheri, ausgesprenget haben:
Aus dem Latein in deudsche Vers durch den Poeten selbst verfasset,*
by Martin Luther and Jesuits, 1568

Chapter Four

The European Reformation: Advocacy of Education and Liberation

Michael Welker

O ver the last few years, forty-seven international Reformation scholars explored the profiles of forty-eight European Reformation cities
and their Reformers to produce a richly illustrated book under the title
Europa Reformata: European Reformation Cities and Their Reformers.[1] Many
of the insights gained are, of course, familiar, at least to many educated
Christians. But we also gained sharper and more illuminating views on
crucial issues of the Reformation. This chapter presents some of these
insights.[2]

A Revolution in Education: The Importance
of the Printing Press for the Reformation

One simply cannot overestimate the enormous cultural impact of what,
at the time, was the still relatively new technology of movable-type
printing for the success of the Reformation, especially in the production of pamphlets and books in the vernacular. Between 1518 and 1530,
no fewer than 457 printings of Luther's writings—with an overall print
run of a half million copies!—appeared in Augsburg alone.[3] Publishers
and printing shops were enormously successful in many, many cities:

---

1. Michael Welker, Michael Beintker, and Albert de Lange, eds., *Europa Reformata: European
Reformation Cities and Their Reformers* (Leipzig: Evangelische Verlagsanstalt, 2016); cf. German
ed., *Europa Reformata: Europäische Reformationsstädte und ihre Reformatoren* (Leipzig: Evangelische
Verlagsanstalt, 2016; 2nd ed. 2017).
2. Many of the following insights are drawn from my introduction to Welker, Beintker,
and Lange [hereafter WBL], *Europa Reformata*, 13–23 (in the English ed.).
3. Cf. Andreas Link, "Augsburg—Wolfgang Musculus," in WBL, *Europa Reformata*, 38.

Basel, Emden, Hamburg, Herborn, Hermannstadt (Sibiu), Kronstadt, Leiden, Nuremberg, Speyer, Stockholm, Ulm, Urach, Vienna, Worms, and others.[4]

Pamphlets, often with gripping illustrations, shook people up. Printed sermons and tractates made it possible to disseminate the Reformation message directly among the people. Catechisms summarized the most important elements of faith and were disseminated far and wide—in part even globally. Translations of the Bible into the language of the people swiftly appeared in many countries. New congregational hymns and even entire hymnals were printed.

A great number of Reformers distinguished themselves through their extraordinary rhetorical and creative talents. Several, often supported by teams of translators, produced Bible translations that in turn determinatively influenced the development of local languages: Martin Luther in Germany, William Tyndale in England, Pierre-Robert Olivétan in France, Casiodoro de Reina in Spain, the Petri brothers in Sweden, Michael Agricola in Finland, Gáspár Károli in Hungary, and Primož Truber in Slovenia. Johannes Bugenhagen's translation of the Bible into Low German provided the model for the Danish Bible. The list of such linguistically seminal accomplishments could easily go on.[5]

Improving Institutionalized Education

The enthusiasm for the Reformation was borne largely by an educated middle class with a pronounced emancipatory disposition. Yet even before the Reformation, larger towns as centers of both news and communication were already providing the backdrop for educational movements: for example, around 40 percent of the population in Nuremberg could read.[6] In some towns, circles of educated persons met who not only were attracted by the humanist ideals of Erasmus of Rotterdam but were

---

4. Thomas Kaufmann, "Die Reformation—ein historischer Überblick," in *Die Weltwirkung der Reformation: Wie der Protestantismus unsere Welt verändert hat*, ed. Udo Di Fabio and Johannes Schilling (Munich: C. H. Beck, 2017), 25–27. Thomas Maissen, *Geschichte der Frühen Neuzeit* (Munich: C. H. Beck, 2013), 22, points out that 250 places of printing in Europe already existed by 1500.

5. Cf. Thomas Söding, "Leuchtfeuer der Reformation—Luthers Bibelübersetzung," in Di Fabio and J. Schilling, *Die Weltwirkung der Reformation*, 79.

6. Berndt Hamm, "Nuremberg—Lazarus Spengler and Andreas Osiander," in WBL, *Europa Reformata*, 302.

also open to the Reformation. As the Göttingen historian Bernd Moeller put it: "Without humanism, no Reformation." These circles, often with a broad network of correspondents, both disseminated and otherwise promoted Reformation doctrine. But it was not just in larger towns that the Reformation was able to gain a foothold. Devout rulers also joined and began supporting it in their own territories. Ultimately the Reformation spread to every class in the population.

As an educational movement, the Reformation put great value in founding schools and *höhere Schulen* (schools of higher learning) and in renewing the educational system in the broader sense from the ground up. The impetus behind this extraordinary commitment was the will to promote universal access to the Bible as the Word of God and, by educating all people—not just the clergy—to promote a sound community in which human freedom could flourish. Portraits of numerous towns vividly illustrate these developments. In Schwäbisch Hall, for example, Johannes Brenz in his own writings taught that children were to be esteemed and respected, and he demanded the development of more empathetic pedagogical methods. Just as Luther himself had proposed in his publication *To the Councilors* (1524), Brenz founded German and Latin schools for both boys and girls of all classes.[7] In 1526 in Nuremberg, similarly inspired by Philipp Melanchthon, Reformers created a new type of school altogether, the *Gymnasium* (secondary school). And finally, in 1541 the Reformer Johannes Honterus founded the first humanist *Gymnasium* in southeastern Europe.[8]

In 1527 Philipp of Hesse, in Marburg, founded the first Protestant university. The *hohe Schule* in Herborn was developed as an educational institution not only for theology but also for philosophical and jurisprudential research and teaching.[9] Dynamic young scholars and erudite teachers from other European countries accepted appointments at the various universities, contributing not inconsiderably to these institutions' ability to attract students from all over Europe and enhancing their interdisciplinary renown. Through these developments, the Reformation provided an enduring source of energy and inspiration for early modern

---

7. Wolfgang Schöllkopf, "Schwäbisch Hall—Johannes Brenz," in WBL, *Europa Reformata*, 366.

8. Andreas Müller, "Kronstadt/Brașov—Johannes Honterus and Valentin Wagner," in WBL, *Europa Reformata*, 221.

9. See Wolf-Friedrich Schäufele, "Marburg—Philipp of Hesse and Adam Krafft," in WBL, *Europa Reformata*, 258; Tobias Sarx, "Herborn—Caspar Olevian," in WBL, *Europa Reformata*, 204.

universities in the fields of theology, philology, historiography, jurisprudence, and political science.

This intensified and enhanced educational climate, together with the will to support and sustain it, similarly contributed to a fortification of people's self-consciousness in the broader sense, which at least over time promoted freedom in the political sphere. Members of the clergy enthusiastically embraced the new ecclesiastical and theological freedoms. Legal scholars sensed the potential of political freedom and were keen on putting these theories into actual practice. Even the mercantile upper classes, tradesmen, and guilds participated in Reformation developments, intent in their own way to help secure and solidify these newly acquired freedoms. At the same time, such developments often served to strengthen previously existing anticlerical attitudes among the various strata of society, with the clergy's political, economic, and taxation privileges now coming under fire or being eliminated entirely. The message was clear: this yearning for a radical renewal of the church could no longer be repressed.

The new technical means of printing and disseminating ideas and the enthusiasm for education and freedom among many people do not alone, however, explain the vigor and the glory of the Reformation. Spiritual and theological messages and insights ignited the fire of the Spirit in Europe.

The Spiritual Basis of the Reformation: Trust in God and God's Revelation

The most famous and most beloved hymn of the Reformation, by Martin Luther, follows Psalm 46. One of more than seventy translations into English[10] reads:

> A mighty fortress is our God,
> a bulwark never failing;
> our helper he amid the flood
> of mortal ills prevailing.
> For still our ancient foe
> doth seek to work us woe;
> his craft and power are great,
> and armed with cruel hate,
> on earth is not his equal.

10. This translation by Frederick H. Hedge, 1853.

The Reformation message is characterized by profound trust in God—the reality of God, not just a God-thought or a God-idea or a religious feeling. God and God's might allow for fearlessness in the face of human power. The priorities and oppositions that the Reformation articulates are quite clear:

- God's word before human words, and if necessary even *against* human words!
- Biblical witnesses before human doctrines!
- God's truth before human certainties or opinions!
- Faith in redemption attained not through one's own actions but rather solely through God, against trust in indulgences and one's own works.[11]

Trust in the Mighty and Merciful Presence of Jesus Christ and His Reign

The famous Reformation hymn continues:

> Did we in our own strength confide,
> our striving would be losing,
> were not the right man on our side,
> the man of God's own choosing.
> Dost ask who that may be?
> Christ Jesus, it is he;
> Lord Sabaoth, his name,
> from age to age the same,
> and he must win the battle.

The Reformation emphasizes that God has turned compassionately toward human beings and that precisely this action on God's part is what is revealed in Jesus Christ and grasped in faith. God, God's word, and God's truth draw near to human beings, seeking to comfort, uplift, and ennoble them.

---

11. Cf. Hamm, "Nuremberg," in WBL, *Europa Reformata*, 305; and Christoph Strohm, "Heidelberg—Petrus Dathenus and Zacharias Ursinus," in WBL, *Europa Reformata*, 189–90.

- God reveals the divine self in the compassionate, suffering human being Jesus Christ, executed on the cross.
- Jesus Christ seizes his witnesses in the power of the Holy Spirit and enables them to partake in his life and authority—even against the power of pope and emperor.[12]

Sharp Reactions against the Disturbing Impacts of the Reformation

As was to be expected, especially where the Reformation did not enjoy the protection of a territorial ruler, various forms of opposition against the Reformation and its followers quickly emerged, including persecution and public executions. The Reformation movement proper was, from the very outset, also a movement of martyrs. Indeed, in some locales, especially in southern Europe (e.g., Seville, Valladolid, Venice), Protestants could sustain their faith only as "crypto-Protestants," that is, as underground Protestants, organizing themselves in secret networks.

The Reformation's stirring theological insights and life-changing energy are today associated especially with the towns of Wittenberg (Martin Luther and Philipp Melanchthon), Zurich (Ulrich Zwingli and Heinrich Bullinger), and Geneva (John Calvin and Theodor Beza), and with the developments commencing after 1517 (when Luther posted or sent out his theses in Wittenberg).

Yet more than a century earlier than the Reformation in Germany, Switzerland, and other European countries, reform initiatives and the articulation of several key Reformation insights had prompted the demand for corresponding reforms, especially in the broader sphere of the universities at Oxford (particularly from John Wycliffe) and Prague (from Jan Hus), and indeed even earlier from Petrus Waldes from Lyon and the Waldensians.[13]

Such Reformation forerunners—whom many today claim deserve more recognition for their achievements—were already emphasizing that God's grace alone constitutes the foundation of human salvation and that the status of the Holy Scriptures is higher than any church doctrine. For just that reason, they argued, not only should the Bible be

12. Cf. Michael Welker, *God the Revealed: Christology* (Grand Rapids: Wm. B. Eerdmans Publishing Co., 2013), 144–51 and 209–16.
13. See Albert de Lange, "Lyon—Waldes and Pierre Viret," in WBL, *Europa Reformata*, 246–47; Martin Ohst, "Oxford—John Wycliffe and William Tyndale," in WBL, *Europa Reformata*, 324–26; Martin Wernisch, "Prague—Jan Hus," in WBL, *Europa Reformata*, 331–34.

made accessible to *all* people, it should also be preached and its teachings communicated in every country's native language. These early reformers emphasized human maturity, human beings having come of age in spiritual matters, and they demanded that the Eucharist be distributed accordingly through the bread and wine to *all* congregants. Even before later Reformation figures, several of these reformers were publicly executed for disseminating these notions, which were indeed liberating but considered heretical.

Reformation and the Sharing of Power

Even before the Reformation, secular authorities were becoming increasingly interested in expanding their oversight and control of ecclesiastical spheres and concerns. Indeed, in some locales, councils received papal support or at least tolerance in this regard. For example, even before the Reformation, the pope had granted the council in Bern the right to appoint ecclesiastical officeholders. In many locales, politicians used Reformation successes to expand the scope of their own power. In Augsburg, for example, where 90 percent of the citizens quickly became Protestant, the town council and laypersons took over the task of appointing ecclesiastical officeholders, adjudicating disputes in matters of faith, and ensuring that sermons adhered to Scripture and had a Protestant orientation.

Some town councils, uncertain of their legal status in the empire (e.g., in Augsburg, Speyer, Worms, though also in certain Swiss towns [Zurich, Bern] and Latvia and Estonia [Riga and Reval/Tallinn]) were in some instances able, through cautious maneuvering, to promote peaceful and even bi-confessional arrangements—situations in which groups and church communities of Protestants coexisted with members of the "old faith"—sometimes even for the long term. In other places, monarchical actions unfortunately hindered the hesitating emergence of a de facto division of power between church and political authorities (as well as between legal and scholarly bodies). In Copenhagen and Stockholm, for example, the king exploited Reformation enthusiasm to rid himself of opponents among the nobility and upper citizenry, or to have himself consecrated in a quasi-religious fashion, arrogating to himself the corresponding authority.

In Lyon, Huguenots under the influence of Pierre Viret tried, through violence, to turn the town into a "second Geneva." Especially among some Roman Catholic authors, such developments fuel the view that the

Reformation utterly disempowered the church and surrendered control to political authorities. What in fact emerged, however, was a gradual process of division of power (religious, political, legal, scholarly, educational) and a commitment to an ecumenical search for truth, which turned out to be quite compatible with a more globally receptive and open piety, on one hand, and an enhanced focus on freedom and democracy, on the other.[14]

Public Theology: The Import of Sermons and Disputations

The Reformation was a "reading and preaching movement."[15] Even the worship service was now to serve spiritual, ethical, and political education. Questions of faith and ecclesiastical-political circumstances were to be stated and discussed freely and openly. Many town councils embraced the Reformation message and accordingly promoted theologically and biblically informed "sermons according to God's word." Public reaction to these developments was strong and positive.

Disputations played an important role in spreading new Reformation ideas. In this regard, Luther's famous Heidelberg Disputation of 1518 can serve as a kind of model. Through this disputation Luther, focusing intently and unswervingly on God's revelation in Jesus Christ, excited and won over numerous future Reformers. Other important disputations in the 1520s included those in Zurich, Breslau, Memmingen, Nuremberg, Hamburg, Stockholm, Bern, Flensburg, and Ulm. "In all public or semipublic disputations during the 1520s, defenders of the old faith inevitably ended up having to withdraw in defeat."[16]

Catechisms, Church Ordinances, Innovations in Ordinary Life

In many towns and cities, adoption of the Reformation was accompanied by the emergence of church ordinances and catechisms designed to provide reliable orientation in both life and doctrine. Over time, Luther's Small and Large Catechisms (1528/29), the Heidelberg Catechism (1563), and later Thomas Cranmer's Book of Common Prayer

---

14. This development is also emphasized by the sociologist Detlef Pollack, "Protestantismus und Moderne," in Di Fabio and J. Schilling, *Die Weltwirkung der Reformation*, 86–88; and the jurist Udo Di Fabio, "Die Dialektik der Neuzeit im Geist der Reformation," in Di Fabio and J. Schilling, *Die Weltwirkung der Reformation*, 150–54.

15. Cf. Hamm, "Nuremberg," in WBL, *Europa Reformata*, 305.

16. Peter Blickle, "Memmingen—Christoph Schappeler," in WBL, *Europa Reformata*, 267.

(1549) all became perennial spiritual bestsellers throughout the world. Yet even catechisms that today remain relatively unknown often exerted enormous influence. The most important of the three catechisms by Johannes Brenz from Schwäbisch Hall (1535) went through five hundred printings.

Reformers focused not merely on renewing church life and doctrine in the narrower sense, but also on improving the culture of social services and assistance, such as care for the poor, services to the ill, and care of orphans. Reformers largely transferred care for the poor from ecclesiastical to secular oversight. In Hamburg and elsewhere, a fund was established to address the needs of the poor and ill, overseen by twelve citizen "deacons." This reorganization of church institutions, school systems, and institutions of social services, including hospitals, was buoyed and sustained by a spirit of Christian fellowship. In Constance, Ambrosius Blarer drafted exemplary ordinances for reorganizing monastic life and implementing worship services commensurate with Scripture.[17] Whether through reorganization of existing structures or adoption of completely new forms, initiatives for concrete aid for the poor emerged in many locales, often as a reaction to acute crises—for example, in connection with the demise of the textile industry (Leiden, Memmingen) or after storm surges (Witmarsum).

Female Reformers, Young Theologians, and Jurists in Leadership Roles

Socially active princesses and educated women from the upper classes of the citizenry made important contributions to the Reformation. The queen of Navarre, Margarete of Angoulême, and her daughter, the duchess of Albret in the principality of Béarn (Pau), Jeanne d'Albret, promoted "simultaneous churches," that is, churches that opened Roman Catholic Church buildings to Protestant preachers. In contact with Reformers in Geneva, they assisted in reforming church institutions and the principality itself as well as in efforts to purify "Roman idol worship." In cosmopolitan Emden, Countess Anna of East Friesland appointed as senior spiritual administrator the Polish humanist and Reformation theologian Johannes à Lasco, charging him with reorganizing the entire church and its institutions in East Friesland. New synodical

---

17. Hermann Ehmer, "Constance—Ambrosius, Margarete and Thomas Blarer," in WBL, *Europa Reformata*, 113.

leadership committees were created, and in Emden itself leaders organized religious colloquies with those who still adhered to the "old faith" and with peaceable Anabaptists.

At the court of Ferrara, Renée de France promoted interest in Protestant ideas in a circle of ladies and gentlemen of the nobility. One of the most genteel families in Constance, the Blarer family, was captivated by the educational ideals of humanism and inspired by the Protestant spirit. The Blarer siblings, acquainted with both Melanchthon and Luther, endeavored not only to renew the church and school system but also to improve care for the poor. Margarete Blarer, whom no less a personage than Erasmus of Rotterdam publicly praised, began a correspondence with Martin Bucer and became personally engaged in behalf of impoverished women and orphans as well as in care for the sick.

In 1523 in Strasbourg, Katharina Zell became not only one of the first wives of Protestant clergy (marrying the preacher at the Strasbourg cathedral) but also a distinguished Reformation writer. She publicly defended the abolition of celibacy as well as the right of women to speak and play a determinative role in spiritual matters—adducing as support the biblical testimony to the effects of the Holy Spirit. She supported refugees of faith not only by providing practical assistance but also through letters of consolation and encouragement. She published a hymnal reflecting the spirituality of the Bohemian Brethren and defended peaceable Anabaptists against public persecution.[18]

The spirit of the Reformation was also characterized, finally, by the considerable influence exerted by energetic young theologians and jurists[19] who, often immediately after concluding their university studies, assumed key leadership roles in doctrinal matters, proclamation, and church administration and governance. Distinguished examples include, of course, Philipp Melanchthon and John Calvin, though also numerous other young Reformers, such as Márton Kálmáncsehi Sánta in Debrecen, Johannes Honterus and Valentin Wagner in Kronstadt, Johannes Brenz in Schwäbisch Hall, Michael Diller in Speyer, Michael Agricola in Turku, Hans Tausen in Viborg, and Ulrich Zwingli and Heinrich Bullinger in Zurich.

---

18. Matthieu Arnold, "Strasbourg—Martin Bucer and Katharina Zell," in WBL, *Europa Reformata*, 405–6.

19. See John Witte Jr., *The Reformation of Rights: Law, Religion, and Human Rights in Early Modern Calvinism* (Cambridge: Cambridge University Press, 2007), esp. 77–80, 134–41, 203–7.

European Internationality

The small town of Wittenberg became the "center of the civilized world"[20] from which a new religious culture radiated out in all directions. The just recently founded university (1502), with its renowned teachers Luther and Melanchthon, attracted more than 4,700 students from all over Europe between 1535 and 1545, making it the most populous university in the empire. Distinguished artists as well, however, especially from the school of Lucas Cranach, similarly extended the Reformation's aura far beyond Germany. Other institutions of higher learning where Reformation doctrine was represented similarly attracted students and scholars from all over Europe. Heidelberg, Marburg, Herborn, and Cambridge were especially successful in this regard.

Alongside the attraction of theological, jurisprudential, and humanist educational opportunities, however, the persecutions and resultant floods of refugees contributed to education and exchange across borders and to the increasingly international interconnectedness of life. Towns such as Emden and Frankfurt am Main, by accepting refugees from other countries, thereby enhanced their own economic and cosmopolitan aura. Students and teachers, yet also persons serving the church who had to flee their country because of issues of faith, acquired cultural and linguistic skills that similarly enabled them to pass along the new ideas in the most varied contexts. Cosmopolitan towns with long-standing local traditions and great power, such as the Republic of Venice or Edinburgh, as well as cities characterized by multiple ethnic groups, such as Kronstadt and Turku, gained new stimulation through their often-contentious exposure to the Reformation spirit, which subjected their tradition and fixed routines to constructive endurance tests.

Thematic Conflicts with the Roman Church

Not surprisingly, copious thematic issues generated conflicts between the Reformation and the Roman Church. Although many people today view the Reformation as having been initiated or set into motion by the sale of indulgences, that particular theme was but one among many. The central theme prompting this new religious embarkation was the Reformation's disagreements with regnant speculative and metaphysical

---

20. Johannes Schilling, "Wittenberg—Martin Luther and Philipp Melanchthon," in WBL, *Europa Reformata*, 467–68.

theology, which understood God as detached and abstract. Luther's Heidelberg Disputation of 1518 broke completely new ground from which to criticize a theology that did *not* grant absolutely normative status to God's revelation in Jesus Christ and to a focused orientation toward the biblical witnesses. Whereas the new theology, oriented toward Jesus Christ and Holy Scriptures, was intent on enabling all people to gain access to the sources of knowledge of God, speculative and metaphysical theology now seemed exposed as the exclusive domain of those who ruled and sought even more power. The new theology also severely called into question the dominant practice of confession as well as celibacy.

Still another controversial topic during the Reformation was the Roman church's refusal to offer the Eucharist to the congregation in its two forms (bread and wine, *sub utraque*). The Reformation objected that this position clearly contradicts the witness of Scripture. The Reformation similarly rejected other themes as being nonbiblical or as exaggerations with little or no direct biblical support, including the cult of Mary and the saints, the transmission of legends of the saints, the rosary, and the doctrine of purgatory. The movement also demanded abolition of the Latin Mass, processions, excessive imagery in churches, and the often numerous secondary altars. Such objections and disputes were often particularly vehement precisely where clerical hegemony entailed unjustified economic privilege and the obvious cultivation of a double morality. Conflicts similarly arose when inadequate leadership of the church contributed to social problems and poor educational opportunities.

The notion of the priesthood of all believers provided support for those who questioned the authority of the pope, the hierarchical organization of the clergy, and the powerful status of monasteries. Teaching and proclamation focused solely on the Holy Scriptures was to expel all obscurantism from the church. The dominance of church jurisdiction was called into question, and in many areas adjudication by secular authorities replaced canonical law and traditional dispensation of justice by the church. Many developments initiated by the Reformation anticipated that a division of power offered a more effective way of promoting individual and societal freedom; people began to see that such freedoms were best served when politics, the administration of justice, science and scholarship, and oversight of church and religious matters were not concentrated in a single entity.

Inner-Protestant Thematic Conflicts

As early as 1520, conflicts arose between Luther and the very man whom, alongside Luther, many between 1518 and 1522 considered one of the most important representatives of Wittenberg's Reformation theology, namely, Luther's own doctoral adviser, Andreas Rudolf Bodenstein, known as Karlstadt, from the Franconian town of Karlstadt. The initial issue concerned the inviolability of the biblical canon. Luther had questioned the canonical validity of the Letter of James, which in Luther's view advocated "righteousness through works." His colleague Karlstadt sensed here a threat to the authority of the Holy Scriptures. The two men also came into conflict over infant baptism and the appropriate age for baptism, as well as over the presence of Jesus Christ in the Eucharist. Karlstadt, influenced by mystical theology, emphasized more radically than Luther the maturity of the individual Christian and the authority of the congregation—even without the crucial prerequisite of education and training that was so important for Melanchthon and Luther. In his church community in Orlamünde, as "Brother Andreas," he developed a ministry that emphasized the importance of all laypersons for all ecclesial activities.[21]

These and other themes generated inner-Protestant conflicts that, along with social conflicts and the accompanying tensions, aggravated and exacerbated the contentious arguments. The dispute concerning Christ's presence in the Eucharist turned into one of the central conflicts between Lutherans and Reformed. In Marburg in 1529, after a debate that had started in 1526 and been carried on in polemic pamphlets, Philipp of Hesse tried to find a middle ground between Lutherans and Zwinglians, albeit without success. Although the Wittenberg Concord of 1536 (Bucer and Melanchthon) took an important step along this path, it was not until the Leuenberg Concord of 1973 that Protestants achieved reconciliation in this matter.

Similarly contentious conflicts arose in connection with spiritualist movements, which referenced the "inner word of the Spirit" in emphasizing the theological authority of the individual Christian (e.g., Sebastian Franck and Caspar von Schwenckfeld in Ulm) and called into question central tenets of faith (e.g., the doctrine of the Trinity and of Christ's divine nature; cf. especially the anti-Trinitarians in Venice, Poland, and

---

21. Thomas Kaufmann, "Orlamünde—Andreas Karlstadt," in WBL, *Europa Reformata*, 316.

Transylvania; and Michael Servetus in Geneva). Conflicts similarly arose over infant baptism and the baptism of adults, which not infrequently was accompanied by a willingness to undergo rebaptism as an adult. These conflicts came to a head within the framework of emancipatory and ultimately violent protest movements that also directed their anger toward oppressive economic and existential abuses and situations of acute distress. Mühlhausen, Münster, Memmingen, and other locales became centers of such radicalization.

In the spring of 1525 in Upper Swabia, in the religious center of gravity, Memmingen, commenced the largest uprising in Europe before the French Revolution of 1789. Some fifty thousand rebellious peasants demanded in "Twelve Articles" the abolition of serfdom, the right of the congregation to choose its own pastor, the replacement of the hegemony of the nobility and ecclesiastical princes by a "common government," and the implementation of other freedoms and privileges. Thousands of peasants perished in battles with troops of the nobility. The Reformation historian Heiko A. Oberman was inclined to assert that Memmingen in fact represented a "fourth center of the Reformation," alongside Wittenberg, Zurich, and Geneva.

Radical Anabaptist movements cropped up—for instance, in Münster, where the tailor Jan van Leiden had himself declared king, abolished money, imposed the death penalty on those who transgressed against the Ten Commandments, instituted polygyny, and even arrogated to himself the right to name every newborn child. While such movements remained isolated, they nonetheless damaged the reputation of the Reformation.[22] Indeed, even today the unresolved relationship between Lutherans and Anabaptists, the Reformation's failure in connection with the peasants, and the stubborn recurrence of anti-Semitism all belong to the darker side of the Reformation.

A movement markedly different from those of the violently inclined peasants and their equally violently inclined opponents is represented by the Mennonites, who even today continue to embody a rigorous and consistent theology and ethics of peace. Reformation highlights include countless other examples of nonviolent resistance and efforts on behalf of peaceful ecumenical coexistence. Many locales, after dramatic show trials, public executions and burnings, and even posthumous condemnations with public burnings of coffins (Antwerp, Augsburg, Edinburgh,

---

22. Hubertus Lutterbach, "Münster—Bernhard Rothmann, Jan Matthys and Jan van Leiden," in WBL, *Europa Reformata*, 288–89.

Ferrara, Oxford, among others), became temporary or even permanent places in which refugees of faith from many different countries could find safe harbor. Protestants in Augsburg, after their churches were confiscated following their impressive initial successes, patiently and peacefully conducted their worship services for fourteen years in the open air. Accounts from other locales similarly relate how Protestants marched "outside [the town gates] to their worship services" (thus as late as 1649 in an engraving of Hernals Castle near Vienna by Matthäus Merian). The turbulent emergence of the Reformation gave way in many countries to long periods of great hardship and suffering. For more than a century, bloody wars took the lives and homelands of millions of people. But the Reformation was also followed by long periods of patience, reconciliation, and growing cooperation—on the road to a peaceful ecumenical life enduringly inspired by the Reformation.

Historiated Title-Page Border, in *Der Stat Nurmberg verneute Reformation*,
by Nuremberg (Germany), 1564

Chapter Five

Faith in Law: The Legal and Political Legacy of the Protestant Reformations

John Witte Jr.

Introduction

The Protestant Reformation erupted with Martin Luther's posting of the Ninety-five Theses on the church door in Wittenberg in 1517 and his burning of the medieval canon lawbooks at the city gates three years later. The Reformation soon split into four main branches—Lutheranism, Anabaptism, Anglicanism, and Calvinism—with ample regional and denominational variation within each branch. Lutheranism spread throughout the northern Holy Roman Empire, Prussia, and Scandinavia and their later colonies, consolidated by Luther's catechisms and the Augsburg Confession (1530), and by local liturgical books and Bible translations. Anabaptists fanned out in small communities throughout Western and Eastern Europe, Russia, and eventually North America, most of them devoted to the founding religious principles of the Schleitheim Confession (1527). Anglicanism, established in England by King Henry VIII and Parliament in the 1530s and consolidated by the Great Bible (1539) and the Book of Common Prayer (1549/1559), spread eventually throughout the vast British Empire in North America, Africa, the Middle East, and India. Calvinist or Reformed communities, modeled on John Calvin's Geneva and anchored by the Geneva Bible and Genevan Academy, spread into portions of the Swiss Confederation, France, the Palatinate, Hungary, Poland, the Lowlands, Scotland, England, and eventually North America and southern Africa. This checkerboard of Protestant communities, living tenuously alongside each other and their Catholic neighbors, was protected for a time by the Peace of Augsburg (1555), the Union of Utrecht (1579), the Edict of Nantes (1598), the

Peace of Westphalia (1648), and other peace treaties, though religious persecution and religious warfare were tragically regular events in early modern Europe.

While new confessions, creeds, and catechisms helped to inspire and integrate these Protestant movements, it was new law that usually set them in motion and consolidated them. Hundreds of local "church ordinances" (*Kirchenordnungen*), or "legal reformations" (*Rechtsreformationen*), were issued by Lutheran German cities, duchies, and principalities after 1520 and were replicated in national church ordinances in Sweden, Denmark, Norway, Finland, and Iceland over the next half century.[1] Local Anabaptist elders issued short "church orders" to establish and govern their small, self-sufficient Anabaptist communities, many of their rules drawn directly from biblical and early apostolic teachings.[2] Parliament's Supremacy Act (1534) declared the English monarch to be "supreme head" and "defender of faith" in the freestanding Church of England (*Anglicana Ecclesiastica*).[3] Geneva's Reformation Edict (1536), modeled on similar edicts passed the decade before in Zurich, Strasbourg, and other Protestant cities, was echoed in scores of European towns and provinces and later North American colonies that accepted Reformed Protestantism.[4]

All these early Protestant legal declarations were, in part, firm rejections of the law and theology of Roman Catholicism. The Catholic Church had been the universal legal authority of the West since the twelfth century. Medieval church authorities claimed exclusive jurisdiction over doctrine, liturgy, clergy, polity, marriage, family, inheritance, trusts, education, charity, contracts, moral crimes, and more. They also claimed concurrent jurisdiction over many other legal subjects, sometimes filling gaps in local civil rules and procedures, but often rivaling local civil authorities in governing the local population. And the church had huge property holdings—more than a quarter of the land in some regions of Europe—all of which remained under exclusive church control and free from secular taxes and regulation. To exercise this power,

1. See Emil Sehling et al., eds., *Evangelischen Kirchenordnungen des XVI. Jahrhunderts*, 24 vols. (Leipzig: O. R. Reisland, 1902–13; new ed., Tübingen: Mohr, 1955–).

2. See illustrative sources in Walter Klaassen, *Anabaptism in Outline: Selected Primary Sources* (Scottdale, PA: Herald Press, 1981).

3. Collected in Carl Stephenson and Frederick G. Marcham, *Sources of English Constitutional History* (New York: Harper & Bros., 1937).

4. Émile Rivoire and Victor van Berchem, eds., *Les sources du droit du canton de Genève*, 4 vols. (Aarau: H. R. Sauerländer, 1927–35).

the medieval church developed an intricate system of canon laws promulgated by the pope, bishops, and church councils, laws enforced by a hierarchy of church courts and clerical officials under the final papal authority of Rome. A vast network of church officials, immune from secular legal control, presided over the medieval church's executive and administrative functions. The church registered its citizens through baptism. It taxed them through tithes. It conscripted them through crusades. It educated them in church schools. It nurtured them in cloisters, monasteries, chantries, hospitals, and guilds. It cared for them and their families even after death through perpetual obits, indulgences, trusts, and foundations. The medieval church was, in F. W. Maitland's apt phrase, "the first true state in the West."[5] Its canon law was the first international law in place since the fall of Rome and its Roman law in the fifth century.

Already in the fourteenth and fifteenth centuries, strong secular rulers started to rebel against the power, prerogatives, and privileges of the medieval church and put in place legal reforms.[6] In fourteenth-century England, several statutes of "provisors" and "praemunire" limited papal control over local clerical appointments, church taxes, and local property disputes. Beginning in 1414, the Holy Roman emperors called a series of great church councils that put limits on the operation of canon law and church courts in the empire and aimed to regularize papal succession and the appointments of bishops, abbots, and abbesses. In the Pragmatic Sanction of Bourges (1438) and again in the Concordat of Bologna (1516), French kings banned various papal taxes, limited appeals to Rome, required election of French bishops by local church councils called by the king, and subjected French clergy and church property to royal controls. Fifteenth-century Spanish monarchs subordinated church courts to civil courts on many legal subjects and assumed political and legal control over the Inquisition. Fifteenth-century German and Scandinavian princes and city councils passed numerous "legal reformations" that placed limits on church property and religious taxation, disciplined wayward clergy and monastics, and curtailed the jurisdiction of church courts over crime, family, inheritance, and contracts. Medieval Reformers like Marsilius of Padua (ca. 1280–ca. 1343), John Wycliffe (ca. 1330–84), Jan Hus

5. F. W. Maitland, quoted by Harold J. Berman, *Law and Revolution: The Formation of the Western Legal Tradition* (Cambridge, MA: Harvard University Press, 1983), 276.

6. See documents in Sidney Z. Ehler and John B. Morrall, eds., *Church and State through the Centuries: A Collection of Historic Documents with Commentaries*, repr. ed. (Getzville, NY: William S. Hein & Co., 2017).

(ca. 1370–1415), and many others pressed for attendant theological reforms, often at the cost of their lives.

The Protestant Reformers built on these late-medieval reforms but went beyond them. The Reformers now called for full freedom from the medieval Catholic legal regime—freedom of the individual conscience from intrusive canon laws, freedom of political officials from clerical power and privilege, freedom of local clergy from centralized papal and conciliar rule. "Freedom of the Christian" was the rallying cry of the early Protestant Reformation. It led the Reformers to denounce canon law and clerical authority altogether and to urge radical legal and political reforms on the strength of the new Protestant theology. Many Reformers burned the church's canon lawbooks and forcibly closed church courts and episcopal offices. They stripped clerics of privileges and immunities and prohibited mendicant begging. They suspended mandatory celibacy and condemned indulgence trafficking. Outlawing annates and tithe payments to Rome or distant bishops, they also severed diplomatic and appellate ties to the pope and his curia. Catholic bishops, priests, and monastics were banished from their homes, sometimes maimed or killed. The church's vast properties and institutions were seized, often with violence and bloodshed, as priceless church art, literature, statuary, and icons were looted, sometimes destroyed. And Protestant authorities confiscated and seized control of church sanctuaries, parsonages, and seminaries.

The Reformers defended this revolutionary purging of the church as a theological necessity. All the early Protestant leaders—Martin Luther (1483–1546), John Calvin (1509–64), Thomas Cranmer (1489–1556), Menno Simons (1496–1561), and others—taught that salvation comes through faith in the gospel, not by works of the law. Each individual was to stand directly before God, to seek God's gracious forgiveness of sin, and to conduct life in accordance with the Bible and Christian conscience. To the Reformers, the Catholic canon law administered by the clergy obstructed the individual's direct relationship with God and obscured simple biblical norms for right living. All the early Reformers further taught that the church was at heart a community of saints, not a corporation of law. Its cardinal signs and callings were to preach the Word, to administer the sacraments, to catechize the young, and to care for the needy. The Catholic clergy's legal rule in Christendom obstructed the church's divine mission and usurped the state's role as God's vice-regent, called to appropriate and apply divine and natural law in the earthly kingdom. Protestants did recognize that the church needed internal rules of order to govern its own polity, teaching, and discipline. Church officials and councils needed to oppose legal injustice and combat political tyranny. But for most early Protestants, law was primarily the province of the state, not of the church—of the magistrate, not of the pastor.

These new Protestant teachings helped to transform Western law in the sixteenth and seventeenth centuries. The Protestant Reformation broke the international rule of the Catholic Church and the canon law, permanently splintering Western Christendom into competing nations and regions, each with its own religious and political rulers. The Protestant Reformation triggered a massive shift of power and property from the church to the state. State rulers now assumed jurisdiction over numerous subjects and persons previously governed by the church and its canon law.

These massive shifts in legal power and property from church to state in Protestant lands did not, however, signal the secularization of law or the cessation of traditional Christian influences on the law. For all of their early attacks on canon law, Protestant leaders eventually transplanted many Catholic canon law rules and procedures directly into the new Protestant state laws—some trimmed of theologically offensive provisions, others reformed in light of new teachings, but many retained largely in their medieval forms, though now administered by the state instead of the church. Moreover, in creating other new state laws, Protestant authorities drew anew on Christianized Roman law and medieval civilian jurisprudence, Christian republican political thought, and biblical and Talmudic law, all of which were staples in the new Protestant law faculties. And Protestant leaders worked hard to convert some of their own distinct new theological teachings into new legal forms, especially rules concerning family, charity, education, and crime. What emerged from the Protestant Reformation were impressive new legal syntheses that skillfully blended classical and biblical, Catholic and Protestant, civilian and canonical teachings.

This chapter summarizes and illustrates these new legal syntheses born of the Protestant Reformation, with a focus on changes in the laws of church-state relations and religious and civil freedom, marriage and family law, education law, and social welfare law, with attention to accompanying changes in legal and political philosophy. Where Lutheranism, Anabaptism, Anglicanism, and Calvinism made distinct contributions, I spell those out separately; where the reforms were comparable across the traditions, I pick illustrative case studies.

The Law of Church-State Relations and Religious Freedom

Lutheranism.[7] The Lutheran Reformation of Germany and Scandinavia territorialized the Christian faith and gave to the local Christian magistrate ample new political power over civil and spiritual affairs. Luther replaced medieval teachings with a new two-kingdoms theory. The invisible church of the heavenly kingdom, he argued, was a perfect community of saints, where all stood equal in dignity before God, all enjoyed perfect Christian liberty, and all governed their affairs in accordance with the gospel. The visible church of this earthly kingdom, however, embraced saints and sinners alike. Its members still stood directly before God and still enjoyed liberty of conscience, including the liberty to leave the visible church itself. But unlike the invisible church, the visible church needed both the gospel and human law to govern its members' relationships with God and with fellow believers. The clergy must administer the gospel. The magistrate must administer the law.

Luther regarded the magistrate as God's vice-regent in the earthly kingdom, called to elaborate and enforce God's Word and will and to reflect God's justice and judgment for earthly citizens. "Law and earthly government are a great gift of God to humankind," Luther wrote. "Earthly authority is an image, shadow, and figure of the dominion of Christ." But magistrates also exercise God's judgment and wrath against human sin. "Princes and magistrates are the bows and arrows of God," equipped to hunt down God's enemies near and far, using military power and criminal punishment. The hand of the Christian magistrate, judge, or soldier "that wields the sword and slays is not man's hand, but God's."[8]

Luther further regarded the magistrate as the "father of the community" (*paterpoliticus*). He was called to care for his political subjects as if

7. For illustrative writings, see Hermann W. Beyer, *Luther und das Recht*, repr. ed. (Paderborn: Salzwasser-Verlag GmbH, 2013); J. M. Porter, ed., *Luther—Selected Political Writings* (Philadelphia: Fortress Press, 1974). For overviews, see Johannes Heckel, *Lex Charitatis: A Juristic Disquisition on Law in the Theology of Martin Luther*, trans. Gottfried G. Krodel (Grand Rapids: Wm. B. Eerdmans Publishing Co., 2010); Martin Heckel, *Martin Luthers Reformation und das Recht* (Tübingen: Mohr Siebeck, 2016); Virpi Mäkinen, ed., *Lutheran Reformation and the Law* (Leiden: Brill, 2006); Mathias Schmoeckel, *Das Recht der Reformation* (Tübingen: Mohr Siebeck, 2014); W. D. J. Cargill Thompson, *The Political Thought of Martin Luther*, ed. Philip Broadhead (Totawa, NJ: Barnes & Noble, 1984); John Witte Jr., *Law and Protestantism: The Legal Teachings of the Lutheran Reformation* (Cambridge: Cambridge University Press, 2002).

8. Quotes are in *LW* 2:139; 13:44; 17:171; 44:92; 45:85; 46:95, 237; WA 6:267; WA 19:626; WA 30/2:554; 31/2:394–95; here and below, WA = Weimarer Ausgabe: *Martin Luthers Werke: Kritische Gesamtausgabe*, 121 vols. (Weimar: Hermann Böhlau / H. Böhlaus Nachfolger, 1883–2009).

they were his children, and his political subjects were to honor and obey him as if he were their parent. Like a loving father, the magistrate was to keep the peace and protect his subjects from threats or violations to their persons, properties, and reputations. He was responsible to deter his subjects from abusing themselves through drunkenness, wastrel living, prostitution, gambling, and other vices. He was to nurture and sustain his subjects through the community chest, the public almshouse, and the state-run hospital. The magistrate was to educate them through the public school, library, and lectern. He was to see to their spiritual needs by supporting the ministry of the locally established church and encouraging their attendance and participation through the laws of Sabbath observance, tithing, and holy days. He was responsible to see to their material needs by reforming inheritance and property laws to ensure more even distribution of the parents' property among all children. The magistrate was to set a moral example of virtue, piety, love, and charity in his own home and private life for his faithful subjects to emulate and respect.

Luther and his colleagues called on Christian magistrates to build their positive laws on the basis of the Ten Commandments, which the Reformers regarded as a universal statement of natural law. "The Decalogue is not the law of Moses," Luther wrote, "but the Decalogue of the whole world, inscribed and engraved in the minds of all men from the foundation of the world."[9] The Christian magistrate is "a voice of the Ten Commandments" within the earthly kingdom, wrote Philipp Melanchthon (1497–1560), a Wittenberg theologian, moralist, educator, and jurist with wide influence in Germany and Scandinavia. "When you think about *Obrigkeit*, about princes or lords, picture in your mind a man holding in one hand the tables of the Ten Commandments and holding in the other a sword."[10]

Melanchthon took this image directly into his theory of political authority and positive law, which he organized by using the two tables of the Decalogue. The first table of the Decalogue, he wrote, undergirded the state's positive laws that govern spiritual morality, the relationship between persons and God. The second table undergirded the state's positive laws that govern civil morality, the relationships between persons. As custodians of the first table of the Decalogue, Melanchthon wrote, the magistrate must not only pass laws against idolatry, blasphemy, and

9. WA 39/1:478.
10. Philipp Melanchthon, *Philippi Melanthonis Opera quae supersunt omnia*, in *Corpus Reformatorum*, ed. G. Bretschneider, 28 vols. (Braunschweig: C. A. Schwetschke, 1834–60), 22:615.

violations of the Sabbath—offenses that the first table prohibits on its face. He must also "establish pure doctrine" and right liturgy, "prohibit all wrong doctrine," "punish the obstinate," and root out the heathen and the heterodox.[11] Melanchthon came to this position reluctantly in the 1530s and 1540s, knowing that he was departing from Luther's early call for universal religious freedom. But Melanchthon lamented the perennial outbreaks of violent antinomianism, spiritual radicalism, and "diabolical rages" by those who took too literally Luther's teaching of free grace. To allow such blasphemy and chaos to continue without firm rejoinder, Melanchthon believed, was ultimately to betray God and to belie the essence of the political office. Magistrates must "maintain external discipline according to *all* the commandments" and thus must "prohibit, abolish, and punish these depravities" and "compel them to accept the Holy Gospel."[12]

This was the theoretical basis for the welter of new religious establishment laws set out in the elaborate church ordinances promulgated in Lutheran and other Protestant lands in the sixteenth and seventeenth centuries. These church ordinances both reflected and directed the resystematization of dogma; the truncation of the sacraments; the reforms of liturgy, devotional life, and the religious calendar; the vernacularization of the Bible, liturgy, and sermon; the expansion of catechesis and religious instruction in schools and universities; the revamping of corporate worship, congregational music, religious symbolism, church art, and architecture; the radical reforms of ecclesiastical discipline and local church administration; the new practices of tithing, baptism, confirmation, weddings, and burial; the new forms of diaconal care, sanctuary, and much more. All these aspects of church and spiritual life, once governed in detail by the medieval church's canon laws and sacramental rules, were now subject to the Protestant state's religious establishment laws. Particularly after the Peace of Augsburg (1555) and the Peace of Westphalia (1648) confirmed the constitutional principle that each civil ruler was free to establish the religion of their own local polity (*cuius regio eius religio*—"whosoever region, his religion"), these religious establishment laws became increasingly detailed, ornate, and routinized. Vestiges of these laws remain in Lutheran lands today, though strong new policies of religious disestablishment are now afoot.

---

11. Ibid., 22:617–18.
12. Philipp Melanchthon, *Melanchthon on Christian Doctrine: Loci Communes, 1555*, trans. and ed. Clyde L. Manschreck (Oxford: Oxford University Press, 1965), 324–36.

While the first table of the Decalogue supported the state's laws governing relations between God and persons, the second table supported state laws governing relations between persons. Melanchthon and Lutheran jurists like Johan Oldendorp (ca. 1486–1567) and Nicolaus Hemming (1513–1600) set out a whole series of state laws under each commandment of the second table. On the basis of the commandment to "Honor thy father and mother," they argued, magistrates were obligated to prohibit and punish disobedience, disrespect, or disdain of authorities such as parents, political rulers, teachers, employers, masters, and others. They were also to issue state laws of authority—constitutional law, administrative law, master-servant laws, and more. The commandment "Thou shalt not kill" undergirded state laws against unlawful killing, violence, assault, battery, wrath, hatred, mercilessness, and other offenses against the bodies of one's neighbors. "Thou shalt not commit adultery" and "Thou shalt not covet thy neighbor's wife or maidservant" were the foundations of laws against sex crimes such as adultery, fornication, prostitution, pornography, obscenity, and similar offenses, as well as positive laws of marital formation, maintenance, and dissolution; child care, custody, and control; parental rights, roles, and responsibilities; and more. The commandment "Thou shalt not steal" supported state laws against theft, burglary, embezzlement, and similar offenses against another's property, as well as waste or noxious or sumptuous use of one's own property. This commandment also supported state laws of real and personal property, its acquisition, use, maintenance, encumbrance, sale, alienation, and more. On the basis of the commandment "Thou shalt not bear false witness," magistrates were to punish all forms of perjury, dishonesty, fraud, defamation, and other violations of a person's reputation or status in the community. And they were to build the state laws of promises and contracts, of keeping one's word to one's neighbor, as well as laws of procedure, evidence, and testimony in court proceedings. Finally, on the basis of the commandment "Thou shalt not covet," magistrates were to punish all attempts to perform offensive acts against another's person, property, reputation, or relationships, and to establish the basic rules protecting the privacy of one's household from the covetous predations of neighbors.

Many of these aspects of social intercourse had been governed by the Catholic Church's canon law and organized in part by the church's seven sacraments. The sacrament of marriage, for example, supported the canon law of sex, marriage, and family life. The sacrament of penance supported the canon law of crimes against the persons, properties, and reputations of others. The sacraments of baptism and confirmation undergirded the constitutional law of natural rights and duties of Christian believers. The sacrament of holy orders supported the law of the clergy. The sacrament of extreme unction supported the canon laws of burial, inheritance, foundations, and trusts. Lutheran jurists used the Ten Commandments, instead of the seven sacraments, to organize the various systems of positive law. Further, they looked to the state, instead of the church, to promulgate and enforce these positive laws on the basis of the Ten Commandments and the biblical and extrabiblical sources of natural law and morality. This way of systematizing and teaching became a standard in many early modern Protestant state laws, eventually on both sides of the Atlantic.

Anabaptism.[13] While Lutherans territorialized the faith, early modern Anabaptists communalized the faith. They did this by expounding a two-kingdoms theory that more fully separated the redeemed realm of religion and the church from the fallen realm of politics and the state. Emerging as a new form of Protestantism in the early 1520s, Anabaptists were scattered into various groups of Amish, Brethren, Hutterites, Mennonites, Baptists, and others. Some of the early splinter groups, like the followers of Thomas Müntzer (1489–1525) and Caspar Schwenckfeld (d. 1561) were politically radical or utopian spiritualists. Others, like the Anabaptist sect in Münster under Jan van Leiden (d. 1536), practiced polygyny for a short time, which they enforced ruthlessly against detractors. But most Anabaptist communities by the mid-sixteenth century were quiet Christian separatists, monogamists, and pacifists, taking their lead from such theologians as Menno Simons, Pilgram Marpeck (d. 1556), Dirk Philips (1504–68), and Peter Riedeman (1506–56), who urged their followers to return to the simple teachings of the New Testament and the apostolic church.

Anabaptist communities ascetically withdrew from civil and political life into small, self-sufficient, intensely democratic communities. These communities were governed internally by biblical principles of discipleship, simplicity, charity, and nonresistance. They set their own standards of worship, liturgy, diet, discipline, dress, and education. They handled

13. For illustrative writings, see Klaassen, *Anabaptism in Outline*. For overviews, see William R. Estep, *The Anabaptist Story: An Introduction to Sixteenth-Century Anabaptism* (Grand Rapids: Wm. B. Eerdmans Publishing Co., 1996); Robert Friedmann, *The Theology of Anabaptism* (1973; repr. ed., Scottdale, PA: Herald Press, 1998); Guy F. Hershberger, ed., *The Recovery of the Anabaptist Vision* (1957; repr. ed., Scottdale, PA: Herald Press, 2001); George Huntston Williams, *The Radical Reformation*, 3rd rev. ed. (Kirksville, MO: Truman State University Press, 2000).

their own internal affairs of property, contracts, commerce, marriage, and inheritance—so far as possible by appeal to biblical laws and practices, not those of the state. And they enforced these internal religious laws not by coercion but by persuasion, and not for the sake of retribution but for the redemption of the sinner and restoration of that person to community. Recalcitrant sinners and community members who grew violent or destructive or persistently betrayed the community's ideals were shunned and, if necessary, banned from the community. Moreover, when Anabaptist communities grew too large or too internally divided, they deliberately colonized themselves, eventually spreading Anabaptists from Russia to Ireland to the furthest frontiers of North America.

The state and its law, most Anabaptists believed, was part of the fallen world, which was to be avoided so far as possible in accordance with biblical injunctions that Christians should not be "of the world" or "conformed" to it. Once the perfect creation of God, the world was now a fallen, sinful regime that lay beyond "the perfection of Christ" and beyond the daily concern of the Christian believer. God had built a "wall of separation" (*paries maceriae*) between the redeemed church and the fallen world, Menno Simons wrote, quoting Ephesians 2:14.[14] God had allowed the world to survive by ordaining magistrates who were empowered by their positive laws to use coercion and violence in maintaining a modicum of order and peace. Christians should obey the laws of political authorities, so far as the Bible commanded: paying their taxes, registering their properties, avoiding theft and homicide, keeping their promises, and testifying truthfully. But Christians should avoid active participation in and unnecessary interaction with the world and the state—avoiding litigation, oath-swearing, state education, banking, large-scale commerce, trade fairs, public festivals, drinking houses, theaters, games, political office, policing, or military service. Most early modern Anabaptists were pacifists, preferring derision, exile, or death to active participation in war or violence. This aversion to common political and civic activities often earned Anabaptists scorn, reprisal, and repression by Catholics and Protestants alike—violent martyrdom in many instances.

While unpopular in its genesis, Anabaptism ultimately proved to be a vital source for Western legal arguments for the separation of church and state and for the protection of the civil and religious liberties of a plurality of all peaceable faiths. Equally important for later legal reforms was the Anabaptist doctrine of adult rather than infant baptism. This

14. Quotes in Klaassen, *Anabaptism in Outline*, 245–57.

doctrine gave new emphasis to religious voluntarism as opposed to traditional theories of birthright or predestined faith, let alone traditional practices of coercing believers to accept the established religious faith or penalizing the wrong religious choices they made. In Anabaptist theology, each adult was called to make a free, conscientious choice to accept the faith—metaphorically, to scale the wall of separation between the fallen world and the realm of religion to come within the perfect realm of Christ. And it was up to God, not to the state or to any other authority, to decide which forms of religion should flourish and which should fade. In the seventeenth and eighteenth centuries, various Free Church followers, in both Europe and North America, converted this cardinal image of separation into a powerful platform of freedom of conscience and free exercise of religion. Particularly in America, diverse leaders like Roger Williams (ca. 1604–84), William Penn (1644–1718), Isaac Backus (1724–1806), and John Leland (1754–1841) grounded their advocacy of religious freedom in these earlier Anabaptist arguments, and their views helped to shape new American constitutional laws that disestablished religion and protected freedom of conscience and free exercise of religion for all.[15]

Anglicanism.[16] Whereas Anabaptism communalized the Protestant faith and Lutheranism territorialized it, Anglicanism nationalized the faith under the final spiritual and political rule of the Christian monarch. King Henry VIII resolved his bitter dispute with the papacy over dissolution of his marriage with Catherine of Aragon from 1527 to 1533 by cutting all legal and political ties with Rome and declaring the Catholic Church in England to be the separate Anglican Church of England. Henry and early Anglican Reformers like Thomas Cranmer and Thomas Cromwell (1485–1540) pushed through Parliament a series of sweeping new laws that rapidly established the new Anglican order in top-down fashion, enforced by brutal execution of scores of dissenters and exile for

---

15. See sources and discussion in John Witte Jr. and Joel A. Nichols, *Religion and the American Constitutional Experiment*, 4th ed. (Oxford: Oxford University Press, 2016), 29–32, 41–63.

16. For illustrative sources, see Stephenson and Marcham, *Sources*; Gerald Lewis Bray, ed., *Documents of the English Reformation, 1526–1701* (Cambridge: James Clarke, 2004). For overviews, see, e.g., A. G. Dickens, *The English Reformation*, 2nd repr. ed. (London: Schocken Books, 2006); Christopher Haigh, *English Reformations: Religion, Society, and Politics under the Tudors* (Oxford: Clarendon Press, 1993); Joseph LeCler, *Toleration and the Reformation*, trans. T. L. Westow, 4 vols. (New York: Association Press, 1960); Diarmaid MacCulloch, *All Things Made New: The Reformation and Its Legacy* (Oxford: Oxford University Press, 2016); Joan Lockwood O'Donovan, *The Theology and Law of the English Reformation* (Grand Rapids: Wm. B. Eerdmans Publishing Co., 1991).

thousands of others. The Supremacy Act (1534) declared the monarch to be the "Supreme Head" of the Church and Commonwealth of England. The Act for the Submission of Clergy and Restraint of Appeals (1534) gave the monarch final authority to appoint, discipline, and dismiss all clergy; to call church councils; to reform the church's doctrine, liturgy, and canon law; and to register church properties and personnel. The Act for First Fruits and Tenths (1534) required church tithes and taxes to be paid to the Crown. The Act Dissolving the Greater Monasteries (1539) and later acts led to the massive seizure and dissolution of monasteries, cloisters, chapels, chantries, guilds, schools, colleges, hospitals, fraternities, almshouses, and other church properties, cutting to the heart of the pre-Reformation church-based systems of welfare and education. Within a decade and a half of the break with Rome, the king and his retinue had replaced the pope and his curia as supreme rulers of the Church of England and, in time, a growing colonial empire.

Having seized the church's institutions and properties, the Anglican Reformers also moved rapidly to establish by law the new Anglican faith and worship, but this proved more difficult. In 1539 Thomas Cranmer did issue, with royal approval, the Great Bible, an English translation based on the earlier masterwork of William Tyndale (1494–1536) and Miles Coverdale (1488–1569). This text was now to be used for Anglican worship and devotional life. Other Bible translations were censored and would remain so until the King James Version (1611) became the authorized English Bible. Parliamentary Acts of Uniformity in 1549 and 1552 further mandated the use of Cranmer's Book of Common Prayer in Anglican worship, with escalating penalties for clergy and laity who deviated from its prayers, liturgy, and sacramental rites. The king also approved the Forty-Two Articles of the Faith, a new creed that, while consonant with medieval Catholic tradition on many matters, included a number of familiar Lutheran and Calvinist teachings about God, sin, salvation, and the sacraments and rejected Anabaptist teachings about adult baptism, biblical asceticism, and separation of church and state.

A more sweeping act titled the "Reformation of the Ecclesiastical Laws of England," however—akin to the many legal reforms passed by Continental Protestants—floundered despite repeated efforts to enact it in 1552, 1559, and 1571. This proposed reform aimed to retain church courts in England and to maintain their traditional jurisdiction over marriage, tithes, inheritance, defamation, and benefices. But the document also envisioned major new Parliamentary reforms of each of these laws and stronger review of church courts by royal courts. It also proposed sweeping reforms of clerical and lay marriage, rights to fault-based divorce and remarriage, and annual conferences and regular democratic meetings between bishops, priests, and laity. None of these changes came to pass in the Reformation era. The structure of the church courts, and of the clerical hierarchy altogether, remained largely unchanged, although appeals from church court judgments now went not to the curia in Rome but to a new Court of Delegates in England, staffed by civilians and canonists. The law administered by these Anglican church courts remained largely the canon law of the medieval Catholic Church, with only minor changes gradually introduced by Parliament and church convocations over the next three centuries.[17]

This Anglican adherence to legal and religious tradition reflected not only inertia but also ample resistance of the English clergy and laity to the Crown's heavy-handed, top-down reformation of church and state. Moreover, Queen Mary (r. 1553–58) sought to return England forcibly to full communion with Rome. In twin acts of 1553 and 1555, Mary aimed to repeal all the Reformation laws and practices of her father, Henry VIII, and her half brother, Edward VI, to repair England's relations with the papacy, and to restore to the Catholic Church and clergy their traditional power, property, and prerogatives. When church and state officials resisted these changes, too, more than 250 Protestants were executed, and thousands more, called the Marian Exiles, fled to the Continent, leaving the English church, state, and society in turmoil.

During Queen Elizabeth's long reign, from 1558 to 1603, England gradually settled on a via media between Roman Catholicism and Continental Protestantism, and this settlement, too, was legally prescribed and judicially enforced. Parliament issued an Act of Uniformity (1559) that clearly reestablished the Anglican doctrine, liturgy, and creed of the church and commonwealth. Communicant status in the Anglican Church now became a condition for citizenship status in the English Commonwealth, holding high political and religious office, acquiring professional licenses and charters, and exercising many other basic rights. Parliamentary acts prohibited papal bulls and "traitorous" worship, publications, or teaching by Catholics and Protestant "sectaries," and these laws were enforced firmly in the Star Chamber, High Commission, and other royal courts in Elizabeth's reign, and even more firmly by her Stuart successors, James I and Charles I. Elizabeth's Parliament further renewed the Act of

---

17. See R. H. Helmholz, *Roman Canon Law in Reformation England* (Cambridge: Cambridge University Press, 1990).

Supremacy (1559), restoring to the Crown final authority over the Angli-can Church's clergy, polity, and property. The English church courts retained their jurisdiction, although new canons introduced piecemeal legal changes in 1571, 1575, 1585, 1597, and 1604. Parliament passed the Poor Relief Act (1598) and Charitable Uses Act (1601) that sought to restore some of the robust pre-Reformation welfare and educational system of England, now largely through Anglican parishes and Crown-chartered private enterprises.

This Elizabethan settlement of church and state, and of law and reli-gion, attracted new political and legal theories from such Anglican divines as John Jewel (1522–71), Edmund Grindal (1519–83), and Richard Ban-croft (1544–1610). The most important defense came in the massive *Laws of Ecclesiastical Polity* by Richard Hooker (1553–1600), who defended the Anglican establishment against more radical Calvinist views of congrega-tional and presbyterian forms of democratic church government. "The powers that be are ordained by God," Hooker quoted from Scripture, and they reflect God's authority as supreme monarch over the entire universe, which God rules by eternal divine law. The Christian monarch on earth embodies God's monarchical government in heaven; indeed, the mon-arch is a "god on earth," as Psalm 82:6 put it. And the monarch embraces God's law for all of religious and civil life. As God's vice-regent, the mon-arch is called to promulgate positive laws to instruct humans on how to live together and to live well in Christian communion. While all human beings have the rational capacity to ascertain the natural law for their pri-vate lives, Hooker wrote, drawing on Thomas Aquinas (1225–74), the monarch's positive laws of church and state must guide and govern their communal spiritual and temporal lives in accordance with the eternal laws of Christ. While different nations have formed their own voluntary com-pacts with God and their political rulers, England and its great common-law tradition had formed a unique covenant, with God's blessing, whereby the people had consented to this Christian monarchical reign of church, state, and society.[18] Hooker's defense of Christian monarchy in a unitary church and commonwealth became more expansive in the theories of "the divine right of kings" and absolute monarchy offered by King James I, Sir Robert Filmer (1588–1653), and others in the seventeenth century—the-ories that John Locke (1632–1704) would later counter directly with his proto-democratic arguments in his *Two Treatises on Government* (1689).

---

18. Richard Hooker, *The Laws of Ecclesiastical Polity*, ed. W. Speed Hill (Cambridge, MA: Harvard University Press, 1977), I.6–11; VIII.2–4.

Calvinism.[19] Calvinists charted a course between Lutherans and Anglicans, who subordinated the church to the state, and Anabaptists, who withdrew the church from the state and society. Like Anabaptists, Calvinists insisted on a basic separation of the offices and operations of church and state, leaving the church to govern its own doctrine and liturgy, polity, and property without interference from the state. Calvin set the foundation for this church-state division in the Ecclesiastical Ordinances (1541/1561) of Geneva, which influenced ordinances in many later Calvinist cities. Like Lutherans, in turn, Calvinists insisted that each local polity be an overtly Christian commonwealth that adhered to the general principles of natural law and translated them into detailed new positive laws of religious worship, Sabbath observance, public morality, marriage and family, crime and tort, contract and business, charity and education. Calvin drafted many such laws for Geneva during his tenure there from 1536 to 1538, and again from 1541 to 1564, drawing rules variously from the Bible and Talmud, classical Roman law and medieval canon law, and local customs and city ordinances. All these piecemeal laws were eventually integrated into the Civil Edict of Geneva (1568), drafted by Calvinist jurist Germain Colladon (1508–94). Many other Calvinist cities, provinces, and colonies issued their own local Christian laws, too, often using Geneva as their model and source.

Unlike Lutherans, Anglicans, and Anabaptists, however, Calvinists stressed that both church and state officials were to play complementary roles in creating the local Christian commonwealth and cultivating the Christian citizen. More fully than other Protestants, Calvinists emphasized the educational use of the natural and positive law. Lutherans stressed the civil and theological uses of the law: the need for law to deter sinners from their excesses and to drive them to repentance. Calvinists emphasized the educational use of the law as well: the need to teach persons both the letter and the spirit of the law, both the civic morality common to all persons and the spiritual morality that becomes the

---

19. For sources, see Rivoire and Berchem, eds., *Les sources du droit*. For overviews, see Philip Benedict, *Christ's Church Purely Reformed: A Social History of Calvinism* (New Haven, CT: Yale University Press, 2002); Matthew J. Tuininga, *Calvin's Political Theology and the Public Engagement of the Church* (Cambridge: Cambridge University Press, 2017); Harro Höpfl, *The Christian Polity of John Calvin* (Cambridge: Cambridge University Press, 1982); Robert M. Kingdon, *Church and State in Reformation Europe* (London: Variorum Reprints, 1985); Christoph Strohm, *Calvinismus und Recht* (Tübingen: Mohr Siebeck, 2008); John Witte Jr., *The Reformation of Rights: Law, Religion, and Human Rights in Early Modern Calvinism* (Cambridge: Cambridge University Press, 2007).

Christian life. It was the church's responsibility to teach aspirational spiritual norms, Calvinists argued. It was the state's responsibility to enforce mandatory civil norms. This division of responsibility was reflected in Geneva in the procedural divisions between the church consistory and the city council. For many nonviolent legal issues, the consistory was the court of first instance; it would call parties to their higher spiritual duties, backing its recommendations with (threats of) spiritual discipline. If such spiritual counsel failed, the consistory referred parties to the city council to compel them, by using civil and criminal sanctions, to honor at least their basic civil duties.

In sixteenth-century Geneva and other Swiss cities, the consistory was an elected body of civil and religious officials, with original jurisdiction over cases of marriage and family life, charity and social welfare, worship and public morality. Among most later Calvinists, the Genevan-style consistory was transformed into the body of pastors, elders, deacons, and teachers that governed each local church congregation but often played a less structured political and legal role in the broader Christian commonwealth. Yet local clergy still had a strong role in advising magistrates on the positive law of the local community, and local churches and their consistories also generally enjoyed autonomy in administering their own doctrine, liturgy, charity, polity, and property and in administering ecclesiastical discipline over their members without interference from the state courts.

In addition to reconstructing the law of church-state relations, Calvinists after 1560 also laid some of the foundations for Western theories of democracy and human rights, as they faced massive repression and genocide that were killing their coreligionists by the many thousands. One method, developed by Calvinist writers like Christopher Goodman (ca. 1530–1603), Theodore Beza (1519–1605), and Johannes Althusius (1557–1638), was to ground fundamental rights in the duties of the Decalogue and other biblical moral teachings. Echoing earlier Protestants, these Calvinist writers argued that the two tables of the Decalogue prescribe duties of love owed to God and to neighbors respectively. But these writers now translated the first-table duties toward God as natural rights that others could not obstruct: the right to religious exercise, the right to honor God and God's name, the right to rest and worship on one's Sabbath, the right to be free from false gods and false oaths. They cast the second-table duties toward a neighbor as the neighbor's right to have those duties discharged. One person's duties not to kill, commit adultery, steal, or bear false witness gives rise to another person's rights to life, property, fidelity, and reputation. Goodman called all of these "unalienable rights" rooted in the natural law of God.[20] Later Calvinists like Beza, John Knox (ca. 1514–72), and Philippe Duplessis-Mornay (1549–1623) argued further that the persistent and pervasive breach of these unalienable rights by a tyrant triggered a further fundamental right to resistance, rebellion, revolution, even regicide.

Another method, developed especially by Dutch and English Calvinists, was to draw out the legal and political implications of the signature Reformation teaching, coined by Luther, that a person is at once sinner and saint (*simul justus et peccator*). On the one hand, they argued, every person is created in the image of God and justified by faith in God. Every person is called to a distinct vocation, which stands equal in dignity and sanctity to all others. Every person is a prophet, priest, and king, responsible to exhort, to minister, and to rule in the community. Every person thus stands equal before God and before the neighbor. Every person is vested with a natural liberty to live, to believe, and to love and serve God and neighbor. Every person is entitled to the vernacular Scripture, to education, to work in a vocation. On the other hand, Protestants argued, every person is sinful and prone to evil and egoism. Every person needs the restraint of the law as a deterrence from evil and a goad to repentance. Every person needs the association of others who exhort, minister, and rule with law and with love. Every person, therefore, is inherently a communal creature, belonging to a family, a church, and a political community.

By the later sixteenth century, Calvinists recast these theological doctrines into proto-democratic norms and forms. Protestant doctrines of the person and society shaped democratic social forms. Since all persons stand equal before God, they must stand equal before God's political agents in the state. Since God has vested all persons with natural liberties of life and belief, the state must ensure all persons of similar civil liberties. Since God has called all persons to be prophets, priests, and kings, the state must protect their constitutional freedoms to speak, to preach, and to rule in the community. Since God has created persons as social creatures, the state must promote and protect a plurality of social institutions, particularly the church and the family.

Protestant doctrines of sin, in turn, shaped democratic political forms. The political office must be protected against the sinfulness of the political

---

20. Christopher Goodman, *How Superior Powers Ought to be Obeyd* [1558], ed. Charles H. McIlwain, facsimile ed. (New York: Columbia University Press, 1931), 147–54.

official. Political power must be distributed among self-checking executive, legislative, and judicial branches. Officials must be elected to limited terms of office. Laws must be clearly codified and discretion closely guarded. Officials must hold regular meetings to give account of themselves and to hear the people's petitions and grievances. If officials abuse their office, they must be disobeyed. If they persist in their abuse, they must be removed, even if by revolutionary force and regicide.

These Protestant teachings were among the driving forces behind the revolts of the French Huguenots, Dutch Pietists, Scottish Presbyterians, and English Puritans against their monarchical oppressors in the later sixteenth and seventeenth centuries. They were also critical weapons in the eventual arsenal of the revolutionaries in eighteenth-century America and France. It is instructive that, by 1650, almost every right listed 150 years later in the United States Bill of Rights (1791) and the French Declaration of the Rights of Man and of the Citizen (1789) had already been defined, defended, and died for by Calvinists on both sides of the Atlantic.

Criminal Law and Procedure

The shift of power from the church to the state led to a dramatic expansion of state criminal law in Protestant lands.[21] Expanding on late-medieval legal reforms of state criminal law, like the *Bambergensis* (1507), as well as earlier efforts to shut down the criminal jurisdiction of manorial, feudal, and mercantile courts, Protestant Reformers called on the state to develop a new systematic and separate body of criminal law to replace both the medieval canon law of crimes and the Catholic Church's penitential rules. The state, Protestants argued, had to prohibit major crimes like treason, murder, rape, theft, burglary, and adultery as it always had done. But the state now also had to prohibit many other major and minor offenses traditionally under church laws and courts. These included religious and ideological offenses—heresy, sorcery, witchcraft, alchemy, blasphemy, sacrilege, Sabbath-breaking, tithe-breaking, false oaths, perjury, contempt, slander, defamation, and more. They included various family and sexual offenses—neglect and abuse of wife and child, malicious desertion,

---

21. For overviews, see Schmoeckel, *Das Recht der Reformation*, 207–37; Heikki Pihlajamäki, "Executor Divinarum et Suarum Legum: Criminal Law and the Lutheran Reformation," in Mäkinen, *Lutheran Reformation and the Law*, 171–204; John H. Langbein, *Prosecuting Crime in the Renaissance: England, Germany, France* (Cambridge, MA: Harvard University Press, 1974).

seduction and fornication, prostitution, pornography, voyeurism, exhibitionism, and more. These criminal laws also included a growing number of offenses against "public morality and policy" (*Polizei*): drunkenness and debauchery; sumptuousness and waste; crimes of trade, labor, and finance; improper conduct in taverns, shops, and lodgings; embezzlement, usury, and banking irregularities; false weights and measures; passport and travel violations; and much more. In Lutheran, Calvinist, and Anglican polities alike, the roll and role of state criminal laws was greatly expanded, even if consistories and church courts still sometimes had a firm hand in enforcing these laws through spiritual means.

Protestant Reformers further called on magistrates to balance firmness and equity, severity and temperance in the administration of this expanded criminal law. In particular, they urged magistrates to stop using torture to extract confessions from defendants. Not only were these coerced confessions often unreliable as evidence in criminal cases, but such confessions also did the defendant's soul no good, Protestants argued. Medieval Catholic authorities regarded confession as an essential first step in receiving the sacrament of penance, without which the sinner faced eternal punishment in hell. A onetime act of bodily torture was thought to be a small price to pay for eternal life of the soul. Protestants rejected the sacrament of penance and the underlying rationale for torture. Every sinner had to confess directly to God, without the mediation, let alone coercion, of church or state authorities. Here was one source, alongside others, for the gradual abolition of torture in early modern criminal law.

Protestants also called on magistrates to draw more refined distinctions between degrees of criminality and to prescribe a broader range of punishments short of execution. The refined differentiation of mortal and venial sins and their punishment that historically had guided the church's sacrament of penance now informed the state's criminal laws and punishments. The Reformers emphasized the importance of rehabilitating convicted defendants, consigning them to public work programs, workhouses, and penitentiaries (*Zuchthausen*), and furnishing them with chaplains, pastors, and teachers to return them to a suitable level of sociability and morality, if not piety and spiritual integrity. These reforms of criminal justice were only partly achieved in sixteenth-century Protestant lands, and they had other sources of inspiration besides Protestant theology—not least legal humanism and new Catholic criminal jurisprudence. But the Reformation was an important source and catalyst for these criminal-law reforms in Protestant lands.

Marriage and Family Law

The Protestant Reformers embraced the familiar medieval idea that God has ordained "three estates" (*drei Stände*) for the governance of human society—the church, the state, and the family. Thus, alongside sweeping reforms of church and state, the Reformers gave high priority to reforming marriage and family law as well. Indeed, almost every new Protestant community had a new marriage ordinance in place within a decade of accepting the Reformation—even though some later Protestants, notably in England, retreated from some of the more radical positions of the early Reformation.[22]

Before the sixteenth century, the Catholic Church regarded marriage as a sacrament, formed by the mutual consent of a fit man and a fit woman in good religious standing. It symbolized the enduring union of Christ and his church, and it conferred sanctifying grace upon the couple and their children. The parties could form this marital union in private, but once properly formed it was an indissoluble bond broken only by the death of one of the parties. As a sacrament, marriage was subject to the jurisdiction of the medieval church. A complex network of canon laws and penitential rules administered by church courts and clergy governed sex, marriage, and family life in detail. The medieval church did not regard the marital family as its most exalted estate, however. Although it was a sacrament and a sound way of Christian living, marriage and its attendant family life were not considered spiritually edifying. Marriage was a remedy for sin, not a recipe for righteousness. Marriage was considered subordinate to celibacy, and clerics and monastics had to forgo marriage as a condition for ecclesiastical service. Those unable to do so were unworthy of the church's holy orders and offices.

Many early Protestant Reformers challenged this medieval theology and law of the marital family. For them, the medieval Catholic Church's jurisdiction over marriage and family life was a particularly flagrant example of the church's usurpation of the state's legal authority. For them, the Catholic sacramental concept of marriage on which the church predicated its jurisdiction was a self-serving theological fiction. For them, the canonical prohibition on marriage of clergy and monastics ignored the Bible's teachings on sexual sin and temptation and the reality that most

---

22. For detailed sources and discussion, see John Witte Jr., *From Sacrament to Contract: Marriage, Religion, and Law in the Western Tradition*, 2nd ed. (Louisville, KY: Westminster John Knox Press, 2012); John Witte Jr. and Robert M. Kingdon, *Sex, Marriage, and Family in John Calvin's Geneva*, 2 vols. (Grand Rapids: Wm. B. Eerdmans Publishing Co., 2006–18).

humans needed the remedial gift of marriage, whatever their vocation. For them, the church's intricate regulations of sexual feelings and practices, even within marriage, were a gratuitous insult to God's blessing of marital love and an unnecessary intrusion on private life and Christian conscience. Moreover, the canon law's long roll of impediments to engagement and marriage, together with its prohibitions against divorce and remarriage, stood in considerable tension with the Protestant understanding of the right of each fit adult to marry and remarry.

Sixteenth-century Protestant political leaders rapidly translated this Protestant critique of canon law into new reforms of state law. Taken together, the new Protestant family laws (1) shifted principal marital jurisdiction from the church to the state; (2) abolished monasteries and cloisters; (3) commended, if not commanded, the marriage of clergy; (4) rejected the sacramentality of marriage and the religious tests and spiritual impediments traditionally imposed on Christian unions; (5) banned secret or private marriages and required the participation of parents, peers, priests, and political officials in the process of marriage formation; (6) sharply curtailed the number of impediments to engagements and marriages that abridged the right to marry or remarry; and (7) introduced fault-based complete divorce with a subsequent right for divorced persons to remarry. These reforms found their strongest legal expression in sixteenth-century Lutheran and Calvinist lands. They took three centuries to soak into the English common law and Anglican theology. Anabaptists largely retained biblical sexual ethics with little formal legal apparatus.

Lutheranism. Lutherans regarded the marital family as a social estate of the earthly kingdom, not a divine sacrament of the heavenly kingdom. They accepted the traditional Catholic teaching that marriage was a natural association created by God for the procreation of children and mutual protection of both parties from sexual sin. They also accepted the traditional canon law teaching that marriage was a contract formed by the mutual consent of a man and woman with the fitness and capacity to marry each other, and once properly formed was a presumptively permanent union. But Lutherans rejected the idea that marriage was a sacrament. Yes, Christian marriages symbolize the "mystery" of Christ's union with the church, as Ephesians 5:32 put it. Yes, the sacrifices that husband and wife make for each other and for their children echo the sacrificial love of Christ on the cross. But these analogies do not make marriage a sacrament on the order of baptism and the Eucharist. Sacraments are God's gifts and signs of grace ensuring Christians of the promise of redemption, which is available only to those who have faith. Marriage carries no such promise and demands no such faith. The Bible teaches that only baptism and the Eucharist confer this promise of grace; nowhere does it ascribe this promise to marriage. Calling marriage a sacrament, Luther charged, is a "fiction" that the church has created to claim jurisdiction over marriage and to fill its coffers with court fees and fines.

Lutherans also rejected the subordination of marriage to celibacy. Most adults, Lutherans argued, were too tempted by sinful passion to forgo God's soothing remedy of marriage. The celibate life had no superior virtue and was no prerequisite for clerical service. It led too easily to fornication and concubinage and too often impeded the access to and activities of the clerical office. Moreover, the marital household, particularly that of the pastor, was a vital model of authority, charity, and pedagogy and a vital source of evangelical and charitable impulses in society.

These new Lutheran teachings influenced the new Protestant state laws of marriage and family life in sixteenth-century Germany and Scandinavia. There the new state laws repeated many of the basics inherited from medieval canon law and the broader *ius commune*—that marriage was formed by a two-step process, first of engagement then of marriage; that a valid engagement and marriage contract required the mutual consent of a man and a woman who had the age, fitness, and capacity to marry each other; that marriage was a presumptively permanent union that triggered mutual obligations of care and support for the other spouse, their children, and their dependents; that marriage often involved complex exchanges of betrothal gifts and dowry and triggered presumptive rights of dower and inheritance for widow(er)s and legitimate children; that marriages could be annulled on the discovery of various impediments and upon litigation before a proper tribunal; and that in the event of dissolution, both parents remained responsible for the maintenance and welfare of their children. All these assumptions remained common both to the new Protestant state law and to medieval Catholic canon law.

But the new Lutheran teachings about the family also yielded crucial legal changes, beyond the critical shift of marital jurisdiction from the church to the state. Because the Reformers rejected the subordination of marriage to celibacy, they rejected laws that forbad clerical and monastic marriage, that denied remarriage to those who had married a cleric or monastic, and that permitted vows of chastity to annul vows of marriage. Because they rejected the sacramental nature of marriage, the Reformers rejected impediments of crime and heresy and prohibitions against divorce and remarriage. For them, marriage was the community of the couple in the present, not their sacramental union in the life to come. Where that community was broken, for one of several specific reasons (such as adultery, desertion, cruelty, or crime), the couple could sue for divorce. Because persons by their lustful natures needed God's remedy of marriage, the Reformers removed numerous legal, spiritual, and consanguineous impediments to marriage not countenanced by Scripture. Because of their emphasis on the godly responsibility of the prince, the pedagogical role of the church and the family, and the priestly calling of all believers, the Reformers insisted that both marriage and divorce be public. The validity of marriage promises depended on parental consent, witnesses, church consecration and registration, and priestly instruction. Couples who wanted to divorce had to announce their intentions in the church and community and petition a civil judge to dissolve the bond. In the process of marriage formation and dissolution, therefore, the couple was subject to God's law, as appropriated in the civil law, and to God's will, as revealed in the admonitions of parents, peers, and pastors.

On account of these legal reforms, marriages in Lutheran lands were easier to enter and exit. Family life was more public and participatory. Children were afforded greater rights and protections. Abused spouses were given a way out of miserable homes. The divorced and widowed could have a chance to start life anew. Ministers were married, rather than single, and better able to exemplify and implement the ideals of Christian marriage and sexual morality.

But not all was sweetness and light in this reformation of domestic life. Yes, the Protestant Reformers did outlaw monasteries and cloisters. But these reforms also ended the vocations of many single women and men, placing a new premium on the vocation of marriage. Ever since, adult Protestant singles have chafed in a sort of pastoral and theological limbo, objects of curiosity and pity, even suspicion and contempt. Yes, the Protestant Reformers did remove clerics as mediators between God and the laity, in expression of St. Peter's teaching of the priesthood of all believers. But they ultimately interposed husbands between God and their wives, in expression of St. Paul's teaching of male headship within the home. Ever since, Protestant married women have been locked in a bitter struggle to gain fundamental equality both within the marital household and beyond.

Calvinism. Building on a generation of Lutheran and other Protestant reforms, Calvinists constructed a comprehensive new family law that made marital formation and dissolution, children's nurture and welfare, family cohesion and support, and sexual sin and crime essential concerns for both church and state. Together, the consistory and the council outlawed monasticism and mandatory clerical celibacy and encouraged marriage for all fit adults. They set clear guidelines for courtship and engagement. They mandated parental consent, peer witness, church consecration, and state registration for valid marriage. They radically reconfigured weddings and wedding feasts. They reformed marital property and inheritance, marital consent and impediments. They created new rights and duties for wives within the bedroom and for children within the household. They streamlined the grounds and procedures for annulment. They introduced fault-based divorce for both husbands and wives on grounds of adultery and desertion. They encouraged the remarriage of the divorced and widowed. They punished rape, fornication, prostitution, sodomy, and other sexual felonies with startling new severity. They put firm new restrictions on dancing, sumptuousness, ribaldry, and obscenity. They put new stock in catechesis and education, and created new schools, curricula, and teaching aids. They provided new sanctuary to illegitimate, abandoned, and abused children. They created new protections for abused wives and impoverished widows. All these reforms were set out in Geneva's Marriage Ordinance (1545), Ecclesiastical Ordinance (1561), and Civil Edict (1568), and the rich case law they inspired; these laws were replicated and elaborated in the laws of other early modern Calvinist polities on both sides of the Atlantic.

Calvinists grounded these legal reforms in the repeated biblical reference to marriage as a covenant, not a sacrament. The idea of covenant, they argued, recognizes better the critical mutuality and consensuality of marriage. The true sacraments of baptism and Eucharist involve God's unilaterally pouring divine grace upon undeserving persons. Marital covenants, on the other hand, are mutual bonds whose validity depends on the mutual consent of both spouses to the natural rights and duties that the marital covenant holds out to them. The idea of covenant also shows better that marriage is enduring but not indissoluble. Sacraments are permanent marks of grace that cannot be erased no matter how the parties behave. But covenants have built-in conditions of mutual performance, whose fundamental breach triggers rights of exit and redress.

For Calvinists, however, marriage was more than a mere contract. "When a covenant of marriage takes place between a man and a woman," John Calvin wrote, "God presides and requires a mutual pledge from both."[23] God participates in the formation of the marital covenant

---

23. Quoted by Witte, *From Sacrament to Contract*, 186.

through God's chosen agents on earth. The couple's parents, as God's "lieutenants" for children, instruct the young couple in the mores and morals of Christian marriage and give their consent to the union. Two witnesses, as "God's priests to their peers," testify to the sincerity and solemnity of the couple's promises and attest to the marriage event. The minister, holding "God's spiritual power of the Word," blesses the union and admonishes the couple and the community of their respective biblical duties and rights. The magistrate, holding "God's temporal power of the sword," registers the parties, ensures the legality of their union, and protects them in their conjoined persons and properties. The involvement of parents, peers, ministers, and magistrates alike represented different dimensions of God's involvement in the marriage covenant. They were essential to the legitimacy of the marriage itself, for to omit any of the parties was, in effect, to omit God from the marriage covenant. Covenant theology thus helped Calvinists integrate the requirements of mutual consent, parental consent, two witnesses, civil registration, and church consecration for a valid marriage. It also provided a standing response to the centuries-long problem of secret marriage. Marriage was, by its covenantal nature, a public institution, involving a variety of parties in the community. To marry secretly or privately was to defy the very nature of marriage.

God participates in the maintenance of the covenant of marriage not only through the onetime actions of these human agents, Calvinists continued, but also through the continuous revelation of the natural law, on which positive family laws are built. Calvinists grounded various biblical rules against illicit sexual unions in the natural structure of the marital covenant as a union of "male and female," who have the physical capacity and natural inclination to come together in love. They condemned sodomy, bestiality, homosexuality, and other "unnatural" acts and alliances. They condemned incestuous engagements and marriages between various blood and family relatives, arguing that God had prohibited such unions to avoid discord, abuse, rivalry, and exploitation among those who were too close. They condemned, at greater length, the traditional Hebrew practice of polygyny, which ignored the creation of marriage as a "two in one flesh" union. Calvinists saved their greatest thunder for the sin of adultery as the most fundamental violation of the created structure of the marital covenant. They read the commandment "Thou shalt not commit adultery" expansively to outlaw various illicit alliances and actions, both within and outside marriage. Calvin in particular stretched the commandment far beyond actual adultery and actual fornication to include lewdness, dancing, bawdy gaming, sexual innuendo, coarse humor, provocative primping, suggestive plays and literature, rowdy wedding parties, and much more.

These Calvinist reforms of sex, marriage, and family law penetrated deeply into the early modern civil law of Protestant lands on the Continent and colonial America. Not so in England, however. While strongly pressed by many Anglican theologians in the sixteenth century, and prominently featured in the proposed Reformation of Ecclesiastical Laws, these Protestant family reforms were rejected by the Crown and Parliament in favor of traditional medieval family law administered by English courts. It took more than three centuries for the English church and state to adopt piecemeal the family law changes that Continental Reformers put in place in a generation.

Education Law

The Protestant Reformers soon extended their reforms to schools as well. Before the sixteenth century, schools were dominated by the church.[24] Cathedrals, monasteries, chantries, ecclesiastical guilds, and large parishes offered the principal forms of lower education, governed by general and local canon law regulations. Gifted graduates were sent on to church-chartered universities for advanced training in the core faculties of law, theology, and medicine. The vast majority of students, however, were trained for clerical and other forms of service in the church.

Building on the ample efforts of fifteenth- and sixteenth-century humanists, Protestants transformed this church-based school system into a new system of public education. They often established new public schools in confiscated monasteries and church schools, with the state now chartering most of the schools and universities and licensing their teachers and tutors. Each citizen, Protestants argued, must be literate enough to read the Bible at home in their own language, to understand the Sunday sermons and catechisms, and to participate actively in church

---

24. For illustrative sources, see F. V. N. Painter, *Luther on Education*, repr. ed. (Eugene, OR: Wipf & Stock, 2001); Frederick Eby, *Early Protestant Educators: The Educational Writings of Martin Luther, John Calvin, and Other Leaders of Protestant Thought*, repr. ed. (New York: AMS Press, 1971). For overviews, see, e.g., Joan Simon, *Education and Society in Tudor England* (Cambridge: Cambridge University Press, 1966); Sebastian Kreiker, *Armut, Schule, Obrigkeit: Armenversorgung und Schulwesen in den evangelischen Kirchenordnungen des 16. Jahrhunderts* (Bielefeld: Verlag für Regionalgeschichte, 1997); Gerald Strauss, *Luther's House of Learning: Indoctrination of the Young in the German Reformation* (Baltimore: Johns Hopkins University Press, 1978).

worship and liturgy. Each citizen must also prepare for the distinct vocation that matches their God-given talents. Church ministry was only one such worthwhile vocation, Protestants insisted, and no better or more virtuous than any other. The vocation of the butcher, farmer, or soldier was just as spiritual and conducive to salvation as the life of the bishop, abbot, or priest. The same devotion and discipline that a cleric directed to spiritual and ecclesiastical ends could now be devoted to secular and material ends as well, with equal assurance of justification by faith in God's grace.

In Lutheran lands, the magistrate, as "father of the community," created a public school system, regulated by detailed new school ordinances (*Schulordnungen*). Mandatory for boys and girls alike, education was to be fiscally and physically accessible to all. It was marked by both formal classroom instruction and civic education through community libraries, lectures, and other media. The curriculum combined biblical values and Lutheran catechisms with humanistic and vocational training. Students were stratified into different classes, according to age and ability, and slowly selected for any number of vocations, with the most precocious tapped for university training. The public school was to be, in Philipp Melanchthon's famous phrase, the "civic seminary"[25] of the commonwealth, designed to combine deep faith and deep learning. This eventually became a model for public schools in many parts of the Christian world.

In Calvinist lands, each city and village was expected to create schools along the same lines. In Calvin's Geneva, the *petite école* that was part of the Collège de Rive in the early days of the Reformation was subsumed in 1559 into the Genevan Academy, which added advanced training in theology, law, and other subjects. In German, French, Dutch, and Scottish Calvinist communities, particularly those that were new, small, or poor, church and state officials often worked together to establish schools, apprenticeships, and vocational training programs for young students, sometimes sharing teachers, space, and resources until an independent school could be built, with gifted students sent to Protestant lower schools and universities elsewhere.

Sixteenth-century Calvinist cities issued detailed edicts on education, collected education taxes and donations, and acquired property for new schools. City councils and consistories worked together to devise curricula, supervise instruction, and discipline students. Similarly and

---

25. Karl Hartfelder, *Philipp Melanchthon als Praeceptor Germaniae* (Munich: Monumenta Germaniae Paedagogica, 1978).

quite early, New England Puritans established Harvard (1636) and Yale (1701) for advanced education, with feeder primary schools attached to churches, charities, and private tutors.

Sixteenth-century Anglican communities initially left a good deal of primary education to the laity, who converted old church buildings into open charity or grammar schools for basic literacy and vocational training. The upper classes of gentry and merchants also established elite private schools and academies to prepare students for advanced studies at Cambridge, Oxford, Edinburgh, St. Andrews, or the Inns of Court. In the larger cities, the Crown looked to the Church of England to establish diocesan schools, staffed by teachers approved and supervised by the local Anglican bishops. During Elizabeth's long reign and those of James I and Charles I, this diocesan-based school system was greatly expanded, and Anglican authorities in church and state sought to impose strict Anglicanism on grammar- and private-school teachers alike. But many of these local schools continued to harbor religious dissenters, particularly Calvinists, whose teachings slowly penetrated into seventeenth-century Anglicanism and helped to fuel the Puritan-led English revolution against Charles I in the 1640s.

Social Welfare Laws

A similar pattern of translating new theological insights into institutional settings occurred as Protestants reformed the laws of poor relief and social welfare.[26] Here the Protestant theological critique of Catholicism was more complicated. The medieval church taught that both poverty and charity were spiritually edifying. Voluntary poverty was a form of Christian sacrifice and self-denial that conferred spiritual benefits on its practitioners and provided spiritual opportunities for others to accord them their charity. Itinerant monks and mendicants in search of alms were the most worthy exemplars of this ideal, but many other deserving poor were at hand as well. Voluntary charity, in turn, conferred spiritual benefits upon its practitioner, particularly when pursued as a work of penance and purgation in the context of the sacraments of penance or extreme unction. To be charitable to others was to serve Christ, who had said, "Inasmuch as ye have done it unto one of the least of these my brethren, ye have done it unto me."[27]

26. See detailed sources in chapter 6 below, by Carter Lindberg.
27. Matt. 25:40 KJV.

These teachings helped to render the medieval church, at least in theory, the primary object and subject of charity and social welfare. To give to the church was the best way to give to Christ, since the church was the body of Christ on earth. The church thus received alms through the collections of its mendicant monks, the charitable offerings from its many pilgrims, the penitential offerings assigned to cancel sins, the final bequests and indulgence payments designed to expedite purgation in the life hereafter, and much more. The church also distributed alms through the diaconal work of the parishes, the hospitality of the monasteries, and the welfare services of the many church-run almshouses, hospitals, schools, chantries, and ecclesiastical guilds. A rich latticework of canon law and confessional rules calibrated these obligations and opportunities of individual and ecclesiastical charity and governed the many charitable corporations, trusts, and foundations under the church's general auspices.

The Protestant Reformation destroyed a good deal of this teaching and practice. Protestant Reformers rejected the spiritual idealization of poverty and the spiritual efficaciousness of charity. All persons were called to do the work of God in the world, they argued. They were not to be idle or to impoverish themselves voluntarily. Voluntary poverty was a form of social parasitism to be punished, not a symbol of spiritual sacrifice to be rewarded. Only the worthy local poor deserved charity, and only if their immediate family could not help them. Charity, in turn, was not a form of spiritual self-enhancement. It was a vocation of the priesthood of believers. Charity brought no immediate spiritual reward to the giver but brought spiritual opportunity to the receiver. The Protestant doctrine of justification by faith alone undercut the spiritual efficacy of charity for the giver; salvation came through faith in Christ, not through charity to one's neighbor. But the Protestant doctrine of the priesthood of all believers enhanced the spiritual efficacy of charity for the receiver. Those already saved by faith became members of the priesthood of all believers, called to love and serve their neighbors charitably in imitation of Christ. Those who received the charity of their neighbors would see in this personal sacrificial act the good works brought by faith, and so be moved to have faith themselves.

These Protestant teachings built on humanist teachings and anti-begging laws already in place before the Reformation. The Protestant Reformers went further, however, in altogether outlawing not just mendicancy but also monasticism. They translated their belief in the spiritual efficacy of the direct personal relationship between the giver and the receiver into a new emphasis on local charity for the local poor, without dense administrative bureaucracies. Particularly the complex tangle of ecclesiastical guilds, endowments, foundations, and other charitable institutions of the medieval church were, for the early Reformers, not only economically inefficient but also a distraction from the church's essential mission. The local church should continue to receive the tithes of its members, as biblical laws taught. It should continue to tend to the immediate needs of its local members, as the apostolic church had done. But most other gifts to the church and the clergy were, in the Reformers' view, misdirected. Most other forms of ecclesiastical charity, particularly those surrounding pilgrimages, penance, and purgation, were, for the Reformers, types of "spiritual bribery," predicated on the fabricated sacraments of penance and extreme unction and on the false teachings of purgatory and works righteousness.

In Lutheran and Calvinist lands, the Reformers instituted a series of local civil institutions of welfare, usually administered directly by local townsfolk. Local welfare systems were centered on the community chest, administered by the local magistrate. These community chest funds at first comprised the church's monastic properties and endowments that had been confiscated, then were eventually supplemented by local taxes and private donations. Larger cities and territories each established several such community chests and closely monitored the poor in the use of their services, often under the watchful eye of both church and state officials. At minimum, this system provided food, clothing, and shelter for the poor, plus emergency relief in times of war, disaster, or pestilence. In larger and wealthier communities, the community chest eventually supported the development of a more comprehensive local welfare system featuring public orphanages, workhouses, boarding schools, vocational centers, hospitals, and more, administered by the local magistrate with the cooperation of the consistory and diaconate.

In England, the rapid and widespread dissolution of monasteries and church-based charities in the early Reformation produced a massive welfare crisis by the mid-sixteenth century. The Privy Council and eventually Elizabeth's Parliament thus passed several laws that placed poor relief and social welfare directly into the hands of individual Anglican parishes, supported by tithe collections and church rates. Anglican church wardens and justices of the peace were now responsible for distributing aid to widows, the disabled, and chronically sick, for finding homes, schools, apprenticeships, and work for orphans and nonmarital children, and more.

In Anabaptist communities, an internal system of community property and of mutual caring and sharing within and across families provided local members with the support they needed from cradle to grave. Anabaptist church orders also instructed the community to offer Christian hospitality to the poor and needy who were "sojourners in their midst."[28] Only in dire emergencies would early modern Anabaptists look to the state or the established church for aid, or turn away a wayfarer or sojourner who had need. These Anabaptist communities were often the closest analogues Protestants had to Catholic monasteries.

Conclusions

The Protestant Reformation had its most direct and enduring impact on early modern laws of church-state relations, religious and civil freedom, marriage and family, education and social welfare. Protestant teachings affected some areas of criminal law and civil law as well. Many of the legal reforms introduced by Protestants built directly on a "legal reformation" movement already afoot on the Continent and in England in the fourteenth and fifteenth centuries. They also drew on pre-Reformation movements of humanism, conciliarism, nominalism, nationalism, and pietism. But the new Protestant teachings helped integrate these pre-Reformation movements and translate them directly into new legal, political, and social norms and forms. With the establishment of the printing press and dozens of new law faculties at Protestant universities, these new Protestant teachings yielded a vast new legal literature that held sway in many Protestant lands until the great codification movements and liberal reforms of the later eighteenth and nineteenth centuries.

28. Cf. Deut. 24:14; Ps. 146:9.

Parable of the Great Banquet, in *Kercken Postilla, dat ys, Vthlegginge der Epistelen vnd Euangelien, an de Söndagen vnde vornemesten Festen,* by Doctor Martin Luther, 1563

Chapter Six

"There Will Be No Poor among You": The Reformation of Charity and Social Welfare

Carter Lindberg

The reformation of charity and social welfare is but one aspect of the larger issue of the Reformation as an agent of social change. But even this one aspect defies brief compass. The medieval worldview formed by the church's "piety of achievement" idealized poverty as the preferred path to salvation actualized by either voluntary poverty or charity focused on alms to the poor. Both paths—identification with the poor through voluntary poverty, as for example the Franciscan order, or patronizing the poor by indiscriminate almsgiving—had little material effect on the causes and conditions of the widespread poverty of the time. Urban efforts to respond constructively to the social conditions causing such poverty were stymied by the religious endorsement of poverty and the concomitant monopoly of charitable institutions by the church—not incidentally a major source of church income.

The Reformation undercut the religious legitimation of poverty by displacing salvation as a human achievement with salvation as a divine gift. The governing authorities of town councils and princes in areas where the Reformation took hold were thereby freed to engage in a new field of discourse regarding social issues such as poverty. With the new theology and active cooperation of Reformers such as Martin Luther and his colleagues, they developed and passed new legislative structures for social welfare. This development was marked by a secularization or laicization and rationalization of social welfare. Although innumerable reformers, ably assisted by lawyers, humanists, and governing authorities throughout Europe and England, contributed to the development of early modern social welfare, the constraints of space limit our focus mainly to Luther (1483–1546), Johannes Bugenhagen (1485–1558),

139

Ulrich Zwingli (1484–1531), Martin Bucer (1491–1551), and John Calvin (1509–64), with some concluding references to the Anabaptists and later influences.

Theology, Charity, and Welfare

By the eve of the Reformation, the increasing population of "have-nots"[1] had become a major social issue rooted in and legitimated by the medieval church's sanctification of poverty as *the* Christian ideal, and exacerbated by the rapid, unregulated growth of the profit economy. The religious vow of poverty gave one a decided edge on the pilgrimage to heaven since the rich, like the proverbial camel, would have to squeeze through the eye of a needle to get there (Mark 10:23–27). On the other hand, the tradition affirmed not only that all things are possible with God, but that Scripture itself (Luke 11:41), especially the apocryphal books of Tobit (12:9) and Ecclesiasticus (Sir. 3:30), provides the solution to the dilemma of the rich: almsgiving atones for sin. Thus a symbiotic relationship of rich and poor developed, in which charity to the poor was perceived as charity to Christ (Matt. 25:31–46, esp. verse 40: "Just as you did it to one of the least of these who are members of my family, you did it me," NRSV Catholic Ed.). The rich atone for their sins by giving alms to the poor, who reciprocate by interceding for the rich and even carry their riches to heaven for them. "To testators, therefore, the outcome of testamentary charity was a win all round—the poor were relieved and the wealthy saved in one transaction."[2] The "pious egoism" of almsgiving and the salvific privileging of poverty was further enhanced by the rise of the mendicant orders, especially the Franciscans. It is not accidental that Francis himself became the patron saint of merchants, for he became the intermediary between the rich and the poor, providing "urban laity with

---

1. "Habnits" and "nihil habens" were late-medieval urban tax categories. Carter Lindberg, *Beyond Charity: Reformation Initiatives for the Poor* (Minneapolis: Fortress Press, 1993), 41.
2. Philippa Maddern, "A Market for Charitable Performances? Bequests to the Poor and Their Recipients in Fifteenth-Century Norwich Wills," in *Experiences of Charity, 1250–1650*, ed. Anne M. Scott (Farnham, Surrey, UK: Ashgate, 2015), 79–103, 82. This "higher hedonism" was already present in the early church and explicitly affirmed by Augustine of Hippo (354–430): "The poor to whom we give alms! With regard to us, what else are they but porters through whom we transfer our goods from earth to heaven?" Lindberg, *Beyond Charity*, 29. See Roman Garrison, *Redemptive Almsgiving in Early Christianity* (London: Bloomsbury Publishing, 1993); and Carlos M. N. Eire, *From Madrid to Purgatory: The Art and Craft of Dying in Sixteenth-Century Spain* (Cambridge: Cambridge University Press, 1995), 232–37.

the tools to work for their own salvation."[3] In brief, the poor were seen by the rising merchant class as a God-ordained investment. The Italian Dominican Giordano da Pisa echoed this ideology of poverty and salvation: "God has ordered that there be rich and poor so that the rich may be served by the poor and the poor may be taken care of by the rich. . . . So that the rich might earn eternal life through them."[4]

The logic of this theology is that of

> a barter economy of gift and reciprocal gift (*"Do ut des,"* I give so that you give). . . . This contractual thinking could strengthen mercantile dealings with God and the next life according to the logic of an exchange of goods, that is, to an economization of the relation to God that without a doubt was not far from the commercial religiosity of the fourteenth and fifteenth centuries. . . . Thus, one reads of "purchasing," "acquiring," "gaining" and "earning" heaven and of satisfying the temporal punishment for sin in this world and in purgatory by setting up charitable foundations and purchasing indulgences.[5]

Scholastic theology gave epigrammatic formulation to the theological construct that made charity a condition of salvation: "faith formed by charity." This "piety of achievement," no matter how grace-assisted, threw the burden of proof for salvation back upon the sinner. Its social

3. David Lesnick, *Preaching in Medieval Florence: The Social World of Franciscan and Dominican Spirituality* (Athens, GA: University of Georgia Press, 1989), 37. For the mediating role of Francis, see Lester K. Little, *Religious Poverty and the Profit Economy in Medieval Europe* (Ithaca, NY: Cornell University Press, 1976), 38, 217; and Kenneth B. Wolf, *The Poverty of Riches: St Francis of Assisi Reconsidered* (Oxford: Oxford University Press, 2003).

4. Lesnick, *Preaching in Medieval Florence*, 126. See also Michel Mollat, *The Poor in the Middle Ages: An Essay in Social History*, trans. Arthur Gold Hammer (New Haven, CT: Yale University Press, 1986); Spencer E. Young, "More Blessed to Give *and* Receive: Charitable Giving in Thirteenth- and Early Fourteenth-Century *Exempla*," in Scott, *Experiences of Charity*, 63–78; Catherine Lis and Hugo Soly, *Poverty and Capitalism in Pre-Industrial Europe* (Atlantic Highlands, NJ: Humanities Press, 1979), 22.

5. Berndt Hamm, "Martin Luther's Revolutionary Theology of Pure Gift without Reciprocation," *Lutheran Quarterly* 29, no. 2 (2015): 125–61, 128, 131–32. See also Hamm, "Den Himmel kaufen: Heilskommerzielle Perspektiven des 14. bis 16. Jahrhunderts," in *Himmel auf Erden / Heaven on Earth*, ed. Rudolf Suntrup and Jan R. Veenstra (Frankfurt am Main: Peter Lang, 2009), 23–56; Jacques Chiffoleau, *La comptabilité de l'au-delà: Les hommes, la mort et la religion dans la région d'Avignon à la fin du Moyen Age (vers 1320–vers 1480)* (Rome: École Française de Rome, 1980); Jacques Le Goff, *Your Money or Your Life: Economy and Religion in the Middle Ages* (New York: Zone Books, 1988); Joel Rosenthal, *The Purchase of Paradise: Gift Giving and the Aristocracy, 1307–1485* (London: Routledge, 1972).

consequences kept the poor in their God-ordained place and provided a cheap labor pool; but begging proliferated not only by the rise of the mendicant orders and the increasing numbers of the "honest poor," but also by the "dishonest poor," who posed as mendicants or more commonly as destitute. By the eve of the Reformation, the social problems associated with begging led to numerous "guides" to expose the tricks of beggars and to warn people about the "embezzlement" of their alms.[6] The nexus of theology, poverty, and the rising profit economy made it difficult for pre-Reformation society to move beyond charitable activities to developing secular (laicized) and rational social welfare policies.

Luther's exegetical discovery that the righteousness of God is "pure gift without reciprocation"[7] shifted the understanding of salvation from a goal to be achieved to that of salvation as the received foundation of life. This was a "paradigm shift *par excellence*,"[8] "a fundamental 'system-crashing' departure from medieval religiosity."[9] "This is the reason why our theology is certain: it snatches us away from ourselves and places us outside ourselves, so that we do not depend on our own strength, conscience, experience, person, or works but depend on that which is outside ourselves, that is, on the promise and truth of God, which cannot deceive."[10] If this is not clear enough, Luther commented on Hebrews 9:17 that God names us in his will and dies to make it effective. "You would have to spend a long time polishing your shoes, preening and primping to attain an inheritance, if you had no letter and seal with which to prove your right to it. But if you have a letter and seal, and believe, desire, and seek it, it must be given to you, even though you were scaly, scabby, stinking, and most filthy."[11] The Christian is now freed from striving for salvation, freed for service to the neighbor:

<hr>

6. One of the most famous of these tracts was the *Liber vagatorum*, in English *The Book of Vagabonds* [New York: Coward-McCann, 1933]). Luther wrote a preface for one of its reprints in 1528 (*LW* 59:236–39); see Lindberg, *Beyond Charity*, 182–85.

7. Hamm, "Luther's Revolutionary Theology," 128: "Wherever the Reformation's exclusive formulae of *sola Scriptura*, *solus Christus*, *sola gratia* and *sola fide* form a common intersection of content, the central theme of theology, proclamation, worship and piety is the exclusive sovereignty of the divine gift without any human cooperation whatsoever."

8. Hans Küng, *Great Christian Thinkers* (New York: Continuum, 1995), 142, emphasis original.

9. Berndt Hamm, *The Early Luther: Stages in a Reformation Reorientation*, trans. Martin Lohrmann (Grand Rapids: Wm. B. Eerdmans Publishing Co., 2014), 31; see also 237, 255. Calvin, too, understood "that salvation is rescue and not achievement." John Leith, *John Calvin's Doctrine of the Christian Life* (Louisville, KY: Westminster/John Knox Press, 1989), 122.

10. *Lectures on Galatians*, 1535; *LW* 26:387.

11. *A Treatise on the New Testament*, 1520; *LW* 35:88.

"Here faith is truly active through love." "We conclude, therefore, that a Christian lives not in himself, but in Christ and in his neighbor."[12] Here is a new ethos of community particularly relevant to the urban developments of the time. The motif of the common good (*gemeinen Nutzen*) versus self-interest and greed (*Eigennutz*) reverberates in the writings of the Reformers. For example, in 1523 Martin Bucer, the Strasbourg reformer strongly influenced by Luther, published his tract *That No One Should Live for Himself, but Rather for Others, and How We May Attain This.*[13] Likewise for Calvin, "social and economic behavior is neither an autonomous sphere of human life, nor just an optional addendum; it is a vital part of the worship of God."[14] Similarly, Luther explicitly tied worship and welfare together: "Now there is no greater service of God [*dienst gottis*, i.e., worship, *Gottesdienst*] than Christian love which helps and serves the needy, as Christ himself will judge and testify at the Last Day, Matthew 25[:31–46]."[15]

The paradigm shift in justification cut the nerve of the medieval ideology of poverty. Since salvation is God's free gift, poverty and almsgiving lose saving significance. Here, too, there is a paradigm shift: the desanctification of poverty enabled movement from charity to consideration of the systemic roots of poverty, to prophylactic action instead of remedial maintenance of the poor. The poor are no longer objects for meritorious charity but neighbors to be served through justice and equity. In Luther's words: "Poverty, I say, is not to be recommended, chosen, or taught; for there is enough of that by itself, as He says (John 12:8): 'The poor you always have with you,' just as you will have all other evils. But constant care should be taken that, since these evils are always in evidence, they are always opposed."[16] Instead of the fatalistic eisegesis of John 12:8, Luther

---

12. *The Freedom of a Christian*, 1520; *LW* 31:365, 371.

13. Cf. Lindberg, *Beyond Charity*, 94.

14. Elsie Anne McKee, "The Character and Significance of John Calvin's Teaching on Social and Economic Issues," in *John Calvin Rediscovered: The Impact of His Social and Economic Thought*, ed. Edward Dommen and James Bratt (Louisville, KY: Westminster John Knox Press, 2007), 3–24, at 6. Cf. Mark Valeri, "Religion, Discipline, and the Economy in Calvin's Geneva," *Sixteenth Century Journal* 28, no. 1 (1997): 123–42, esp. 126, 136, 141–42.

15. Preface to the Leisnig Order, 1523; *LW* 45:172. See Carter Lindberg, "Luther's Concept of Offering," *Dialog* 35, no. 4 (1996): 251–57, at 256; Lindberg, *Beyond Charity*, 136, 163–65. Luther had already distinguished true and false worship in his tracts on usury. See WA 6:7–8; WA 6:59, as referenced in Michael Beyer, "Wirtschaftsethik bei Martin Luther," in *Wirtschaft und Ethik in theologischer Perspektive*, ed. Udo Kern (Münster: LIT, 2002), 85–110, at 109; here and below, WA = Weimarer Ausgabe: *Martin Luthers Werke: Kritische Gesamtausgabe*, 121 vols. (Weimar: Hermann Böhlau / H. Böhlaus Nachfolger, 1883–2009).

16. *Lectures on Deuteronomy*, 1525; *LW* 9:148.

and his colleagues turned to the Deuteronomic rubric "There will be no poor among you" (Deut. 15:4 RSV).[17] The Reformers thereby moved in alliance with local governments to establish and legislate government social welfare programs designed to prevent as well as remedy poverty. "For so to help a man that he does not need to become a beggar is just as much of a good work and a virtue as to give alms to a man who has already become a beggar."[18]

Welfare Legislation through Common Chest Ordinances

The Wittenberg Town Council, with Luther's assistance, passed the first social welfare legislation, the "Common Purse," in late 1520 or early 1521. The purpose was to collect resources such as grain and firewood for distribution to those in need. The council followed this with the Wittenberg Order of January 1522. It is known as the Common Chest because a heavy strongbox with three separate locks was commissioned and placed in the parish church for the weekly collection and disbursement of funds.[19] Four stewards were elected on the basis of their knowledge of the town and its inhabitants. The criterion for loans and outright gifts was the need of the recipient. The funds initially came from expropriated ecclesiastical endowments and then from taxes, gifts, and wills. The order's prohibition of begging was directed mainly at the mendicant orders and swindlers. The Common Chest provided interest-free loans to artisans (to be repaid if possible); funds for orphans, children of the

---

17. *Lectures on Deuteronomy*, 1525; *LW* 9:147–48; *To the Christian Nobility*, 1520; *LW* 44:189–91. In 1522, Luther's Wittenberg colleague Andreas Bodenstein von Karlstadt published an extensive tract on this text that focused on the abolition of both images and begging. See Carter Lindberg, "'There Should Be No Beggars among Christians': An Early Reformation Tract on Social Welfare by Andreas Karlstadt," in *Piety, Politics, and Ethics: Reformation Studies in Honor of George Wolfgang Forell*, ed. Carter Lindberg (Kirksville, MO: Sixteenth Century Journal Publishers, 1984), 157–66. The link between iconoclasm and poor relief reflects the convictions of Luther, Zwingli, and Calvin that images are not only against the First Commandment but also "voracious idols" devouring money and resources that ought to go to the poor. See Lee Palmer Wandel, *Voracious Idols and Violent Hands: Iconoclasm in Zurich, Strasbourg and Basel* (Cambridge: Cambridge University Press, 1995); and Wandel, *Always among Us: Images of the Poor in Zwingli's Zurich* (Cambridge: Cambridge University Press, 1990). Money invested in church ornamentation and indulgences removed resources from the community; cf. Philipp Rössner, "Burying Money? Monetary Origins and Afterlives of Luther's Reformation," *History of Political Economy* 48, no. 2 (2016): 225–63.

18. *Commentary on Psalm 82*, 1530; *LW* 13:54. This commentary, like those Luther wrote on Ps. 101 and the Magnificat, is known as a *Fürstenspiegel*, that is, a "mirror for princes" that speaks truth to power by candidly addressing religious and ethical issues.

19. This original Common Chest is on display in the Luther Museum in Wittenberg.

poor, and women in need of dowries; refinancing of high-interest loans at 4 percent for burdened citizens; education and training for poor children; and vocational retraining for underemployed artisans.[20] In addition, the town engaged Melchior Fendt, professor on the Wittenberg University medical faculty, as town physician for the poor, thus a precursor to socialized medicine.[21] The Common Chest functioned as a kind of central bank responsible to the whole community for communal poor relief.

The concept of the Wittenberg Common Chest, rapidly spread by printing, quickly attracted the attention of preachers and cities influenced by Luther.[22] Within a few years it was emulated in Leisnig, Augsburg, Nuremberg,[23] Altenburg, Kitzingen, Strasbourg, Breslau, Regensburg, Schwabach, and the area of Hesse.[24] Under the influence of the reformer Ulrich Zwingli, Zurich established an Order for Poor Relief in 1525 that echoed some of the Lutheran orders, such as that in Nuremberg, in terms of a common chest, funding, aid criteria, and prohibition of begging as well as the communalizing and rationalizing of poor relief. The Zurich order is significant not only as an expression of Zwingli's clear social orientation but as one of the earliest orders from the Reformed sphere of the Reformation.[25] Luther's Wittenberg colleague and pastor, Johannes

20. Lindberg, *Beyond Charity*, 200–202.

21. Stefan Oehmig, "Der Wittenberger Gemeine Kasten in den ersten zweieinhalb Jahrzeiten seines Bestehens (1522/23 bis 1547)," *Jahrbuch für Geschichte des Feudalismus* 13 (1989):141–45; Robert Jütte, "Die Sorge für Kranke und Gebrechliche in den Almosen- und Kastenordnungen des 16. Jahrhunderts," in *Medizin und Sozialwesen in Mitteldeutschland zur Reformationszeit*, ed. Stefan Oehmig (Leipzig: Evangelischen Verlagsanstalt, 2007), 9–21.

22. Very likely also influential in England; see Nicholas Dean Brodie, "A History of the English Parochial Poor Box c. 1547," in Scott, *Experiences of Charity*, 215–37, 227.

23. "An outpost of Wittenberg in southern Germany," where "the new alms ordinance in the year 1522 . . . clearly betrayed the influence of Lutheran preaching." Gottfried Seebass, "The Reformation in Nürnberg," in *The Social History of the Reformation*, ed. Lawrence Buck and Jonathan Zophy (Columbus: Ohio State University Press, 1972), 17–40, at 18, 25.

24. Luther himself assisted the town council of Leisnig in establishing a common chest (*LW* 45:159–94). The standard multivolume collection of the numerous common-chest orders is that of Emil Sehling et al., eds., *Die evangelischen Kirchenordnung des XVI. Jahrhunderts* (Leipzig: Riesland, 1902–), now continued by the Heidelberg Akademie der Wissenschaften. See also Anneliese Sprengler-Ruppenthal, "Zur Entstehungsgeschichte der Reformatorischen Kirchen- und Armenordnung im 16. Jahrhundert: Eine Dokumentation," in *Kleine Essays und Nachträge zu den Kirchenordnungen des 16. Jahrhunderts* (Hamburg: Selbstverl, 2011), 66–148.

25. An English translation with introduction is in *Some Early Tracts on Poor Relief*, ed. F. R. Salter (London: Methuen, 1926), 96–103; and a modern German edition with an introduction by Michael Klein is in *Die Entstehung einer sozialen Ordnung Europas*, ed. Theodore Strohm and Michael Klein, 2 vols. (Heidelberg: Universitätsverlag, 2004), 2:100–107. See also Wandel, *Always among Us*.

Bugenhagen, further developed and spread the ideas of the Wittenberg Common Chest.[26] In constant demand throughout northern Europe, Bugenhagen wrote or edited church orders for Braunschweig (1528),[27] Hamburg (1529), Lübeck (1531), Pomerania (1535), Denmark-Norway (1537), Schleswig-Holstein (1542), Braunschweig-Wolfenbüttel (1543), and Hildesheim (1544). He also influenced developments in southern Germany through the work of the Strasbourg reformer Martin Bucer, who in turn influenced John Calvin during Calvin's three-year exile in Strasbourg. Bugenhagen's work was rooted in Luther's theology. "Faith active in love is the theological basis and practical motivation for the care of the poor in Bugenhagen's theology. He . . . maintains that caring for the poor is not a matter of free choice for the Christian but a clear expectation."[28] One of Bugenhagen's contributions was to separate funds for poor relief from funds for schools, pastors' salaries, and church maintenance so that when pastors appealed for social welfare, people would know that the pastors were supported by salaries and not lining their own pockets.

Rooted in evangelical preaching and teaching, the legal establishment of the Reformation through these church ordinances and their provisions for social welfare and schools was the work of jurists.[29] One example is Johannes Eisermann, also known as Ferrarius, a student of Luther's colleague Philipp Melanchthon. Eisermann studied theology, medicine, and the classics at the University of Wittenberg before receiving his law degree there in 1532. He went into the service of Landgrave Philip of Hesse and was the founding law professor of the new Lutheran University of Marburg. Eisermann's tract *On the Common Good* developed some of Luther's theological themes and went through several editions and translations, including into English. "Eisermann contemplated

26. See Tim Lorentzen, *Johannes Bugenhagen als Reformator der öffentlichen Fürsorge* (Tübingen: Mohr, 2008); and Lorentzen, "Theologie und Ökonomie in Bugenhagens Fürsorgekonzept," in *Der späte Bugenhagen*, ed. Irene Dingel and Stefan Rhein (Leipzig: Evangelische Verlagsanstalt, 2011), 151–74; Kurt Hendel, "Johannes Bugenhagen, Organizer of the Lutheran Reformation," *Lutheran Quarterly* 18, no. 1 (2004): 43–75; Hendel, "Paul and the Care of the Poor during the Sixteenth Century: A Case Study," in *A Companion to Paul in the Reformation*, ed. Ward Holder (Leiden: Brill, 2009), 541–71.

27. An English translation of the Braunschweig "Order of the Poor Chest" is in *Johannes Bugenhagen: Selected Writings*, ed. and trans. Kurt Hendel (Minneapolis: Fortress Press, 2015), 2:1390–99.

28. Kurt Hendel, "The Care of the Poor: An Evangelical Perspective," *Currents in Theology and Mission* 15 (1988): 526–32, at 527.

29. See John Witte Jr., *Law and Protestantism: The Legal Teachings of the Lutheran Reformation* (Cambridge: Cambridge University Press, 2002).

an active Christian magistrate at the core of an active Christian welfare state: '. . . to enlarge the common good, to relieve the poor, to defend the orphan and the widow, to promote virtue, to administer justice, to keep the law.'"[30]

Luther used the pulpit and his extensive writings to remind and exhort political authorities that they were responsible not only for defending their people but also especially for the nurture and education of their people. The second virtue of a prince after securing justice "is to help the poor, the orphans, and the widows to justice and to further their cause."[31] In his explanation of the fourth petition of the Lord's Prayer in his Large Catechism, Luther wrote: "It would therefore be fitting if the coat of arms of every upright prince were emblazoned with a loaf of bread instead of a lion or a wreath of rue, or if a loaf of bread were stamped on coins, in order to remind both princes and subjects that it is through the princes' office that we enjoy protection and peace and that without them we would neither eat nor preserve the precious gift of bread."[32]

In his advocacy for the "least of these" (Matt. 25:40),[33] Luther asserted that the exhortation of secular authorities to establish civil justice is a function of the preaching office "in the congregation," "openly and boldly before God and men." It is God's will, Luther continues, "that those who are in the office [of ministry] and are called to do so shall rebuke their gods [rulers] boldly and openly. . . . To rebuke rulers is not seditious, provided it is done . . . by the office by which God has committed that duty, and through God's Word, spoken publicly, boldly, and honestly." Indeed, Luther continues, "every prince should have painted on the wall of his chamber, on his bed, over his table, and on his garments" the three

30. John Witte Jr., "An Evangelical Commonwealth: Johannes Eisermann on Law and the Common Good," in *Caritas et Reformatio: Essays on Church and Society in Honor of Carter Lindberg*, ed. David M. Whitford (St. Louis: Concordia Publishing House, 2002), 73–87, 83. See also Winfried Schulze, "Vom Gemeinnutz zum Eigennutz," *Historische Zeitschrift* 243 (1986): 591–626, at 598. Two other important advisers were the Lutherans Johann Feige and Adam Kraft. See William J. Wright, "Reformation Contributions to the Development of Welfare Policy in Hesse," *Journal of Modern History* 49, no. 2 (1977): D1145–79; Wright, *Capitalism, the State, and the Lutheran Reformation: Sixteenth-Century Hesse* (Athens: Ohio University Press, 1988); Hans Liermann, "Protestant Endowment Law in the Franconian Church Ordinances of the Sixteenth Century," in Buck and Zophy, *Social History of the Reformation*, 340–54.
31. *Commentary on Psalm 82*, 1530; *LW* 13:53.
32. Robert Kolb and Timothy J. Wengert, eds., *The Book of Concord* [hereafter *BC*] (Minneapolis: Fortress Press, 2000), 450. See Albrecht Peters, *Kommentar zu Luthers Katechismen*, vol. 3, *Das Vaterunser* (Göttingen: Vandenhoeck & Ruprecht, 1992), 128–30.
33. *Whether One May Flee from a Deadly Plague*, 1527; *LW* 43:130.

virtues emphasized in Psalm 82: to secure justice, to further the cause of the poor, and to make peace.[34]

Luther's influence on Martin Bucer may be seen not only in Bucer's ministry in Strasbourg but also in his 1550 treatise for the young successor to Henry VIII, Edward VI of England: *De Regno Christ* (*On the Kingdom of Christ*).[35] Thus chapter 14 of book 1, "Care for the Needy," begins with the reference to Deuteronomy 15:4: "For the Lord expressly forbids his people to allow anyone among them to be in need."[36] Bucer then summarizes the main ideas of Reformation poor relief, including the common chest and prohibition of begging. Bucer also expands and elaborates this program in book 2, chapter 14: "The Sixth Law: Poor Relief." A difference from Luther that will also be seen in Calvin's understanding of ministry is Bucer's emphasis upon the ministerial office of deacon. "Your majesty will see to it that each church has its deacons in charge of providing for the poor."[37]

Whether Calvin was influenced by Bucer while in exile in Strasbourg or developed his own ideas on the role of deacons through his theological-exegetical studies or observation of the operation of Geneva's General Hospital, Calvin was convinced that "the diaconate should be a lay ministry devoted solely to aiding the poor."[38] There is no doubt that Calvin built on the Reformation principles of the laicization and rationalization of poor relief. This civic responsibility was put to the test as Geneva was flooded with waves of French religious refugees that doubled the city population within a decade. Sometime between 1545 and 1550, a special fund, the *Bourse française*, was established to aid all these foreigners. "One distinguishing feature of the *Bourse française* was that it served people who were not native to Geneva—the foreign poor, unlike most social welfare systems of the era that preferred to concentrate on the local poor."[39] In Calvin's dedication of his commentary on the Gospel of

34. *Commentary on Psalm 82*, 1530; *LW* 13:49–59.

35. English translation and introduction by Wilhelm Pauck, *Melanchthon and Bucer* (Philadelphia: Westminster Press, 1969), 155–394, at 256–59, 306–15, 307.

36. Ibid., 256.

37. Ibid., 307.

38. Robert M. Kingdon, "Social Welfare in Calvin's Geneva," *American Historical Review* 76, no. 1 (1971): 50–69, 60; Kingdon, "Calvin's Ideas about the Diaconate: Social or Theological in Origin?," in Lindberg, *Piety, Politics, and Ethics*, 167–180. See also Elsie Anne McKee, *John Calvin on the Diaconate and Liturgical Almsgiving* (Geneva: Droz, 1984); and Wulfert de Greef, *The Writings of John Calvin*, expanded ed. (Louisville, KY: Westminster John Knox Press, 2008), 132. Luther made the same point (*LW* 75:325–26).

39. Jeannine Olson, *Calvin and Social Welfare: Deacons and the Bourse Française* (Selinsgrove, PA: Susquehanna University Press, 1989), 182.

John to the Council of Geneva, he refers to Geneva as a refugee center. "That is significant in light of Christ's statement that he regards the taking in of strangers as something done personally to him. In the midst of confusion, may the Council know that Christ will be nearby, protecting the cities where the gospel can be proclaimed and his people are allowed to live."[40] Such aid to the local and foreign poor certainly contributed to John Knox's praise for Geneva as "the most perfect school of Christ that ever was in the earth since the days of the Apostles."[41]

Welfare and the Profit Economy

The upheavals of the Reformation certainly exacerbated poverty, but one of the root causes for widespread European economic insecurity was the late-medieval development of early capitalism. Thus the major Reformers directed attention not only to social-welfare legislation but also to government regulation of the early profit economy. Luther, from the start of his reforming career, directly engaged with the burning financial as well as welfare issues of the day, repeatedly calling for government regulation of business and banking. He attacked profiteering in the *Short Sermon on Usury* (1519), which appeared in three editions, and in the *Long Sermon on Usury* (1520). He incorporated both of these works into his major attack on early capitalism in *Trade and Usury* (1524),[42] which appeared in seven editions. People began looking to him for guidance. In 1525 the Danzig town council requested his advice on profiteering and legitimate interest rates.[43] In response, he emphasized equity and a limit of 5 percent interest. In the meantime, he published *To the Christian Nobility of the German Nation* (1520), stating that taking interest is the work of the devil and the greatest misfortune of the German nation.[44] The drumbeat continued with his exposition of the Seventh Commandment ("Thou shalt not steal") in his *Treatise on Good Works* (1520),[45] his Large Catechism (1529),[46] and his biblical commentaries. Finally, toward the end of his life he wrote the explosive tract that exhorts pastors to excommunicate usurers, *An*

40. Greef, *The Writings of John Calvin*, 82–83.
41. Cited by Kingdon, "Calvin's Ideas about the Diaconate," 180.
42. *LW* 45:2–310.
43. WA Br 3:483–86; Br = Briefe/Briefwechsel [Correspondence].
44. *LW* 44:115–217.
45. *LW* 44:14–114.
46. *BC* 416–20.

die Pfarrherrn wider den Wucher zu predigen, Vermahnung,[47] which went
through four editions and a translation into Latin. The significance
of Luther's writing these tracts in German "for the laity," as he said,
rather than in Latin for fellow academics, cannot be overestimated: he
intended to demystify religious, political, and economic systems that
controlled people.[48] That Luther's writings on economics were important to his contemporaries is evident in the large number of tracts and
their reprints that critiqued merchants not as traders but as financiers
profiting in the world of money markets at the expense of the community at large.

The idea that money can make money was relatively recent by the
Reformation. The medieval church's condemnation of the profit economy, termed "usury" in theology and canon law, was reiterated as late as
the Fifth Lateran Council in 1515. By then, however, the entrepreneur
was well established. Hence the popular contemporary saying that loan
sharks should be strangled or hanged.[49] Luther was convinced that the
new profit economy divorced money from use for human needs, necessi-
tated an economy of acquisition, fed the mortal sin of avarice, and eroded
the common good. "After the devil there is no greater human enemy on
earth than a miser and usurer for he desires to be God over everyone.
Turks, soldiers, and tyrants are also evil men, yet they must allow the
people to live; . . . indeed, they must now and then be somewhat merciful. But a usurer and miser-belly desires that the entire world be ruined
in order that there be hunger, thirst, misery, and need so that he can have
everything and so that everyone must depend upon him and be his slave
as if he were God."[50] "The poor are defrauded every day, and new burdens and higher prices are imposed. They all misuse the market in their
own arbitrary, defiant, arrogant way, as if it were their privilege and right
to sell their goods as high as they please without any criticism."[51]

The "lust for profit," Luther observed, had many clever expressions:
selling on time and credit, manipulating the market by withholding or

47. WA 51:325–424.

48. Vitor Westhelle, "Communication and the Transgression of Language in Martin Luther,"
in *The Pastoral Luther: Essays on Martin Luther's Practical Theology*, ed. Timothy J. Wengert
(Grand Rapids: Wm. B. Eerdmans Publishing Co., 2009), 59–84, at 64.

49. *Trade and Usury*, 1524; *LW* 45:253.

50. WA 51:396–97. See Ricardo Rieth, "Luther on Greed," in *Harvesting Martin Luther's
Reflections on Theology, Ethics, and the Church*, ed. Timothy J. Wengert (Grand Rapids: Wm. B.
Eerdmans Publishing Co., 2004), 152–68.

51. *BC* 418.

dumping goods, developing cartels and monopolies, falsifying bankrupt-cies, and just plain misrepresenting goods.[52] Luther's shorthand for these practices was "usury," the common medieval term for lending at inter-est. Yet the focus of Luther's attack was not usury per se but the finan-cial practices related to large-scale national and international commerce. This "modern" usury, Luther charged, affects everyone. "The usury that occurs in Leipzig, Augsburg, Frankfurt, and other comparable cities is felt in our market and our kitchen. The usurers are eating our food and drink." Even worse, however, is that by manipulating prices, "usury lives off the bodies of the poor."[53] Later, Calvin would make a similar charge: "The houses of the rich are the butchering places of the poor."[54] Luther exploded: "The world is one big whorehouse, completely submerged in greed," where the "big thieves hang the little thieves."[55] In the Large Catechism, Luther wrote: "Yes, we might well keep quiet here about individual petty thieves since we ought to be attacking the great, powerful archthieves with whom the lords and princes consort and who daily plun-der not just a city or two, but all of Germany. . . . Those who can steal and rob openly are safe and free, unpunished by anyone, even desiring to be honored."[56] When Luther exhorted pastors to condemn usury as stealing and murder, and to refuse absolution, the sacrament, and Chris-tian burial to usurers unless they repented, he had in mind these "great, powerful archthieves," not the "petty thieves" who fill prisons. Practicing what he preached, Luther himself excluded a nobleman from commu-nion for exacting 30 percent interest.[57] "Even today, the radical nature of these late statements by Luther on economic questions has not yet been fully apprehended."[58] While Calvin was less linguistically colorful than Luther, he too condemned any business that exploited people. "Calvin warned that the tendency of usury is always to oppress one's neighbor. In other words, the spirit of neighborly love must dominate such business transactions as the lending of money. For this reason he refused to set any

52. *Trade and Usury*, 1524; *LW* 45:231–310.
53. WA 51:417.
54. Cited by Alberto Bondolfi, "Die Debatte um die Reform der Armenpflege im Europa des 16. Jahrhunderts," in T. Strohm and Klein, *Die Entstehung einer sozialen Ordnung Europas*, 1:105–45, 126.
55. *Commentary on the Sermon on the Mount*, 1532; *LW* 21:180; *Lectures on Romans*, 1516; *LW* 25:172.
56. *BC* 417.
57. WA 51:367–68, 422.
58. Martin Brecht, *Martin Luther: The Preservation of the Church, 1532–1546* (Minneapolis: Fortress Press, 1993), 258–61.

one rate as legitimate interest. Each case must be judged separately and in the case of the poor and needy all interest is wrong when it oppresses people."[59] "The Genevan catechism, reprinted throughout Europe, instructed children in the evils of 'making a living from our neighbor, be it by fraud or violence' or any 'schemes, designs, and deliberations' to 'enrich ourselves at our neighbor's expense.'"[60]

A dearth of food and consequent steep rise in food prices in Wittenberg owing to rodent and drought damages to crops in 1538–39 prompted Luther's sharp attack on profiteers who were holding grain off the market to gain higher profits. Luther requested communal assistance from the town council and was told it was not responsible. He then appealed to Prince Johann Friedrich, pointing out that grain was being kept off the market "to the ruin of your electoral grace's land and people."[61] In this context, Luther argued that pastors were to preach against the "great sin and shame" of usury ruining Germany. They were to make it clear that those who take more than 5 percent profit are idolatrous servants of mammon. Preachers should stand firm against the rejoinder that if the taking of interest is condemned, then "nearly the whole world would be damned." One is not to preach according to the customs of the world but according to what God's law demands. In the case of famine, the civil authority must intervene, for refusing to sell grain is equivalent to stealing and robbing. Luther did not naively assume that the CEOs of his day would easily change their ways. "We preachers can easily counsel but no one or few follow." It may be true that the world cannot do without usury, but as Christ said, woe to the person by whom offense comes. Luther concluded, "There must be usury, but woe to the usurer!"[62]

The issue was not just an individual's use of money but also the structural social damage inherent in the idolatry of the "laws" of the market. Luther demanded that the economy be ruled by love of the neighbor through the principles of equity and reason.[63] He saw ideas of an impersonal market and autonomous laws of economics as idolatrous and socially

59. Leith, *Calvin's Doctrine of the Christian Life*, 196.
60. Valeri, "Religion, Discipline, and the Economy in Calvin's Geneva," 140.
61. WA Br 8:403–5.
62. WA 51:325, 332–36, 353–54.
63. Andreas Pawlas, "Ist 'kaufhandel' immer 'Wucher'? Luther zu kaufmännischen Handel und Wucher als Beitrag zu einer evangelischen Wirtschaftsethik," *Kerygma und Dogma* 40 (1994): 282–304, at 289. See Michael Lapp, "'Denn es ist geld ein ungewis, wanckelbar ding': Die Wirtschaftsethik Martin Luthers anhand seiner Schriften gegen den Wucher," *Luther: Zeitschrift der Luther-Gesellschaft* 83, no. 2 (2012): 91–107; Matthieu Arnold, "La notion d'*epieikeia* chez Martin Luther," *Revue d'histoire et de philosophie religieuses* 79, no. 2 (1999): 187–208.

destructive. Luther observed that the entire community was endangered by the financial power of a few great economic centers. His concern is reflected in a saying of the time that "a bit should be placed in the mouth of the Fuggers," the central bank of the empire at that time.[64] The new profit economy was beginning to absorb urban and local economies and to threaten increased opposition between rich and poor. He saw economic coercion immune to normal jurisdiction and thus perceived early capitalism as a "weapon of mass destruction," aimed at the common good, the ethos of community.

Calvin shared Luther's antipathy toward Europe's great commercial centers.[65] To both reformers, early capitalism not only exploited people but also did so by deceiving people about its voracious nature. Luther and then Calvin appealed for government regulation of business practices and interest rates. Although Calvin wrote far less than Luther on the topic of usury, they struck the same notes. Usurers, Calvin stated, should be "chased from every country" because they often are cruel and fraudulent, deceiving and preying upon the poor. Like Luther, Calvin asserted that commerce is not evil in itself but should be regulated on the basis of equity and service to the common good.[66] "Calvin never hesitated to denounce fraudulent and oppressive business transactions in his sermons. . . . He regarded economic injustices as a serious matter both for the Christian community and for the Christian individual."[67]

While Luther's efforts to develop welfare legislation were well received in the cities and territories that accepted the Reformation, his efforts to encourage civic control of capitalism did not gain comparable support. He aimed his criticism of capitalism at far more than exorbitant interest rates. Luther argued that social need always stood above personal gain. "In a well-arranged commonwealth the debts of the poor who are in need ought to be cancelled, and they ought to be helped; hence the action of collecting has its place only against the lazy and the ne'er-do-well."[68] But the common good was being undermined by the activities of large businesses that even the emperor could not hold to account.

Luther experienced that it is easier to motivate assistance to individuals than to curb the economic practices that create their need. Poverty's

64. *To the Christian Nobility; LW* 44:213.
65. Valeri, "Religion, Discipline, and the Economy in Calvin's Geneva," 137.
66. Calvin, "On Usury," in *Calvin's Ecclesiastical Advice*, trans. and ed. Mary Beaty and Benjamin W. Farley (Louisville, KY: Westminster/John Knox Press, 1991), 139–43, 161, 168.
67. Leith, *Calvin's Doctrine of the Christian Life*, 192.
68. *Lectures on Deuteronomy; LW* 9:243.

squalor calls out for redress, whereas the attractive trappings of business muffle criticism. "How skillfully Sir Greed can dress up to look like a pious man if that seems to be what the occasion requires, while he is actually a double scoundrel and a liar. . . . There is no room for anyone next to these griffins and lions, who monopolize every kind of business. And meanwhile they want to be called pious and honorable people."[69] "God opposes usury and greed, yet no one realizes this because it is not simple murder and robbery. Rather, usury is a more diverse, insatiable murder and robbery. . . . Thus everyone should see to his worldly and spiritual office as commanded to punish the wicked and protect the pious."[70]

Public goods, Luther asserted, are for everyone. For example, quality public education should be available for all. In response to the perennial complaint that public education is expensive, Luther replied: "My dear sirs, if we have to spend such large sums every year on guns, roads, bridges, dams, and countless similar items to insure the temporal peace and prosperity of a city, why should not much more be devoted to our poor neglected youth."[71] He was convinced that government and society cannot continue without educated leaders and citizens. The young must be trained not just for the sake of employers but also to benefit and serve the world through training in history, the arts, languages, science, and mathematics. "The devil very much prefers coarse blockheads and ne'er-do-wells, lest men get along too well on earth." Schools should be supplemented by publicly maintained libraries. "For if the gospel and all the arts are to be preserved, they must be set down and held fast in books and writings."[72] The world, Luther argued, needs educated leaders capable of restraining evil and promoting the common good. "If there were no worldly government, one man could not stand before another; each would necessarily devour the other, as irrational beasts devour one another. Therefore . . . it is the function and honor of worldly government to make men out of wild beasts and to prevent men from becoming wild beasts." Without a capable and wise government, society would devolve to the survival of the fittest, the wealthiest. "For if men were to rule solely by the fist, the end result would surely be a bestial kind of existence: whoever could get the better of another would simply toss

69. *Commentary on the Sermon on the Mount; LW* 21:183–84.
70. WA 51:422–23.
71. *To the Councilmen of All Cities in Germany That They Establish and Maintain Christian Schools*, 1524; *LW* 45:350.
72. *To the Councilmen; LW* 45:371, 373.

him into the discard pile."[73] The "preferential option for the poor," well known in our time from the writings of Latin American liberation theologians, was already established in the theory and praxis of the Magisterial Reformers of the Reformation.[74]

Anabaptist "Community of Goods"

The social reforms of Luther, Zwingli, and Calvin remained unsatisfactory to their contemporaries searching for a more radical renewal of church and society and yearning for a more spiritual Christianity. The diversity of these more radical movements, their leaders, and their geographical settings complicates assessment and has prompted a number of designations: Radical Reformation, Left Wing of the Reformation, Nonconformists, Dissidents, or more generically, Anabaptists. No one of these designations is totally satisfactory. The Anabaptists proper encompassed the Swiss Brethren, the Mennonites, and the Hutterites, who practiced believers' baptism, created distinct communities separate from the Magisterial Reformations, and existed on the margins of society. A complex movement with differing tendencies, Anabaptism promoted a vision of restoring the primitive Christian community, a counterculture separate from the world, as the prototype of a better society.

Around 1530, figures appeared who influenced the evolution of the movement. Pilgram Marpeck (ca. 1495–1556), a Tyrolean engineer, animated the Anabaptist circle in Strasbourg until 1532, and then was active in Grisons and Augsburg. Jakob Hutter (ca. 1500–1536), also from Tyrol and then Moravia, exerted such a major influence that some followers were called Hutterites. Another key figure was the furrier Melchior Hoffman (ca. 1495–1543), active in Livonia, Stockholm, Lübeck, Schleswig-Holstein, eastern Frisia, the Low Countries, and finally Strasbourg. He strongly opposed the "papalism" of the Wittenberg reformers and called his followers to prepare for the imminent arrival of the heavenly Jerusalem. Caspar Schwenckfeld (1489–1561), a Silesian nobleman, was influential among the upper classes. Sebastian Franck (1499–1542) emphasized inner illumination and the relativization of all churches. After 1530, Anabaptism in Switzerland took form with the Schleitheim Confession (1527).

Moravia provided a certain amount of toleration for Anabaptist communities. The Anabaptist refugees there were decisively influenced by

---

73. *A Sermon on Keeping Children in School*, 1530; *LW* 46:237–38.
74. Lorentzen, *Johannes Bugenhagen*, 174.

Hutter. To subsist, they held their goods in common, following the teaching of Acts 2:42–47; convinced of apostolic mission, they advanced disciplinary measures for purifying and organizing the community. Luther, Zwingli, and Calvin, to mention only these major reformers, argued that the Anabaptist interpretation of the famous Acts passages was a false extrapolation from an early church emergency measure, and they endorsed private property insofar as it did not lead to oppression.[75]

The most characteristic element in the Hutterites' life, distinguishing them from other Anabaptists, was the practice of communal property, production, daily life and meals, and education of children. When a member died, his tools, clothing, and other possessions returned to the community. The Hutterites lived together in collective farms directed by an elder responsible for its economy and discipline. Along with farming, the Hutterites practiced various trades such as carpentry, woodworking, stonemasonry, shoe-making, and clock-making. Each group had its master to oversee the work, procure materials, and sell the products. The simplified production and free labor contributed to lower prices. Hutterite zeal and professional efficiency were widely recognized, but at the same time their success created jealousy among the outside population. The economic prosperity of the Hutterite communities attracted many new arrivals and served as a solid basis for active missionizing.

The Hutterites, like other Anabaptists, were part of a movement of protest against the large commercial companies and against the practice of lending at interest. Frequently the Anabaptists viewed engaging in commerce itself as sinful. The Swiss Brethren put it most succinctly by proclaiming in 1578 that the children of God must live by honest work rather than the ruses of commerce.[76]

Conclusions

Luther's paradigm shift on justification introduced a new social ethic that facilitated the rationalization and secularization of social welfare, which continues into the development of the modern welfare state. The gospel

75. See, e.g., Luther's rejection of holding all things in common (*LW* 35:363; *LW* 44:357). On Calvin, see Leith, *Calvin's Doctrine of the Christian Life*, 194.

76. See James M. Stayer, "Community of Goods," in *The Oxford Encyclopedia of the Reformation*, ed. Hans J. Hillerbrand, 4 vols. (New York: Oxford University Press, 1996), 1:389–92; Marc Lienhard, "Les Anabaptistes," and Marc Venard, "Les Questions Éthiques," in Marc Venard et al., *Le temps des confessions (1530–1620/30)*, vol. 8 of *Histoire du Christianisme des origines à nos jours* (Paris: Desclée, 1992), 119–81, 1121–41.

of salvation by grace alone, apart from works, cut the nerve of the medieval ideology of poverty that fatalistically presented poverty and wealth as God's plan. By despiritualizing poverty, Luther and his colleagues revealed poverty as a social and personal evil to be combated for the sake of the common good. The incipient conception of the welfare state framed the acceptance of support not as receiving charity but as a social right that contributed to the common good. The Reformation initiated a comprehensive renewal and reconception of welfare, creating a regulated, centralized poor relief administered by the community. Luther also recognized the systemic injustice of the capitalism of his day and called for government regulation of banks and businesses.

Reformation contributions to social welfare continued through the social and economic upheavals of the Thirty Years' War (1618–48), Pietism, and on into urban development and the rise of industrialization. Institutions for the poor, the orphaned, the ill, and the elderly and for vocational training were established in Frankfurt (1679), Berlin (1702), and elsewhere through the influence of the Pietist leader Philipp Jakob Spener (1635–1705). One of Spener's followers, August Hermann Francke (1663–1727), diverged from Spener's emphasis on state responsibility for social welfare when Francke established the famous Halle institutions, including an orphanage as a private institution. Spener and Francke as well as other Pietist leaders viewed education as crucial for fighting poverty and understood poverty in terms of the larger social context rather than individual failings. The Awakening and Inner Mission movements of the nineteenth century strove to respond to challenges of industrialization and worker alienation from a church seen as allied with industry and government ("throne and altar" ideology). Johann Hinrich Wichern (1808–81) developed a male diaconate from the Hamburg Rescue Home he established for street gangs. His call to the church to influence government and society through social services, what he called Inner Mission, was endorsed at the 1848 Wittenberg Kirchentag with the mandate that Wichern form the Central Committee for the Inner Mission. Like Luther and Spener, Wichern realized that mass poverty was not the sum of individual failings but a sickness of the whole society. He called for government redress of the systemic injustices of economic and political structures and advocated self-help associations such as trade unions. So many pastors and social reformers echoed this call that by the 1890s, this "Christian Socialism" was denounced by Kaiser Wilhelm II, who told pastors to stick with preaching and pastoral care and avoid addressing political and social problems.

Yet the realization that poverty was not a moral defect but a consequence of economic contexts continued to spur reformers toward the goal of social welfare. Venues for this included not only the diaconal movements but also associations such as the Evangelical Social Congress, long led by Adolf von Harnack (1851–1920). Implementation of these goals has been most successful in Germany and the Nordic countries, especially following World War II.[77] These developments were not without controversy, but recent studies argue that Reformation motifs such as vocation informed public discourse leading to these welfare states. In contrast, the American ideology of limited government, private property, and individual freedom over communitarian values has confined Protestant social contributions to the realm of philanthropical organizations. Nonetheless, the fundamental Reformation diaconal motif of faith active in love manifests itself through numerous Protestant social services in America.

77. See Foster R. McCurley, ed., *Social Ministry in the Lutheran Tradition* (Minneapolis: Fortress Press, 2008); Antti Raunio, "Luther's Social Theology in the Contemporary World," in *The Global Luther—A Theologian for Modern Times*, ed. Christine Helmer (Minneapolis: Fortress Press, 2009), 210–27; Carter Lindberg and Paul Wee, eds., *The Forgotten Luther: Reclaiming the Socio-Economic Dimension of the Reformation* (Minneapolis: Lutheran University Press, 2016). A connection yet to be fully explored is that of the Freiburg School. See Freiburger Bonhoeffer-Kreis, *In der Stunde Null: Die Denkschrift des Freiburger "Bonhoeffer Kreises" Politische Gemeinschaftsordnung; Ein Versuch zur Selbstbesinnung des christlichen Gewissens in den politischen Nöten unserer Zeit* (Tübingen: Mohr, 1979); Günter Brakelmann and Traugott Jähnichen, *Die protestantischen Wurzeln der Sozialen Marktwirtschaft* (Gütersloh: Gütersloher Verlagshaus, 1994); Nils Goldschmidt, "Die Entstehung der Freiburger Kreise," *Historisch-Politische Mitteilungen* 4, no. 1 (1997): 1–17; Stephan Holthaus, *Zwischen Gewissen und Gewinn: Die Wirtschafts- und Sozialordnung der "Freiburger Denkschrift" und die Anfänge der Sozialen Marktwirtschaft* (Berlin: LIT, 2015).

Er hat funden ym tēpel vorkauffer/schaff/ochßen vñ tawben vñ wechßler sitzen/vñ hat gleich ern geyssel gemacht vō stricke alle schaff/ochssen/taube vñ wechßler außem tempell trieben/ das gelt verschüt/die zall bredt vmkart vñ zu den die tawben vorkaufften gesprochen. Hebt euch hin mit diesen auß meins vatern hauß/solt ir nit ein kauffhauß mache. Joh. z. Ir habts vmb sunst/darüb gebts vmb sunst. Mat. 10. Dein gelt sey mit dir yn verdammuß. Act. 8

Contrast in Attitudes toward Money and Religion, in *Passional Christi und Antichristi*, by Lucas Cranach the Elder, 1521

Chapter Seven

Worldly Worship: The Reformation and Economic Ethics

Wolfgang Huber

W hen scholars consider the legacy of the Reformation, they often overlook one particular topic: the Reformers' influence and relevance for economic ethics. Yet this aspect of the Reformers' work is of central importance, as I hope to demonstrate. One reason for the usual disregard for their contributions to economic ethics is that the concept does not immediately call to mind the names of Luther or Calvin, Bucer or Zwingli. Rather, the name invoked most often is that of Max Weber, who provides a good starting point for my argument.

The Weber Thesis

At the turn of the twentieth century, Max Weber was one of the key figures in the emergence of sociology, including the sociology of religion. His contribution to understanding the relevance of the Reformation for economic ethics is so well known, even today, that it has been recognized at the German carnival in Cologne. Some years ago, one of the leading bands of that carnival put together a song that begins: "Max Weber once said, that only labor is important, / that God gives grace to those who don't forget their duties. / Idleness and carnival are a waste of time. / The one who earns a lot on earth, gets the best seat near to God."[1] The refrain

---

1. Jürgen Becker, *Ich bin so froh, dass ich nicht evangelisch bin* (Cologne: Record Co., 2006), https://gloria.tv/video/KmSpotP1kJHN4yHXSL9mxNdfy:

> Max Weber hat gesagt, dass nur die Arbeit wichtig ist,
> dass der Herrgott den begnadigt, der die Pflichten nicht vergisst.
> Müßiggang und Karneval, das ist für die Katz,
> wer auf Erden viel verdient, hat bei Gott den besten Platz.

begins with the words, "I am so happy that I'm not a Protestant, / they have nothing in mind but to work."[2]

In this carnival song, we find the well-known elements of an ethic of work and capital accumulation characteristically considered key to Protestant economic ethics. Not only the carnival clowns of Cologne but also many intellectuals, economists, and politicians around the globe hold Max Weber responsible for our knowledge of this Protestant ethic.

Let me illustrate this fact with a very different example. A decade ago I visited the Chinese Office for Religious Affairs, eager to learn more about the official concept of the Chinese government's approach to religion. Quickly I was told that the ideal combination of basic elements necessary for the fabric of the gigantic Chinese empire included Marxism, capitalism, Protestantism, and Confucianism. Marxism was named as justification for a one-party system, capitalism as the engine for economic growth, Protestantism as the legitimation of capital accumulation and commitment, and Confucianism as the basis for obedience and a sense of duty and order. Jim Yong Kim, the Korean-born American president of the World Bank, also mentioned this specific connection between Protestantism and Confucianism in an interview in 2014, when he emphasized the so-called Weber thesis. He added that not only Protestantism but Confucianism as well could initiate economic dynamics, as the example of South Korea demonstrates.[3] It appears that even in East Asian intellectual circles, Protestantism is more often identified with the name of Max Weber than with the names of Martin Luther or John Calvin.

Although the Weber thesis has long been criticized as historically invalid, it gained new vigor after World War II to explain the strength of the United States in managing its economy so successfully. The unity between a committed Christian lifestyle and success in business was seen as a marker of the uniqueness of the American way. In the Weber thesis, according to this view, worldly asceticism led to high esteem for

---

Ich bin so froh, dass ich nicht evangelisch bin,
die haben doch nichts anderes als arbeiten im Sinn.
Als Katholik da kannste pfuschen, dat eine is jewiss,
am Samstag gehste beichten und fott is der janze Driss.

2. Joachim Radkau, "Leidenschaft im Eisschrank: Die lustvolle Qual Weberscher Wissenschaft; oder, Die Aktualität Max Webers," *Evangelischer Pressedienst Dokumentation* [epd] 35 (August 29, 2014): 23–28.

3. Jim Yong Kim, "Wir arbeiten weiter und beten für die Mädchen," interview with Jim Yong Kim and Gerd Müller by Manfred Schäfers, *Frankfurter Allgemeine Zeitung* (May 17, 2014): 21.

benefactors of various kinds, for philanthropic foundations, for cultural sponsorships, and so on. Some years ago, Niall Ferguson even used this concept to explain the success of the U.S. economy compared to a perceived decline in the economies of middle and northwestern Europe in the early years of the twenty-first century. He attributed the European economic decline to a falling off of Protestantism there, signaled also by a degradation of the work ethic, which he measured by hours worked per year and years worked per lifetime. Evidently he believed that the longer working hours in the United States had nothing to do with weak labor unions; rather, the longer working time indicated the strength of Protestantism in the Weberian sense.[4] Ten years later, in *Civilization: The West and the Rest*, Ferguson included the United States in his gloomy prediction about the demise of the West and did not hesitate to compare his analysis to Oswald Spengler's *The Decline of the West* (*Der Untergang des Abendlandes*, 1918). Where Spengler had discerned a cultural decline in the West, Ferguson argues in economic terms. Among the success factors of the West, he emphasizes technological innovation and medical progress, but he points to the work ethic and consumerism as two central elements of economic growth. These last two factors he finds more and more neglected in the West, including the United States. Therefore, he expects that sooner or later the West will be surpassed economically by East Asia, especially China.[5] Ferguson foresees a time when China will replace the United States as the biggest national economy in terms of GDP (gross domestic product). In 2013 he expected that to happen in 2017;[6] in the meantime, however, other analysts doubt whether this is likely in the near future. In a change from his earlier interpretations, Ferguson in 2013 relativized his former high esteem of the "God factor," but as far as the role of the work ethic is concerned, he still implicitly employed a Weberian analysis.

Nowadays the Weber thesis is even applied with a completely contrary intention. What I mean is that the thesis has been inverted to investigate contemporary finance-dominated capitalism and its destructive consequences for workers or debtors dependent on it. Kathryn Tanner

---

4. Niall Ferguson, "Why America Outpaces Europe (Clue: The God Factor)," *New York Times*, June 8, 2003, http://www.nytimes.com/2003/06/08/weekinreview/the-world-why-america-outpaces-europe-clue-the-god-factor.html.

5. Niall Ferguson, *Civilization: The West and the Rest* (New York: Penguin, 2011).

6. Niall Ferguson, "Wir löschen unseren Erfolg," *Die Zeit*, May 8, 2013, www.zeit.de/2013/20/der-niedergang-des-westens/komplettansicht.

devoted her 2016 Gifford Lectures to the topic "Christianity and the New Spirit of Capitalism." Her title itself indicates her intention to challenge Weber with his own arguments. She proposes that the pervasive force of finance-dominated capitalism "might be countered by Christian beliefs and practices with a comparable capacity to shape people. Thus, these lectures reverse the project of . . . Max Weber, . . . while employing much the same methods as he used. Weber showed how Christian beliefs and practices could form persons in line with what capitalism required of them." Tanner seeks instead to "demonstrate the capacity of Christian beliefs and practices to help people resist the dictates of capitalism in its present, finance-dominated configuration."[7] Her use of "Weber's method" indicates that she also finds a causal relationship between religious conviction and the structuring of the economy. She sees the "formation of persons" as key to the transformation of the economy. Whereas according to the Weber thesis the image of the Puritan personality and its worldly asceticism furthered the spread of the capitalist spirit, Tanner counters the cultural forms of finance-dominated capitalism. For her, Christian beliefs and practices have the capacity to help people "resist the dictates of capitalism."

An approach comparable to Tanner's project was presented in a campaign under the title *Radicalizing Reformation*. The authors summarize their concept in ninety-four theses, beginning with this one: "At least two billion people are impoverished by the domination of money. That is the contemporary expression of Mammon and therefore the central challenge for faith."[8] The consequence is "to drop out on a daily basis personally and socially from the destructive domination of money and to live—confident in the liberating justice of God—in compassion and solidarity in just relationships with other humans and creatures."[9] Rather than articulating maxims for action by those with economic responsibility, or global regulations of a globalized economy, the authors suggest that the right strategy is for individuals and groups to withdraw from the present state of affairs. This kind of withdrawal from the ruling system requires a personal dedication. As historical examples

---

7. Kathryn Tanner, "Christianity and the New Spirit of Capitalism: An Introduction" (lecture), videostream of the first of the 2016 Gifford Lectures, "Christianity and the New Spirit of Capitalism," at the University of Edinburgh, https://www.giffordlectures.org/lectures /christianity-and-new-spirit-capitalism.

8. Ulrich Duchrow, Daniel Beros, Martin Hoffmann, and Hans G. Ulrich, eds., *Die Reformation radikalisieren / Radicalizing Reformation*, 5 vols. (Berlin: LIT, 2015), 5:24.

9. Ibid., 1:28.

show, this approach might become an important pioneering action, but it cannot be generalized as a moral standard for economically responsible subjects or for the regulation of the economy by legal rules. It is highly questionable whether the challenges related to a globalized and finance-dominated economy can be met by instruments of personal or group withdrawal. Thus there are obvious limits to an inverse use of the Weber thesis.

Regarding the causal interpretation of this thesis, Weber himself was, at least in a part of his formulations, quite careful, even to the point of compromising clarity. For instance, he described the relation between ascetic Protestantism and capitalism as *Wahlverwandtschaft* (elective affinity)—an expression that allows for the vagueness about who elected whom and in which way. The focus of this essay does not permit describing and critically analyzing Weber's famous essays, first published in 1904–5, with later additions and revisions.[10] Instead, I will concentrate on one aspect of Weber's implicit theology.

Weber takes up a lay-theological interpretation of the teaching of John Calvin, the central figure of the second-generation Reformers of the sixteenth century, and his Puritan followers in Britain and the British colonies on the American continent. According to this Calvinist interpretation, the election of the individual Christian for eternal salvation is immediately evident in the person's relationship to temporal, mundane realities. Already in the second part of his studies on Protestantism, in the essay "Protestant Sects and the Spirit of Capitalism," Weber emphasized the question of the *Heilsprämie* (salvation premium) as the central point of his research. In the later revision of his text, he formally regretted that his critics had not sufficiently taken this point into account. He emphasized that "not the ethical doctrine of a religion, but that form of ethical conduct upon which premiums are placed . . . matters."[11] For Calvinism, the salvation premium, the bonus in Weber's understanding, has a specific form related to the doctrine of double predestination, which says that individual human beings are destined by divine providence either to salvation or to damnation. Men and women, however, cannot live in absolute uncertainty about their eternal future. They need at least

---

10. See Max Weber, *Asketischer Protestantismus und Kapitalismus: Schriften und Reden 1904–1911*; and Weber, *Die protestantische Ethik und der Geist des Kapitalismus: Die protestantischen Sekten und der Geist des Kapitalismus; Schriften, 1904–1920*, ed. Wolfgang Schluchter and Ursula Bube (Tübingen: Mohr Siebeck, 2014, 2016).

11. Adam B. Seligman, "Introduction," in *Religion and the Rise of Capitalism*, by Richard H. Tawney (New Brunswick, NJ: Transaction Publishers, 1998), xi–xl, at xxxii.

"symptoms" of their election. And such symptoms are to be found in the positive results of worldly asceticism in terms of economic success, which give the certainty of belonging to a "salvation aristocracy."

That is, of course, a very brief summary of Weber's concept of salvation bonuses. More important than a detailed description and interpretation of his text, however, is understanding that Weber never presented sufficient historical evidence that this lay theology shaped Puritan ethical culture. The thesis about the influence of this ethic on emerging capitalism is thus implausible. There is insufficient reason to believe that the doctrine of double predestination created a kind of uncertainty that had to be or was indeed balanced by the concept of a salvation bonus for worldly asceticism. At the least, this bonus was not consistently acknowledged. Successful bankers in the Netherlands, for example, had no guarantee that they would not be excluded from the Eucharist as sinners simply because of their capitalist success—an idea that had caused some amusement in Catholic Italy.[12] Nor was there sufficient support for the assumption that Puritan capitalists became acquisitive virtuosos because they were simultaneously religious virtuosos who aspired to be members of a salvation aristocracy. The combination of financial bonuses and salvation bonuses had no solid foundation. Finally, recent research finds no plausibility in the idea that this kind of worldly asceticism can explain "the shift of the focus of mercantile activity and entrepreneurial innovation from the Mediterranean to the northwest of the European continent" in the post-Reformation era. The history of European wars, the emergence of the Ottoman Turks, and the marginalized social position of dissenters who sought recognition are examples of alternative explanations.[13]

As Ernst Troeltsch, a close colleague and friend of Max Weber, stated in Weber's own lifetime, it was then commonly understood that the big economic and social transformations of the sixteenth century had happened independently of the religious movements of the era. The religious movements reacted to these transformations more or less reluctantly and adapted to the new situation at differing tempos. Interestingly, in

---

12. Wolfgang Reinhard, "Die Bejahung des gewöhnlichen Lebens," in *Die kulturellen Werte Europas*, ed. Hans Joas and Klaus Wiegandt (Frankfurt am Main: Fischer, 2005), 265–303, at 283.

13. Alexandra Walsham, "Reformation Legacies," in *The Oxford Illustrated History of the Reformation*, ed. Peter Marshall (Oxford: Oxford University Press, 2015), 227–68, at 241–42.

this regard Troeltsch saw the Catholic Church as more flexible than the Lutheran Church.[14]

Even if Weber's thesis had had some validity, we would at least have to admit that, over time, the link between financial success and certainty of election lost all plausibility. Weber had anticipated that to a certain extent. He assumed that established capitalism reduces the spirit to the form. Later capitalism no longer needs a cultural basis as early capitalism did. But there is yet another reason why the thesis became less believable: the theory of double predestination itself lost its credibility, even for Calvinists or Presbyterians. Around the world, wherever you meet a Calvinist, you will not easily come across anyone really passionate about this doctrine. This is even more true in the broader stream of Protestantism. Just as problematic as the historical argument is the general assumption that what Protestantism contributed to the development of capitalism was the spirit of the salvation bonus. Thus we are forced to take a step further in our theological analysis.

The Concept of Vocation

Despite the implausibility of the link between a salvation ethic and acquisitive capitalism, there are still good reasons to see a "Protestant work ethic" at work in Reformation theology. For the Reformation developed its own clear concept of the value of human labor. This concept arose from a central theological interpretation of the standing of the human person before God. The concept of justification by God's grace alone, already formulated by the apostle Paul in the New Testament and rediscovered by Martin Luther, had answered the question of the status of people before God. This belief is completely incompatible with the idea of a salvation bonus, but it leads to a different theological and ethical understanding of work.

A central question prompted by the valuing of human labor refers to the place of human action with regard to grace. The Reformers consistently argue that the quality of human deeds cannot be seen as a precondition for divine grace. Measured against the criterion of God's will, no individuals will overcome their sinfulness by their own deeds; on the contrary, such an effort will lead a person even deeper into sinful

14. Ernst Troeltsch, *The Social Teaching of the Christian Churches*, 2 vols. (Louisville, KY: Westminster/John Knox Press, 1992), 2:869–70.

self-centeredness. Worldly activities are not the means for making God gracious toward humans; rather, human action responds to the gift of divine grace. Understanding Christian freedom as the liberation from self-centered, anxious worry about one's own salvation opens the way to a relational concept of the human person: one is related to God in faith, and to one's neighbor as to oneself in love. The human person is constituted by faith, producing deeds measured by love.

To illustrate this understanding of the interaction between faith and deeds, Luther uses the image of the tree and its fruits. It is not the fruit that makes a tree good. Instead, it is the good tree that makes good fruits possible. The fruits follow the tree as the good works (Luther does not hesitate to use the term) follow faith. In this sense, and in this sequence, together faith and works constitute the whole of Christian life as a life in freedom.

In Luther's understanding, all worldly activity follows a divine calling and is, in this sense, a vocation. Luther prefers the word *Beruf* over *Ruf* or *Berufung*; in his understanding *Beruf* can be translated as "vocation" or "calling" as well as "profession." This use of the word has precedents in the Middle Ages and is already reflected in Luther's translation of the New Testament of 1522. He develops this understanding further in criticizing monastic vows (1522) and in his sermons from 1522 onward.[15] In Christianity he finds unacceptable the notion of a special status arising out of an inner vocation that is distinguished from all other statuses, because divine justification addresses every person similarly—as a child of God, gifted with God's justifying grace. With equal status in relation to God and to the world, every person thus has both an internal and an external vocation.

The inner vocation calls for unity of faith in God and of love to the neighbor as to oneself; the outer vocation expresses itself in a concrete mandate to a worldly activity in one of the major fields: in the language of the time, either the polity, the economy (including the family), or the church. There is no longer any hierarchy among these fields. Whether a person works in politics, in the economy and family, or in the church does not matter. Each profession has dignity equal to the others and has to be respected in its usefulness for other individuals, for the greater community, and for the common good.

---

15. Andreas Stegmann, *Luthers Auffassung vom christlichen Leben* (Tübingen: Mohr Siebeck, 2014), 360–90.

Interestingly, finding the value of human life in justification by grace alone also creates a fundamental equality among the different tasks of persons in their daily responsibilities. Whether simple support tasks in agriculture or family, the work of a merchant or a banker, the political responsibility of a prince, or the spiritual responsibility of a pastor—in all these cases persons are following their vocation. The concept includes paid as well as voluntary work, the unpaid work of a mother as well as the paid work of a servant.

Work as vocation: that is the specific approach of the Reformation to economic ethics. This approach includes the responsibility of the entrepreneur as well as of the laborer, and it includes the employee as well as the employer. On the basis of this understanding of *Beruf*, the core of what is called the Protestant work ethic may be defined as follows: Human labor is the use of one's talents and opportunities to fulfill useful and honest tasks productively, not only to one's own benefit but also to the benefit of others and the community. To make use of one's talents and opportunities, one needs appropriate education and formation. Therefore it was not at all accidental that the Reformation turned out to be, at its center, an education movement. The structure of Christian freedom—liberation from self-justification by God's grace and therefore liberation to serve fellow human beings and the common good—is reflected in the understanding of vocation. Vocation is the predominant place for responsible freedom.

Undoubtedly Luther's concept of work as vocation emphasizes the command to stay in the status into which one is called. Compared to the rather static character of Luther's concept, Calvin seems to present a more dynamic approach.

Calvin's ethics can generally be understood as an "ethics of gratitude." The Heidelberg Catechism, one of the central confessional documents of the early Reformed churches, summarized Calvin's intention very well in the section on Christian life under the heading "On Gratitude." Calvin himself emphasizes enjoying and using the divine gifts of creation as features of Christian life. Because these gifts carry the danger of misuse, either by excess or by exaggerated frugality, using them prudently and measuredly is decisive. This emphasis follows from Christian freedom, which in Calvin's understanding comprises three elements: freedom from judgment by the divine law, freedom to consciously love God and fellow humans as oneself, and freedom to deal independently with the so-called adiaphora, matters for which no clear advice or commandment exists.[16] Issues related to ecclesial ceremonies, lifestyle, or eating habits, as well as questions of prudence in economic affairs belong to this "middle ground" of adiaphora, which must be dealt with consciously and deliberately while taking into account the need for Christian responsibility.

In his understanding of work and profession, Calvin took more seriously than Luther the dynamics of economic development.[17] But the idea that success in a profession and its monetary rewards guarantee certain salvation occurs neither in Calvin's work nor in Luther's. That absence is not astonishing, because for Calvin the bold theory of a double predestination—either for salvation or for damnation—means, first and foremost, that God's transcendence has to be respected, and God's grace should not be misunderstood as "cheap grace."[18] In Calvin's view, the intention to gain salvation would even be annulled by the expectation of finding certainty about one's salvation from the success of one's own working life. For a Christian, the certainty of salvation lies in Christ and not in the merit of one's own deeds. At its heart, Calvin's understanding of work as calling is consistent with Luther's insight into the relevance of justification by grace alone for the understanding of human deeds.

It is notable that the high premium placed on work has consequences for dealing with poverty. The Reformers criticize any spiritual elevation of poverty, and in opposition to mendicant orders they assert the duty of everyone to take care of their own basic needs. Regarding spiritual status, there is no exception to the preference of work over living from alms. At the same time, however, the Reformers distinguish "between the deserving and undeserving poor, between those able but unwilling to work and those incapacitated by illness or other circumstances beyond their control."[19] They emphasize the responsibility of the political body to care for those unable to find their own livelihood. This is the starting point for a political concept of social welfare. Neither orders nor brotherhoods but municipalities must care for the poor and the needy within their walls. They are not obliged, however, to give access to beggars, including mendicants, from outside their borders. Care for the poor

16. John Calvin, *Institutes of the Christian Religion*, trans. John Allen, 2 vols. (Philadelphia: Presbyterian Board of Christian Education, 1936), 2:76–92.

17. See Alister McGrath, "Calvin and the Christian Calling," *First Things* 94 (1999): 31–35.

18. Dietrich Bonhoeffer, *Discipleship*, trans. Barbara Green and Reinhard Krauss, vol. 4 of *Dietrich Bonhoeffer Works* (Minneapolis: Fortress Press, 2001), 43–44.

19. Walsham, "Reformation Legacies," 242.

became organized in the form of publicly administered funds (*Gemeiner Kasten*), prompted especially by the secularization of church treasuries. This consequence of the Protestant work ethic regarding care for poor people followed remarkably quickly in many places.

The Distinction between Interest and Usury as Touchstone

The high valuation of work had implications for how the Reformers thought about poverty. Among other things, their thinking about work led to a "preferential option for the poor" as a very important criterion for questions of economic ethics. It also had another specific consequence of great importance to the Reformers: the distinction between interest and usury in moneylending.[20]

This distinction had been unheard of in earlier theologians, who took literally a biblical commandment that forbade taking interest, at least in dealing with your own people, your own community (Deut. 23:19–20). The Reformers had to address the worry and distrust attendant to a period of significant transition from a home economy to a monetary economy. Luther became a leading spokesperson for men and women caught up in the economic disruptions of this period, and usury therefore formed a core issue during his career as a public writer.

Luther argued against the tendency to raise extreme profits while professing love for fellow humans. Where interest was concerned, he confronted creditors with the Golden Rule—to treat the other as you wished to be treated yourself—and asked whether a creditor would judge the imposed interest as fair if he himself were the debtor. Remembering the biblical commandment, Luther wanted to open a space for critical evaluation of a form of behavior already viewed as normal in his day. He insisted on asking whether interest on loans or purchases served both sides of the transaction best. He dramatically challenged the asymmetric relationship in which creditors acquire riches within a very short period to the extent that they easily "surpass kings and emperors," while others fall deeper and deeper into debt. Yet he combined this sharp criticism with practical suggestions for a fair distribution of risk and a limitation of the interest rate.

With the distinction between interest and usury, the Reformers accepted the functional use of interest that allowed for a temporal

---

20. Benjamin Nelson, *The Idea of Usury: From Tribal Brotherhood to Universal Otherhood*, 2nd ed. (Chicago: University of Chicago Press, 1969).

difference between buying and paying. In this respect, Calvin was more consistent than Luther. He summarized his insights in a famous letter to Claude de Sachins in 1545,[21] in which he argued for a hermeneutical procedure to understand the religious and ethical impulse of the biblical commandment in its inner sense rather than in its literal proposal, and to use this inner sense as a criterion for dealing with the inherent logic of economic thinking.[22] He thus interpreted the biblical commandment not as a general prohibition against interest as such. Instead, he sought to avoid the detrimental effects that interest could have on a community, when one person's misfortune so easily turns into another's benefit in circumstances that foster exploitation. So long as the commandment not to take interest is merely repeated again and again, this core issue goes unaddressed. The critical question is which rules will prevent the exploitation of misfortunes or emergencies. The pragmatic usefulness of charging interest has to be balanced against respect for the other person, who like every human being is created in the image of God, and whose destiny has therefore to be taken into account.

This reflection leads Calvin, as other Reformers, to distinguish between interest and usury in a manner not previously employed. In this view, the rate of interest and other conditions related to lending had to stay within the bounds of equity; in contrast, the Reformers understood usury as an exploitation of emergencies without respect for the integrity of persons. To stay within given legal restrictions, to apply equity in conditions of economic exchange, and to respect the destiny of the poor—these are the main criteria by which the Reformers accepted interest as an instrument of economic exchange.

Conclusions

This brief sketch of the Reformers' thinking has led our reflection from worldly asceticism to worldly worship in the form of vocation as the Reformers understood it, and from a preferential option for the poor to the Reformers' use of it in differentiating between interest and usury.

21. John Calvin, *Tractatum Theologicorum Appendix*, vol. 10/1 of *Opera quae supersunt omnia*, *Corpus Reformatorum* 38/1, repr. ed. (1871; New York: Johnson Reprint Corporation, 1964), 246–49.

22. Nelson, *The Idea of Usury*, 75–82; James B. Sauer, *Faithful Ethics according to John Calvin: The Teachability of the Heart* (Lewiston, NY: Edwin Mellen, 1997); see also Sauer, "Christian Faith, Economy, and Economics: What Do Christian Ethics Contribute to Understanding Economy?," *Faith and Economics* 42 (2003): 17–25.

The possible consequences of their economic ethics for our day can be approached either descriptively or constructively.

Descriptively speaking, I restrict myself only to one example: the preparation that led to the model of a social-market economy developed in West Germany after World War II. Among those preparatory steps were remarkable contributions emerging from Catholic social teachings, on one hand, and from Social Protestantism on the other. Catholic social teachings emphasized the social character of the human person in arguing for institutions that respect the person and promote solidarity and subsidiarity. Social Protestantism strongly underlined personal freedom as a central value for human existence. This personal freedom, however, is inseparable from responsibility not only for oneself, but also for other persons, and even for nature and for future generations. Both the Catholic and the Social Protestant perspectives emphasized the preference for a market economy, but with the condition of a regulatory framework that would guarantee fair competition among participants in the market, fair procedures for negotiating working conditions, and finally sufficient measures of social justice and social security.[23] It is evident, then, that the milieus of Social Protestantism and Social Catholicism nurtured the emergence of a social-market economy, even though the conceptual strengths and weaknesses of both sides differed considerably. As far as the Protestant arguments are concerned, more rigorous research shows that their protagonists had neither a homogeneous understanding of their Protestant religious identity nor a convergent concept for the order of a market economy. On one hand, they emphasized an order *by* competition, and on the other an order *of* competition. A comparable ambiguity appears with respect to the relationship between the economic and the political order.[24]

The development of a social-market economy began nearly seventy years ago. In the meantime, the fairness of competition was endangered by other developments that could not be anticipated at the time. Working conditions became fragile and precarious for a whole series of reasons, among which the growth of a global labor market is of specific

23. See Traugott Jähnichen, "Das wirtschaftsethische Profil des sozialen Protestantismus: Zu den gesellschafts- und ordnungspolitischen Grundentscheidungen der Sozialen Marktwirtschaft," *Jahrbuch Sozialer Protestantismus* 4 (2010): 18–45.

24. Hans-Richard Reuter, "Die Religion der Sozialen Marktwirtschaft: Zur ordoliberalen Weltanschauung bei Walter Eucken und Alexander Rüstow," *Jahrbuch Sozialer Protestantismus* 4 (2010): 46–76.

importance. At the same time, globalization challenged more local understandings of justice, which now must take account of persons and responsibilities beyond the seemingly closed national society.

Since the Social Protestant project appears to be waning, however, I argue for not giving up on the potential for the concept of vocation, and specifically for a broadened understanding of the concept, which would view human existence as active, creative, and productive life.[25] In this broad sense activity is a form of self-realization, but also a source of social recognition. The meaning of work changes but does not disappear. At a time when we observe growing unemployment worldwide, and when employment is becoming increasingly precarious, indifference toward the value of work conflicts with the demands of justice. The Protestant doctrine of the equal freedom of every person, which undergirds the sense of individual responsibility as well as social justice, thus proves its relevance even under the conditions of our time.

That assertion, of course, raises the question of what we mean by justice, understood in this case as the primary virtue of institutions.[26] Rawls understands justice as a system of equal freedoms. Given that those equal freedoms are always realized in unequal ways, Rawls insists on a rule that clarifies which differences are acceptable and which are not. According to his difference principle, inequalities must be seen from the perspective that grants a prerogative to those worst off.[27]

What can a society do to improve the situation of worst-off persons and to put in practice, in this sense, a "preferential option for the poor"? Classical concepts answer that where commutative justice is insufficient, society must implement distributive justice, which puts in place means to effect transfers from the rich to the poor. Such distributive actions help alleviate poverty, but they are not sufficient to overcome it. They often end up creating a kind of revolving door, through which those who pass tend to do it repetitively. Therefore, another kind of justice has to come into consideration, for which the Catholic bishops in the United States coined the term "contributive justice"—that is, a justice that enables people to contribute actively in society and to use their gifts and talents, their

25. See Torsten Meireis, *Tätigkeit und Erfüllung: Protestantische Ethik im Umbruch der Arbeitsgesellschaft* (Tübingen: Mohr Siebeck, 2008); Meireis, "Was ist und worauf zielt sozialer Protestantismus," *Jahrbuch Sozialer Protestantismus* 4 (2010): 231–41.

26. John Rawls, *A Theory of Justice*, rev., 2nd ed. (Cambridge, MA: Harvard University Press, 1999), 3.

27. Ibid., 52–78.

opportunities and social conditions to live an active and productive life.[28] I prefer to call this participatory justice.

The elements of contributive or participatory justice are manifold.[29] Among them, one element of central importance has recently been termed "enabling justice."[30] This approach applies the insights of the "capabilities approach" in the theory of justice developed primarily by Martha Nussbaum and Amartya Sen.[31] "Enabling justice" refers to all measures that promote the capabilities of persons to shape their own lives—through their health conditions or their self-confidence, their ability to play or their formation and education, through their belonging to communities or their ability to control their environment.[32] Education and formation play a central role in enabling justice.[33]

A further element of contributive justice is accessibility to meaningful work. The conditions for accessibility have changed with every step in recent transformations of work, most notably through new technology. An example is the process of digitization of labor, which poses the alternatives of a "disruptive" versus an "organic" transition to labor 4.0. The question is, what drives—and what should drive—this transition? From the perspective of participatory justice, there is a clear preference for an "organic" transition, which requires decisive effort to enable vulnerable people and not to lose them. A more disruptive approach to the digital transformation of labor could leave the vulnerable behind. Consequently, a debate has risen whether citizens should be guaranteed an unconditional basic income, financed by the surplus wealth generated through disruptive digitization. This debate exemplifies the urgent need for a

28. United States Catholic Bishops, *Economic Justice for All: Pastoral Letter on Catholic Social Teaching and the U.S. Economy* (Washington, DC: National Conference of Catholic Bishops, 1986), 17, §71, http://www.usccb.org/upload/economic_justice_for_all.pdf; cf. Heinrich Bedford-Strohm, *Vorrang für die Armen: Auf dem Weg zu einer theologischen Theorie der Gerechtigkeit* (Gütersloh: Kaiser, 1993), 88–106.

29. Evangelische Kirche in Deutschland [EKD], *Evangelische Kirche und freiheitliche Demokratie: Der Staat des Grundgesetzes als Angebot und Aufgabe; Eine Denkschrift der Evangelischen Kirche in Deutschland* (Gütersloh: Mohn, 1985), 43–45.

30. Peter Dabrock, *Befähigungsgerechtigkeit: Ein Grundkonzept konkreter Ethik in fundamentaltheologischer Perspektive* (Gütersloh: Gütersloher Verlagshaus, 2012), 138–218.

31. See Martha Nussbaum, *Frontiers of Justice: Disability, Nationality, Species Membership* (Cambridge, MA: Harvard University Press, 2007); Amartya Sen, *Development as Freedom* (Oxford: Oxford University Press, 1999).

32. Nussbaum, *Frontiers of Justice*, 70–78.

33. See EKD, *Demokratie*; also Dabrock, *Befähigungsgerechtigkeit*.

thorough public discussion. One proposal favors a basic income without labor to alleviate the possible consequences of unemployment resulting from the digitization of labor. But the proposal stands in clear opposition to the conviction that active participation in society includes the possibility of earning one's livelihood through one's talents and opportunities. It stands opposed, in other words, to the tenets of inclusion and contributive justice. I argue that instead of a guaranteed income paid for by the information technology revolution, society should respond to the digitization of labor by generating new ideas and initiatives to create new jobs. Once again, as the Reformers emphasized, education and formation are essential to enable people to come through this difficult and demanding process of transformation. Contributive justice thus includes enabling justice.[34]

To enable people to contribute actively to the economy, the economy itself should be in the service of people rather than people being in service to the economy. Amartya Sen, the 1998 Nobel Laureate in economic sciences, has insisted that an economy in service of human beings is a precondition for promoting freedom on a global scale.[35] The coincidence between the insights of an Indian economist and an impulse leading back to Christian values as reflected in the Reformation tradition is, in my view, stunningly impressive.

To summarize: The critique of an exploitative use of misfortunes and poverty, as formulated by the Reformers, is based on the conviction that all humans are equal in dignity and should therefore have access to the opportunity to contribute productively to the common life of society and to the best of its members. Following such a line of thought, contributive justice is a central criterion for the regulation of the economy. Practical knowledge is needed to institutionalize this contributive justice by means

---

34. The concept of contributive justice was first formulated in the pastoral letter on Catholic social teaching and the U.S. economy: U.S. Catholic Bishops, *Economic Justice for All*. In the bishops' understanding, contributive justice includes duties of the individuals on one side and duties of the society on the other:

> *Social justice implies that persons have an obligation to be active and productive participants in the life of society and that society has a duty to enable them to participate in this way.* . . . The meaning of social justice also includes a duty to organize economic and social institutions so that people can contribute to society in ways that respect their freedom and the dignity of their labor. Work should enable the working person to become "more a human being," more capable of acting intelligently, freely, and in ways that lead to self-realization. (§71)

35. Sen, *Development as Freedom*.

of education, formation, training, and the organization of just participation in society.

This kind of evaluation needs a practice of reflexive equilibrium between the principles of a Christian (or other) ethics and the rules of economy. That practice would exactly fulfill what Shmuel Eisenstadt once called *Wirtschaftsethik*, which evaluates the economic institutional sphere on the premises of a specific religious or other ethical orientation.[36] This kind of equilibrium could be a form of economic ethics suitable to our times.

---

36. Shmuel N. Eisenstadt, "Some Observations on Structuralism in Sociology, with Special, and Paradoxical, Reference to Max Weber," in *Continuities in Structural Inquiry*, ed. Peter M. Blau and Robert K. Merton (Beverly Hills, CA: Sage Publications, 1981), 165–76, at 172.

Mundi negocia.

Eſt, cui nil cœlum debet, labor irritus omnis.

C.

HÆc, quæ mundus agit, tibi parvula monſtrat imago,
    Nempe tenet cunctos anxia cura lucri.
Hoſpes ab extructis ſibi comparat ædibus aurum,
    Inſtitor a variis mercibus auget opes,
Alter agros, alius vites, ille excolit hortos,
    Quis ſua pro numis bajula terga locat.
Hunc quoque, qui tot equis ad Regum ducitur aulas,
    Tecta premit meriti ſollicitudo ſui.
Gratis nemo, ſed heu fruſtra quot ubique, laborant.
    Cælum, ni merces ſit tua, fine cares.

Business World, in *Ethica naturalis, seu Documenta moralia e variis rerum
naturalium proprietatib[us] virtutum vitiorumq[ue] symbolicis imaginibus collecta,
a Christophoro Weigelio,* by Christoph Weigel, ca. 1700

Chapter Eight

The Protestant Ethic
and the Spirit of Consumerism

Jonathan L. Walton

The ascendancy of Donald J. Trump represents one of the more curious phenomena in the intersecting spheres of religion, ethics, and politics. Trump's stunning rise from real-estate developer to reality television star to so-called leader of the free world has left more than a few social scientists and scholars of religion dumbfounded. His victory is due in large part to the support he received from a critical mass of white conservative evangelicals. Postelection polls indicated that he garnered as much as 80 percent of the white evangelical vote. We also know that high-profile leaders of this particular religious subculture, such as James Dobson, head of Focus on the Family, and Jerry Falwell Jr., president of Liberty University, were more than distant supporters. They were active surrogates on the campaign trail. There were even moments during the campaign when their full-throated endorsements of Trump placed them at odds with segments of their constituencies.[1] It seems for now, however, that the reward was worth the risk. As I write, it appears that Falwell will be part of a White House initiative to review higher education.[2]

---

1. T. Rees Shapiro et al., "Liberty University Students Protest Association with Trump," *Washington Post*, October 13, 2016, www.washingtonpost.com/news/grade-point/wp/2016/10/12/liberty-is-not-trump-u-students-protest-donald-trump/?utm_term=.4ef6b1e4d004. Samantha Schmidt and Amy B. Wang, "Jerry Falwell Jr. Keeps Defending Trump as Liberty University Grads Return Diplomas," *Washington Post*, August 21, 2017, www.washingtonpost.com/news/morning-mix/wp/2017/08/21/liberty-university-graduates-return-diplomas-because-of-support-for-trump-by-jerry-falwell-jr/?utm_term=.20a14e4a8b77.

2. Andrew Kreighbaum, "Falwell Higher Ed Task Force Won't Happen," *Inside Higher Ed*, June 9, 2017, www.insidehighered.com/news/2017/06/09/liberty-university-president-wont-be-leading-task-force-higher-ed-regulation-after.

179

This story would be straightforward if it were just about power and politics. Any suggestion that millions of self-professed evangelicals supported Donald Trump so that a few of their more high-profile personalities might attain access to the halls of power is too supercilious and cynical a read. The same is true of theories suggesting that (1) support for Donald Trump among evangelicals tends to come from those who are not consistent churchgoers and have lower levels of education, and/or (2) they are evangelicals more concerned with economic issues than moral issues, and thus are not "real Christians."[3]

I find both responses more knee-jerk than scientific. The same claims about the "less educated" among white evangelicals sound very similar to the claims many made about the group as a whole for most of the previous century. From popular commentators like H. L. Mencken to more recent scholars who write about evangelicals as if they are uneducated, duped subjects trapped in the cultivated psychosis of false consciousness, this is an old yet enduring trope. We pathologize what we do not understand. Nor do I think claims of orthodoxy get us very far. Social, political, and economic concerns informed by the presence of empire have always shaped how and why people embrace the Christian faith. From Paul and Priscilla to Luther and Calvin to Sojourner Truth and Fannie Lou Hamer, the critical interlace of ethnicity, economics, gender, and race are the "moral" issues of Christianity. Those who have the power to determine which of those critical issues needs to recede into the background to concretize the status quo are most often the ones who can establish "the real Christians." In fact, this is why we commemorate the spirit of those who dared to protest any such universal view of the faith. As the late televangelist Reverend Ike used to tell me, "Be careful who you condemn. Remember, everybody is somebody's heretic."

Nevertheless, the question remains: How is it that a group that privileges traditional family values and is known for its conservative stances on marriage, sexuality, and cultural sobriety opted for a thrice-married man who flaunts his indulgent views regarding women and wealth like a drunk King Solomon on a bad day?

---

3. Alvin Chang, "Donald Trump's Poll Numbers Show a Big Divide between Christians and Churchgoing Christians," *Vox*, March 7, 2016, www.vox.com/policy-and-politics/2016/3/7/11174064/do-christians-really-favor-trump. Geoffrey Layman, "Where Is Trump's Evangelical Base? Not in Church," *Washington Post*, March 29, 2016, www.washingtonpost.com/news/monkey-cage/wp/2016/03/29/where-is-trumps-evangelical-base-not-in-church/?utm_term=.e6c40ce5ed49.

Some have attributed Donald Trump's cultural resonance to the spread of the prosperity gospel in America, a particular strand of Neo-charismatic revivalism that blends elements of late-nineteenth-century New Thought metaphysics, Pentecostalism, and twentieth-century post-war healing revivalism.[4] The similarities are undoubtedly unmistakable and undeniable. Trump grew up attending Marble Collegiate Church in New York. This church is where Norman Vincent Peale injected Presbyterianism with positive-thinking psychology—a staple of the health and wealth movement. Like Word of Faith founder Kenneth Hagin of Broken Arrow, Oklahoma, in the 1950s, Peale put a quintessentially postwar American spin on Proverbs 18 ("The power of life and death are in the tongue" [cf. 18:21]) and Proverbs 23 ("As a man thinketh, so is he" [cf. 23:7]). Donald Trump surrounds himself with televangelists and mega-church pastors who adhere to the theological tenets of the prosperity gospel. For instance, one of his spiritual advisers, Paula White, owns a residence in his New York City Trump Tower. And watching a Donald Trump press conference is very much like watching a Christian network telethon. He is an unapologetic showman who understands the power of deflection via cultural signification. Life is a stage, including one's own body, and one ought to make sure that one's props are situated intentionally and appropriately.

As one who has written extensively on the prosperity gospel, I get it. I have made the connection between prosperity gospel televangelists and Donald Trump in my own work.[5] In recent years, however, I have begun to reexamine this obvious cultural connection. In fact, I have started to wonder if it is too apparent and thus also too easy. That is the best-case scenario. The worst-case scenario is that the comparison reinforces epistemological and cultural biases that place all "bad religion" at the feet of those who have been historically alienated from the sources of social power and denied cultural capital. There is a disturbing trend. Those who have written about the prosperity gospel in recent years, myself included, have contributed to a particular etiology and narrow historiography. It is the account that I noted previously: nineteenth-century New Thought metaphysics blending with Pentecostalism and postwar healing revivalism. This account is not wrong: it is just mainly focused in a manner

---

4. "Why Evangelicals Love Donald Trump: The Secret Lies in the Prosperity Gospel," *The Economist*, May 18, 2017, www.economist.com/news/united-states/21722172-secret-lies-prosperity-gospel-why-evangelicals-love-donald-trump.

5. Jonathan L. Walton, *Watch This! The Ethics and Aesthetics of Black Televangelism* (New York: New York University Press, 2009), 58, 96.

that reveals the implicit regional, racial, class, and gender biases of the academic study of religion. In the process, all that is viewed as excessive, self-indulgent, conspicuous, and decadent, whether particular religious forms or the forty-fifth president of the United States, is traced to white-working-class, female-led, or multiracial religious movements typically associated with the southern region of the country—again, the very constituencies traditionally relegated to the margins of North American culture. This narrative has caused me to wonder if such an analysis is akin to diagnosing symptoms rather than disease, the cough of the environmentally impacted rather than the pollutants in the cultural air.

As we observe the five hundredth anniversary of the Protestant Reformation, I want to take a somewhat different approach than the learned and stimulating chapters elsewhere in this volume. For one thing, I am a scholar of North American religions with particular training in Christian social ethics, and my research interest is more limited chronologically and geographically than that of many of my cocontributors. For another, I am not trained to debate the original theological intent of Luther, Calvin, Zwingli, or any other Protestant reformer.

Yet I do want to consider the prevailing representations of Protestantism in this country. This analysis will thus take me back and forth over the previous three centuries and, I believe, help me expand the prevailing narrative about religion, cultural anxiety, and consumerism that we now see manifest in the religious and even political phenomena that we call the prosperity gospel, broadly construed.

Such treatment must begin with what many in my field regard as one of the most important essays of the previous century, Max Weber's *Protestant Ethic and the Spirit of Capitalism* (German, 1905; English, 1930). Weber was among the earliest scholars to examine the relationship between Protestantism and modern capitalism in the Western world. He proffered an ideal type of person who embodied what he called "the spirit of capitalism." This person adheres to an ethic insofar as the highest good is the making of money coupled with a strict asceticism. "Indeed," Weber wrote, "it is so completely devoid of all eudaemonistic, let alone hedonist, motives, so much purely thought of as an end itself."[6] This ideal capitalist finds no pleasure in wealth and seeks no personal material benefit. Rather, pure delight comes from the knowledge of fulfilling a task faithfully and well.

6. Max Weber, *The Protestant Ethic and the Spirit of Capitalism: And Other Writings*, ed. Peter Baehr and Gordon C. Wells (New York: Penguin Books, 2002), 12.

The moral exemplar here is Benjamin Franklin. Though Franklin was a "nonsectarian Deist," Weber contends that Franklin derived his commitment to a vocation from his strict Calvinist father. For Weber, Calvinism proved the critical linchpin that transformed the relationship between asceticism and labor—a critical point of Weber's thesis, which emerges from his developmental model of vocation. In the Middle Ages the ascetic was largely contained within the monastic order. There was an "otherworldly asceticism" among those who renounced all material pleasures and financial profit. The Protestant Reformation disrupted this narrow conception of religious obligation. Martin Luther's notion of "calling" extended beyond the confines of monastic life. Christians were to approach their secular callings as the highest level of moral activity. Labor in a secular role became the outward expression of Christian piety and charity: everyone is to work for one another.

Weber claimed that Calvinism, not Lutheranism, catalyzed the notion of calling to have social and political implications. The Calvinist idea of predestination and election had everybody on a collective counseling couch of worry and anxiety. The church could not answer whether one was damned or saved. Nor could one find solace in the rituals or sacraments. Although Calvin himself believed that such knowledge remains restricted to God, his followers in the late sixteenth and early seventeenth centuries took matters into their own hands: one could prove oneself by working in the world. Everyone must now exercise in worldly affairs the same level of discipline and self-control demonstrated by the medieval monks. The otherworldly asceticism of the Middle Ages had now become a worldly asceticism of modernity. As Weber described it, "God helps those who help themselves."[7] This is how Weber explains the genesis of English Protestantism. And this is how Philadelphia ends up with the moral archetype, the ideal capitalist Benjamin Franklin. The calling—this Protestant ethic—becomes the ultimate good. In the process, the ideal capitalist reaps and then resows wealth beneath his humble feet. Inevitably, however, the pursuit of external goods replaced the internal call to honor God. What the ideal capitalist should wear around his shoulders like a light cloak became a steel shell of imprisonment.

As Bishop Huber points out in this volume (chap. 7), no credible scholar views Weber's developmental model as historically reliable. Almost immediately critics pointed out several fallacies. Capitalism, for

---

7. Ibid., 79.

instance, developed in Holland well before Calvinism was introduced—and many of the capitalists were and remained Catholic. Other scholars traced notions of the calling back to the New Testament and the early church. Thus we cannot take seriously the notion that Luther's innovative idea revolutionized the relationship between asceticism and labor.

These problems are why I wonder whether we might look at the success and enduring power of Weber's thesis in another light: not by viewing it as credible historiography or a theologically sound reading of Luther and Calvin, but by asking what it means to read Weber's essay as an ideological project of its era—an ideological project that helped to shape and solidify conceptual and physical structures of dominance in the twentieth-century United States. What if it were an ideological project that had the unintended consequence of fostering the very sort of iron-cage-inducing ethic that its author found abhorrent? The Protestant ethic as it developed in the United States may have exacerbated social anxieties and civic customs that, I argue, cultivated a spirit of consumerism.

In identifying Weber's thesis as an ideological project, I especially note two features: First, even if its history was askew, Weber's Protestant ethic was very much one with its age. In the nineteenth century there was a trend to moralize economic behaviors along the lines of virtue and vice, productive and unproductive. For instance, William Thompson's 1824 text *An Inquiry into the Principles of the Distribution of Wealth* bemoaned luxurious spending since it did not add to production. Whereas the poor consume for subsistence and thus contribute to their productive capacity, those who consume for the pursuit of novelty devour without a return contribution. Similarly in 1848, John Stuart Mill's *Principles of Political Economy* condemned the unproductive consumer as one who contributes nothing directly or indirectly to production. Money spent on luxury goods redirected resources away from improving the health and expanding the capacities of productive laborers. Both Thompson and Mill represent a broader moral sensibility of Victorian liberalism that many felt was threatened by the moral decay in what Thorstein Veblen famously referred to as a culture of "conspicuous consumption" in his 1899 classic, *The Theory of the Leisure Class.* One can see where Weber seems to hold a similar moral outlook—an outlook that he baptized in Calvinism and mapped back onto the previous century.

So not only was Weber's essay one with its age, but it is also replete with the sort of value-laden binaries that tend to prove culturally resonant for educated readers in general, and for nascent social-science programs at Harvard, the University of Pennsylvania, and the University of Chicago. You have your ideal exemplars in the Calvinists, Benjamin Franklin, and Richard Baxter over against your morally deficient Catholics, Lutherans, and emotional German Pietists. You have a high cultural moment of sober English Puritans who embrace their calling with zeal and selflessness. This gives way to a narrative of decline. We are thus left with a prophetic warning regarding the dangers of self-indulgent hedonism. We must reclaim the sense of purpose and piety of Franklin and his father. For in their Calvinism is the valuable ethic, "the Protestant ethic," which produces this nation's capitalist economy.

The problem with ideologies, however, is that all ideologies willfully obscure as much as they convey. And while the Protestant ethic as a cultural trope and political ideology has done much to encourage thrift, sobriety, and the disciplines essential for success, it has also willfully ignored how the promulgated ideal works to regulate and reify class hierarchies and distinctions based on cultural capital and tastes.

Here I am thinking of Pierre Bourdieu's classic social critique *Distinction* and applying it to Weber's essay. In Bourdieu's thinking, not unlike Weber's, social stratum or class cannot be reduced to a mere economic position. For Bourdieu, people draw on economic, social, and cultural capital to compete for symbolic capital, or status. Unlike the income level one earns or the social networks one is part of, cultural capital signifies the knowledge base, appropriate behaviors, styles, and tastes that one chooses. Whether embodied (knowledge), objectified (goods), or institutionalized (diplomas that certify embodied form), status is cultivated and maintained within the domain of the elites. This elite structure of feeling or habitus dictates the preferences and tastes in each field of our society (politics, religion, art) more than any particular acquired good. In Bourdieu's words, "Taste classifies, and it classifies the classifier."[8]

This reading of Bourdieu is why, in part, I have begun to read Weber's essay as an ideological project that helped to establish in the United States a particular ethic of liberal Protestantism that renounced excess, even as it maintained concrete class distinctions. This is to say, sobriety, thrift, and labor as vocation were hoisted up as the preferred taste of a privileged

8. Pierre Bourdieu, *Distinction: A Social Critique of the Judgement of Taste*, ed. and trans. Richard Nice (Cambridge, MA: Harvard University Press, 1984), 6.

section of white, male elites at the very moment most Americans entering the labor force—European and Asian immigrants, Southern white working class, the formerly enslaved, indigenous populations, and women—were too far removed from the sources of economic production for those professed values to be of much good. In fact, as historians such as William Leach and Lizbeth Cohen have effectively argued, the same captains of industry often responsible for extolling the virtues of labor as vocation and the simple life were usually the same titans that merged the spheres of media, politics, advertising, and, I would add, religion to promote the twentieth-century conception that linked citizenship with consumerism.[9] This is America. We shop, and thus we are.

Let me provide two brief examples to illustrate my point: one example from the eighteenth century and one from the twentieth. We can start with Weber's own ideal capitalist, Benjamin Franklin. In his 1748 piece "Advice to a Young Tradesman," Franklin declares: "The Way to Wealth, if you desire it, is as plain as the Way to Market. It depends chiefly on two Words, Industry and Frugality; i.e., Waste neither Time nor Money, but make the best Use of both. He that gets all he can honestly, and saves all he gets (necessary Expences excepted) will certainly become Rich."[10]

This was the very sort of homespun advice and practical wisdom that Franklin dispensed in his *Poor Richard's Almanack* under the pseudonym Richard Saunders, a name he "borrowed" from a physician and astrologer in London who published his own very successful almanac in the late seventeenth century throughout Europe. Some of Franklin's phrases have become staples of American vernacular: "At the working man's house hunger looks in but dares not enter." "If you lie down with dogs, you will come up with fleas." And "God helps those who help themselves." As the late sociologist Robert Bellah argued in his classic *Habits of the Heart: Individualism and Commitment in American Life*, Poor Richard helped to shape an individualist framework for American society that emphasized individual pursuit and gains as the best way to bring about the social good.[11] This may be why in one curious reinterpretation of the Great

9. William Leach, *Land of Desire: Merchants, Power, and the Rise of a New American Culture* (New York: Vintage, 1994).

10. Benjamin Franklin, "Advice to a Young Tradesman," July 21, 1748, in *The American Instructor: or, Young Man's Best Companion*, ed. George Fisher, 9th ed. (Philadelphia: B. Franklin & D. Hall, 1748), 375–77, founders.archives.gov/documents/Franklin/01-03-02-0130.

11. Robert N. Bellah et al., *Habits of the Heart: Individualism and Commitment in American Life* (Berkeley: University of California Press, 1985), 33–34.

Commandment, Poor Richard declares, "Love your neighbor, yet don't pull down your hedge."[12]

It appears that Franklin discovered early on that it was financially lucrative and politically expedient to conceal his worldview through a populist doppelgänger intended to represent the conventional wisdom of the masses. Franklin is promoting this moral framework of rugged individualism and personal piety as the surest path to success under the guise of "Poor Richard" at the very moment Franklin is emerging among a colonial aristocracy that is systematically seizing the vast majority of property and power in the colonies.

Contemplate the contradictions. While the colonies framed themselves as egalitarian, free of the abuses of Europe, men of influence like Franklin were receiving vast land grants from the British Crown and profiting from the slave trade by running human-sale advertisements in his *Philadelphia Gazette*. To illustrate this point, by 1760 fewer than five hundred men in five colonial cities controlled commerce, shipping, and manufacturing on the eastern seaboard. And following the Revolution, the so-called founding fathers arranged it so that only property-owning white men could vote in twelve of the original thirteen states. This group constituted a mere 10 percent of the total population. Women, Native Americans, and African peoples, as well as non–property-holding white men, were denied a political voice. So while Poor Richard demonized caste systems, his brain trust Benjamin Franklin was remixing and redeeming Europe's aristocratic model for the benefit of the colonial elite. Might we think Benjamin Franklin was successful and made an impact on American religious life? Well, according to one recent study, 75 percent of American Protestants believe that the Bible teaches, "God helps those who help themselves."[13] For men like Franklin, the invisible, enslaved, and exploited labor that made his existence possible provided him with the privilege to embrace the cultural tastes of perceived sobriety.

Or consider twentieth-century department-store magnate John Wanamaker. On one hand, Wanamaker, a devout Presbyterian, helped to build one of the largest Sunday school classes in the country at his local Bethany Presbyterian Church. He drew a crowd of nearly two thousand each Sunday. Central to this Sunday school was a men's group that he named

---

12. Benjamin Franklin, *Poor Richard's Almanac: The Wit and Wisdom of Benjamin Franklin* (Lexington, KY: Seven Treasures Publications, 2008), 111 of 774.

13. Barna Research Group, "Beliefs Held by Americans in Regard to the Bible," ed. Barna Research Online, www.bibleteachingnotes.com/templates/System/details.asp?fetch=7872.

the Roman Legion, many of whom were employees of his store. Wanamaker taught on themes of hard work and human flourishing through an evangelical frame.[14]

He was also a devotee of the philosophy of the simple life promoted by the French clergyman and best-selling author Charles Wagner. Wanamaker hosted Wagner during his visit to America and organized a lunch for Wagner with President Theodore Roosevelt and leading American clergy, such as the Rev. Russell Conwell of *Acres of Diamonds* fame. Wanamaker purchased thousands of copies of *The Simple Life* to distribute to his employees and promote the virtues of living simple, plain, and virtuous lives. Wanamaker even built a "simple" cabin next to his Pennsylvania mansion to host Wagner and experience the simple life himself whenever he felt the need.[15]

On the other hand, Wanamaker is credited with helping make the transition in American culture from the Protestant ethic virtues of thrift, saving, and reinvestment to an ethic predicated on desire, acquisition, and consumption—what historian William Leach describes as "the cult of the new."[16] Wanamaker outfitted his stores with a traditional aesthetic that would remind people of their local cathedral. His department stores contained stained-glass windows, and in 1909 he purchased the ten-thousand-pipe organ from the 1904 St. Louis World's Fair for his Philadelphia store. This organ provided shoppers with the feeling that their shopping experience was indeed a sacred endeavor. The ability to consume was offered as a sign of sanctification, a gift of grace, a sure sign of one's standing in the kingdoms of both God and man. It seems, once again, the mass-consumption practices of everyday people provided Wanamaker with the economic resources to embrace the tastes of Weber's Protestant ethic. The simple life was expensive for Wanamaker, although it was much more costly for the laborers who stocked shelves in Wanamaker's stores.

In conclusion, let me reiterate my thesis and make clear my ethical concern. By using Bourdieu's theory of distinction, I am suggesting that it is possible to read Max Weber's *Protestant Ethic and Spirit of Capitalism* as an ideological project, a professed description that concealed a normative prescription concerning the ideal capitalist and the ideal Protestant.

14. William R. Glass, "Liberal Means to Conservative Ends: Bethany Presbyterian Church, John Wanamaker, and the Institutional Church Movement," *American Presbyterians* 68, no. 3 (1990): 181.

15. Leach, *Land of Desire*, 206–8.

16. Ibid., 4.

And I suggest that this ruling ideal proved beneficial to those who could afford to perform the worldly aesthetic tastes, while simultaneously presenting their wealth as a sign of God's favor. For the vast majority of those unable to achieve either the tastes of simplicity or the security of immense wealth, signs of prosperity may have become the next best thing. Thus, rather than locating the contemporary phenomena of the gospel of prosperity with Pentecostals and working-class constituencies, I am starting to believe that there is enough evidence among the scions of American liberal Protestantism for us to reconsider what the Protestant ethic has come to mean.

Paſſional Chriſti und
Antichriſti.
Chriſtus.
Do Jheſus innen wardt/das ſie kommen wurden und yhnen tzum könig machen/iſt er abermals uffin bergk geflohen/ er allein. Johan.6. Mein reich iſt nicht võ diſzer welt. Joh.18. Die könnige der welt hirſchen yr/unnd die gewaldt haben/ werden gnedige hern genandt/yr aber nicht alſzo/ſonder der do groſſer iſt unther euch/ſall ſich nydern/als der weniger. Luce.22.
Antichriſtus.
Auß obirkayt die wir ſonder tzweiffell tzum keyſzerthũb haben/ und auſz unſer gewalt/ ſeynt wir des keyſertumbs/ ſo ſich das vorledigt/ein rechter erbe.cle.paſtoralis ad fi. de ſen.et re.iudi. Sũma ſummarũ. Nichts anders iſt in des Bapſts geyſtlichẽ rechte tzu finden/dan das es ſeynen abgot und Antichriſt ubir alle keyſzer/könig uñ furſten yrhebet/als Petrus vorgeſagt hat. Es werden kõmen unuorſchambte Biſchoff die die weltlich herſchafft werden vorachten.2.Pet.2. A ij

Contrast in Use of Power, in *Passional Christi und Antichristi*,
by Lucas Cranach the Elder, 1521

Chapter Nine

The Reformation and the Future of Europe

Graham Tomlin

The future of Europe is a matter of common interest to all the churches of the West, particularly those on that continent. We live in a time when Europe needs a new vision. The Brexit vote—the 2016 referendum for the United Kingdom to leave the European Union—dealt a severe blow to the European dream of ever-increasing integration and unity. While Britain flounders to work out what Brexit will mean for British society and economy, and the European Union tries to respond and discourage other populist movements from taking root across the Continent, Europe itself faces an uncertain future.

The European Union (EU) in its origins was inspired by a Christian vision, one that emerged from the Christian Democratic movements of the 1940s and 1950s. The architects of the early EU—people like Robert Schuman, Alcide de Gasperi, and Konrad Adenauer—were all key figures in the European Christian Democratic movement. They shared a Christian perspective on the world, so much so that on the eve of the crucial Paris conference of 1951, which started what became the Common Market and eventually the EU, they retreated to a Benedictine monastery on the Rhine to pray. The goals of the emerging union, including an end to war, interdependence between neighboring nations, and compassion for the poor of the world, were all inspired by their Christian social vision.

Since those times, the threat of war has receded. In recent years doubts have set in as a result of national debates over the euro, the economic travails of 2008 and beyond, and the migrant crisis, which all began to threaten European stability and prosperity. By the fateful referendum of 2016, all that was left was a rather narrow bureaucratic vision of standardized practice and personal prosperity. What the British rejected was a vision of Europe that no longer really inspired anyone. The original Christian vision of Europe had evaporated, and the question now was this: what actually holds Europe together? If the only values that hold European countries together are rather thin and vague notions of tolerance, individual freedom, and human rights, then it is arguable that these do not carry the strength to provide a coherent social vision.

Tolerance is a good thing, yet not robust enough to provide true social cohesion. If I say to my neighbor, "I tolerate you," that does not exactly establish a good and healthy relationship of mutual engagement! In our current climate, human rights do not provide a defined and clear picture either since it is hard to establish what does and does not count as a human right: if a person claims something as a right, there are no criteria by which to judge whether it counts or not. Similarly, notions of personal freedom to do as we choose with our time, talents, and property, as long as we do not impose on the freedoms of others, simply set up relationships of opposition and conflict. Such a vision of freedom sees the other at best as a limitation, or at worst as a threat to my freedom, not a neighbor given to me as a gift to enable me to become all that I have the potential to be, as I have argued elsewhere.[1]

By an irony of history, this crisis in European identity coincided with the five hundredth anniversary of the Reformation. In preparation for the referendum on Britain's future with the European Union, there was a debate in print between Giles Fraser and the historian Diarmaid MacCulloch on the significance of the Reformation for the Brexit question. Fraser, in favor of Brexit, argued that the English Reformation was a classic "leave" moment. It was Britain taking its leave of a bureaucratic, centralized, domineering European institution—the Catholic Church—and going it alone on its independent way. MacCulloch, wanting a "remain" vote, argued on the contrary that the Reformation was a very distinctly *European* event, with the Reformers very conscious of their links with others, links that crossed national boundaries in a pan-European movement.

Both sides of the argument have some force. Yet while Fraser's take on the English Reformation as an independence movement from European control has some merit, if I had to plump for one or the other, I would side with McCulloch's vision of the European character of the Reformation as a whole. Although the Reformation had its national champions and took a different form in Germany than it did in England, France, or Scandinavia, the Reformers had in mind a renewed church in Europe,

---

1. Graham Tomlin, *Bound to Be Free: The Paradox of Freedom* (London: Bloomsbury, 2017).

not just new national churches. A glance at the correspondence of figures such as John Calvin or Martin Bucer shows the extraordinarily wide
range of contacts they held and sought to maintain across the Continent.

As an example, it is significant that the Lutherans made particular efforts to reach out to the Orthodox churches of the East. During
Luther's controversy with the papacy leading up to his excommunication
by the pope in 1520 and his expulsion from the Holy Roman Empire
by Charles V in 1521, he was struck by the significance of the existence
of the Orthodox churches of the East. They seemed to him to belie the
claim of the bishop of Rome to be the vicar of Christ on earth, as they
represented significant, deeply rooted, and historic Christian churches
that owed no particular allegiance to the pope. In his *Defence and Explanation of All the Articles*, which were condemned in the papal bull that
excommunicated him in 1520, Luther responded to the claim that the
papacy was the rock upon which the church was built. He argued, "For all
Christendom has fallen away from the Pope; for example, the Greeks, the
Bohemians, Africa, and the whole Orient! Or to be more accurate, they
were never built upon this rock."[2]

A few years after Luther died, in 1559 Philip Melanchthon sent a copy
of the Augsburg Confession (translated into Greek) with a personal letter
addressed to Jeremiah II, the patriarch of Constantinople, to be delivered by an elderly cleric from Montenegro called Demetrius, who had
made favorable impressions in Lutheran circles. Demetrius arrived in
Constantinople at the end of 1559 to deliver his package. The Greeks
were clearly not particularly impressed by the Lutheran Confession,
however, and responded with discreet diplomatic silence. Melanchthon's
letter was carefully and deliberately lost, and Demetrius never returned
to Wittenberg.

Luther occasionally mused on the possibility of an alliance with the
Greeks that would help reform the Western church, and this venture
by Melanchthon was presumably fruit of that desire when the opportunity offered itself. The ultimate failure of Melanchthon's effort does
not negate the fact, however, that the Reformation saw itself as a movement seeking to bring a new vision, not just to individual nations but to
the whole of Europe. In this essay, I argue that the Reformation, while
flawed, was a vision of a renewed Christian Europe, with an attempt to
address a number of significant social and economic issues facing Europe
at the time. In particular, I identify four factors in late-medieval Europe

2. *LW* 32:69.

that the Reformation sought to address, each of which has significant resonance in our time as well.

The Rise of Individualism

The Reformation is often identified as a key influence in the rise of Western individualism. However, there is much to suggest that the shift to the primacy of the individual rather than the community took place much earlier. The Renaissance had already begun to give birth to a new culture and enabled the rise of a new wealthy elite in the cities across Europe. These were sophisticated, educated people, often driven by a desire to display their newfound wealth and learning ostentatiously, through patronage of the arts or letters or new buildings that expressed connection with the classical past. Leo X, the pope who excommunicated Luther in 1520, was exactly this kind of person, a nobly born Italian known as a patron of artists, including figures such as Raphael. Along with these new Renaissance men and women, new money houses arose—the banks, of which the famous Fugger financial house, based in Augsburg, was the most prominent in the German-speaking lands. Replacing the Medici as the central financial power in the Holy Roman Empire, for around 150 years Fugger banking dominated financial transactions across Europe.

The result of these social changes was an erosion of some of the older social structures that held together a feudal society, and many historians have argued that this left the individual alone and exposed. Small-business people, artisans, and peasants felt left out of this newly emerging mercantile class. These early stages of capitalism freed individuals from economic and social ties that bound them to a particular status in society, allowing for much greater social mobility, but at the same time eroding the security given by those ties. The Peasants' Revolt of 1524–25 was one result of this sense of disillusionment and alienation: those who felt left out of the emerging new social structures struck a blow for their own future and survival.

This was a world in which personal value seemed to rest upon reputation, wealth, or education. The theology and spirituality of the late-medieval church did not always help either. It implied that the individual was alone before God, needing to prove worthy of divine grace by performing religious actions such as attending Mass, going on pilgrimage, buying indulgences, and the like. Popular theology seemed to suggest that if you did your best and turned to God through the sacramental life of the church, God would give you grace to enable you to become good and ultimately merit salvation. Both the economics and the theology of the time left individuals alone and uncertain, unsure of their status in society or their standing before God.[3]

Martin Luther was very aware of both of these factors. His father was a part owner of a mining business in Thuringia, and Martin had spent his childhood moving from town to town according to the fluctuating fortunes of his father's small-business ventures, so he was aware of the social instability caused by these new social arrangements. As a particularly sensitive and thoughtful son of the church, he was also very conscious of the level of personal uncertainty left by the late-medieval spirituality in which he was nurtured.

The doctrine of justification by faith alone can be seen as an answer to these questions of personal worth and status that were alive in early-sixteenth-century Europe. This doctrine told people that they were justified not by what they did or achieved, not by their wealth or status in society, in fact not by their own merits at all, but instead by the merits of Christ. Luther relocated the grounds for God's justification from an *internal* righteousness—a goodness or holiness generated within, albeit with the help of divine grace—to an *external* righteousness, something located outside the individual and entirely independent of personal achievement or social standing. All that was required was simply to believe the promise of divine favor, offered in Christ through the word of absolution or of preaching, in the bread and wine of the Lord's Supper, or in the water of baptism.

This doctrine proved to be a profound answer to the questions of value and self-worth that stalked late-medieval society. The individual may stand alone before God, but this was a God of mercy and grace rather than a God of judgment, who did not demand righteousness but gave it in the person of Christ. Justification by faith offered an unshaken sense of value and worth because it was located in Christ rather than in the self.

For Luther, this new view of justification gave him a God he could love. Luther once wrote, "From childhood on, I knew I had to turn pale and be terror-stricken when I heard the name of Christ; for I was taught only to perceive him as a strict and wrathful judge." Rather than the Christ whom he was taught to fear as the one presiding over the condemnation of the guilty and the acquittal of the good, God was now a generous giver, supplying the righteousness that was required rather than demanding it,

---

3. For more discussion of this, see Graham Tomlin, *Luther's Gospel: Reimagining the World* (London: T&T Clark, 2017).

and not to good people but to sinners—those profoundly aware of their own lack of status or moral achievement.

The doctrine also led to a new view of the neighbor. Rather than a self-absorbed spirituality, requiring constant examining of oneself and whether one had performed enough religious works, pilgrimages, indulgences, Masses, and prayers, Luther instead proposed an externally focused spirituality, where all the spiritual energy and resources formerly spent on religious activity could be spent in love toward one's neighbor. As he put it in *The Freedom of a Christian* in 1520:

> My God has given me in Christ all the riches of righteousness and salvation without any merit on my part, out of pure free mercy, so that from now on I need nothing except faith which believes that this is true. Why should I not therefore freely, joyfully, with all my heart and with an eager will, do all things which I know are pleasing and acceptable to such a Father who has overwhelmed me with his inestimable riches? I will therefore give myself as a Christ to my neighbor just as Christ offered himself to me; I will do nothing in this life except what I see is necessary, profitable, and salutary to my neighbour, since that through faith I have an abundance of all good things in Christ.[4]

Not everyone believed this, of course. There were always doubts about the relationship between faith and works in Reformation doctrine, and Luther's polemics did not always help the Reformation cause. Yet this doctrine had a profound impact upon the early modern world, creating a new way of life that affected people all across Europe right into the present day.

Poverty and the Migrant Crisis

Sixteenth-century Europe was full of displaced people. Conflicts such as the Peasants' Revolt and the religious squabbles that broke into local violence often meant that people had to leave home to find security elsewhere. Increasing numbers of religious refugees either were forced or chose to leave home for territories more sympathetic to their religious views.[5]

---

4. *LW* 31:367.
5. See, e.g., Otfried Czaika and Heinrich Holze, eds., *Migration und Kulturtransfer im Ostseeraum während der Frühen Neuzeit* (Stockholm: Kungliga biblioteket, 2012).

This was also a period when poverty was obvious and endemic. Some within the medieval church—in particular the Franciscans, who had taken vows of poverty—were devoted to the service of the poor. The difficulty was that efforts to restrain begging, whether by the economically destitute or by mendicant monks, who had begun to be a scandal in many cities across the empire, were hampered by a theology that valued alms-giving as meritorious. The medieval view of the relief of poverty posed a paradox. When you gave to the poor, were you doing so genuinely to relieve the poor person's situation, or were you doing it to acquire merit before God, and therefore contribute to your own salvation? Was it an altruistic or a selfish act? There was a sense that the poor were necessary: otherwise, good Christians could not practice virtue by giving to them; if Christians could not practice virtue, they could not acquire merit and therefore could not be saved. Poverty was of course also one of the vows taken by medieval monks, which gave poverty a particular status within the medieval structure of religious life. Poverty was therefore bound up in the system of salvation in late-medieval Catholicism.[6]

Luther's doctrine of justification by faith alone changed this. Acts of charity no longer were considered meritorious before God or contributed to salvation in any way: that came only through faith in the word of promise given in Christ. Almsgiving was entirely removed from the doctrine of salvation. Poverty had no particular status for salvation either, as monastic vows were deemed merely human promises, not binding for life. The Reformers were also suspicious of the new banking arrangements. Although Calvin was more sympathetic to the practice of usury, Luther opposed charging excessive interest and wanted to curb the influence of banking houses such as the Fuggers. He had a very suspicious attitude to wealth, expressed in his quip "Money is one of the least of God's gifts. Therefore, he commonly gives it to those to whom he means no good."[7]

In Wittenberg, one of the first acts of the Reformation was to disband the brotherhoods arranged to collect money to endow Masses said for the repose of the souls of their members. Instead, the money collected was to be distributed to the poor. Johannes Bugenhagen, the pastor of the city church in Wittenberg from 1523, had a genius for organization and the praxis of Christian theology. For him, the true worship of God was to help the poor. He urged the people of Wittenberg to stop leaving money in their wills for Masses or vigils for their dead souls. Instead,

6. See Carter Lindberg, *The European Reformations* (Oxford: Blackwell, 1996), chap. 5.
7. *LW* 54:452.

they should provide for their families or give to the destitute. Energy and resources formerly given to religious practices were instead to be freed up for social welfare. For example, the question soon arose about what to do with the assets of monasteries once they were disbanded. In his preface to the Leisnig congregation's 1523 Ordinance of a Common Chest, Luther argued that the city should "devote all the remaining property to the common fund of a common chest, out of which gifts and loans could be made in Christian love to all the needy in the land, be they nobles or commoners. . . . Now there is no greater service of God than Christian love which helps and serves the needy."[8]

In cities shaped by the Reformation, new patterns of social welfare were established. In Geneva, for example, begging was outlawed as a demeaning and inefficient way of supporting the poor. Instead, a new church order was established. Rather than bishops, priests, and deacons, there was to be the fourfold order of pastors, elders, doctors, and deacons. The deacons are most interesting in this regard. There were to be two kinds. One had the responsibility of caring for the sick in the new Geneva hospital (a remodeled convent, which had been closed down under the influence of Calvin's teaching). The other kind of deacon had the responsibility of managing church funds and providing for the poor. Geneva also had a significant refugee problem, with many exiled Protestants finding their way to the city as a beacon of hope for their new faith. One historian has described the role of the deacon like this: "Deacons found places for people to stay and jobs for them. The deacons employed people to care for the sick, wet nurses for infants and foster homes for orphans. The deacons gave and lent clothing and bedding. They gave money to the poor and lent money, especially if someone needed tools or was trying to set up a business."[9]

While aiming to relieve poverty, Calvin's Geneva also sought to restrict the show of ostentatious wealth. In 1560 a comprehensive ordinance was issued, going into detail on questions like how many rings could be worn, banning gold and silver chains or gilding of hair, and prescribing the number of courses at public banquets. We might find such regulations overly restrictive and intrusive, but in the context, it was an attempt to provide some form of social leveling to narrow the obvious gap between rich and poor in the city.

---

8. *LW* 45:172.

9. Donald Keith McKim, *The Cambridge Companion to Martin Luther* (Cambridge: Cambridge University Press, 2003), 166.

It has been said that Calvin's Geneva was one of the first attempts to establish a welfare state in modern Europe without the need for begging. Other Reformation cities also seriously attempted to banish poverty. The attempts did not always succeed, and sometimes they betrayed a fussy and intrusive form of social control, but they were nonetheless theologically motivated programs to eliminate destitution and poverty in favor of a much more egalitarian view of social life.

The Revolt against the Elites

As already noted, a sense of disfranchisement was common in the sixteenth century. Whether it was the rise of the new educated humanist elites, the distant power of Rome, or the financial houses that concentrated economic power in a very few hands, many people in late-medieval Europe felt distanced from the centers of power and decision making. At imperial diets of the Holy Roman Empire, a tradition had developed that enumerated the grievances of the nation in the *gravamina nationis germanicae*, or "grievances of the German nation," over against the papacy. These complaints focused on papal taxation and appointments to benefices. Paradoxically, the famous Diet of Worms in 1521, while condemning Martin Luther for his refusal to back down from his attack on Roman doctrine, at the same time drew up a new list of 102 papal abuses as a verbal act of resistance to the distant power of Rome.

Luther's doctrine of justification by faith implicitly and explicitly led in a more egalitarian direction. For Luther, Christian faith has at its heart trust in the promise of God. Although he still held a place for pastors and ministers for the sake of good order, in a sense it no longer mattered who uttered the promise, whether in verbal or sacramental form; the crucial thing was whether the Christian believed the Word when it was offered.

In addition, Luther gradually became aware of the reality that the priests, bishops, and cardinals were not going to reform the church, and therefore he began to argue that laypeople had as much right to reform it as the clerics, based on their common baptism. This then led to Luther's doctrine of the priesthood of the baptized and the idea that every Christian has the responsibility to stand in the place of Christ, offering to fellow Christians advice, assistance, and a reminder of the promise of forgiveness—what later became known as the priesthood of all believers. This doctrine leveled social distinctions, not so much eliminating the priesthood as exalting the laity to the level of priestly ministry. Certainly this conclusion was drawn by the peasants, who began to demand social transformation in the early 1520s in the name of Luther's teaching. Luther of course was not so keen. He rejected such calls for social revolution, drawing back from some of the more radical implications of his earlier calls for lay-led reform, but the underlying trajectory of his Reformation program was unmistakable and appealed particularly to those who felt left out, left behind, and abandoned by social and economic trends of the time.

In the early days of the Reformation, Luther harnessed this popular sense of disfranchisement and dissatisfaction to gain strength for his move to independence from papal authority. While he resisted the Peasants' Revolt, at the same time he expressed his genius for popular communication in his use of the new technology of printing and his new German Bible. Printing had democratized knowledge. Beforehand, the dissemination of information was in the hands of the state, the church, or the monasteries. Now anyone could open a printing shop and publish whatever they felt the public would buy. Luther's Reformation in Wittenberg is unthinkable without the printing shops of Johann Grünenberg and Melchior Lotther.

Luther harnessed all this as a genius at popular communication. The seminal year of 1520 marked a shift in his writing from the predominant use of Latin, the rarefied language of academic debate and ecclesiastical pronouncement, to German, so much so that from then on, 88 percent of his work was published in German. It is estimated that between 1510 and 1530, some 20 percent of all German publications were written by Martin Luther. The public could not get their hands quickly enough on anything that flowed from the pen or mouth of Luther, whether or not he had authorized its publication.

In particular, his approach to Bible translation appealed—bypassing academics, clerics, and the educated elites—to "ordinary" Germans. After his appearance at the Diet of Worms in 1521, he was hustled away for safekeeping by his sovereign, Frederick the Wise, into the Wartburg, a castle in the hills near one of his childhood homes in Eisenach. Bored, frustrated, and troubled by stomach problems, he decided to translate the Bible into German. This was not the first German Bible—several others had appeared in the previous fifty years—but Luther's took a radically new approach to translation. Not only was it directly translated from the original Hebrew and Greek rather than the Latin Vulgate; it also aimed to use idiomatic and popular German. As Luther wrote later: "I wanted to speak German, not Latin or Greek, since it was German I had undertaken to speak in the translation. We do not have to inquire of the literal

Latin, how we are to speak German as these asses do. Rather we must inquire about this of the mother in the home, the children on the street, the common man in the market-place. We must be guided by their language, the way they speak, and do our translating accordingly."[10]

Luther's was not a word-for-word translation. He felt free to depart from the original at times to give the sense of a passage to its readers and to ensure it was expressed in a language that ordinary Germans would use. Unlike the King James Version of the next century, this was no attempt to speak in exact literary terminology, but an effort to make the prophets sound like German artisans, and the apostles like Saxon peasants. He argued that the key requirement in a translator is not so much knowledge of the original donor languages but a good profound knowledge of the receptor language, the language used by the intended readers of a text.

As a result, this translation profoundly shaped modern German, drawing a number of distinct dialects into one common language. Luther was a master at popular language and communication, with the ability to express the gospel in terms that could be understood precisely by those who had felt left out of some of the social developments of recent years.

At times the Reformation was an unashamedly populist movement, not particularly concerned with appealing to the highbrow or the educated elites. Again, it did not always manage to communicate with simplicity, but in its radical shift to the vernacular language, the Reformation moved Europe in a more dispersed and democratized direction, opening the treasures of the Bible to a much wider group of people, and taking the risk of allowing them to read it for themselves. It chimed in with the disfranchised and appealed directly to those who felt left out of the prosperity and power that seemed to be concentrated in the hands of those who spoke and read Latin, who held positions of authority, or whose wealth took them out of the experiences of the ordinary people.

The Rise of Islam

Constantinople had fallen to the Turks in 1453, and in the following decades, Muslim armies had consolidated their power and presence northward to the Danube River. In 1520 the Ottomans captured Belgrade, and in 1526 they won the decisive battle of Mohacs in Hungary. The victory of the forces of Suleiman the Magnificent over the armies of Louis II of Hungary and Bohemia (who died in the battle) not only

10. *LW* 35:189.

put an end to the Hungarian nation as a united entity but also sent shock waves through Europe: it seemed that the Islamic forces of the Turk were on the verge of invading the rest of the continent. Three years later, in 1529, Suleiman laid siege to Vienna, and it seemed to many that European capitulation to an Islamic invasion was inevitable. Europe had been weakened and divided by the religious disputes of the Reformation, and a common fear was expressed in the literature of the time that Europe was about to turn Muslim.

As it happened, the siege of Vienna was the pinnacle of the Ottoman advance westward, and despite another attempt in 1532, Suleiman's armies were resisted and turned their attention elsewhere. Throughout the 1520s, the Turkish threat paradoxically helped the spread of the Reformation because the Turks preoccupied Charles V. Not until the Ottomans had begun to retreat, around the turn of the decade, was Charles able to turn his attention again to resisting the growth of the evangelical movement, by belatedly implementing the Edict of Worms in the late 1520s. Nonetheless, the fear of an Islamic takeover was very real in Europe during the decade when the Reformation took hold. It was a live question as to whether a new crusade needed to be launched against the Islamic threat, and whether military or diplomatic solutions should be sought.

On a number of occasions Luther himself shared his own resigned sense of it being quite possible that Europe's future would be Islamic. He expressed a grudging admiration for Islam, owing to its disciplined and ordered piety and the fervency of its adherents, even if he saw it as ultimately destructive of the three estates of the church, temporal government, and marriage and the family. He was pessimistic about the resilience of European Christianity and its ability to survive a hostile takeover by Islam. The flabby spiritual state of Europe had been weakened, as he saw it, by centuries of papal teaching and theological and pastoral neglect. Partly because of this pessimism, he backed a proposal for a translation of the Qur'an into Latin by Thomas Bibliander in 1542, not so that Islam could spread in Europe, but so that Christian scholars could more ably refute Islamic claims.

In 1529, during the siege of Vienna, Luther wrote a brief treatise titled *On War against the Turk*, published the next year. He responded to calls for a Christian army to defeat the Turks militarily with the argument that the pope certainly should not be engaged in such a venture, and that if Charles V were to do so, he should do it firmly in his capacity as emperor rather than in his capacity as a Christian. There should be no crusade against Islam in the name of Christianity. This of course is an application of Luther's doctrine of the two kingdoms, which says that Christians may act with one set of rules as public officials charged with the protection and health of society, and with another set of rules in the realm of faith and personal piety, which has no place for force or violence. Most significantly, however, he urged that individual Christians should not resist the threatened Islamic takeover by meeting violence with violence, but instead should respond with prayer, fasting, and repentance.

Luther saw the Turk as God's judgment on a spiritually lax Europe, and he believed that Christendom must endure this divine verdict, opposing Islam not with violence but with the spiritual weapons God has given. His doctrine of justification by faith persuaded him that attempting to force belief on anyone was a waste of time. In the realm of faith, force achieves nothing. As he writes in this treatise: "I fear the sword will accomplish little. Now the Christian is not to fight physically with the Turk, as the pope and his followers teach; nor is he to resist the Turk with the fist, but he is to recognize the Turk as God's rod and wrath which Christians must either suffer, if God visits their sins upon them, or fight against and drive away with repentance, tears, and prayer."[11]

In response to the threat of Islam and the prospect of Europe being dominated by a growing Muslim presence, the Reformers urged not so much a military response, but renewal of Christian life and discipline. While Luther envisaged the possibility of a military response, a defensive war of resistance against Islamic invasion, his response to the rise of Islam was not what we would call Islamophobia, or a call for armed resistance to Islam in the name of Christian Europe, but instead a call for renewing the wellsprings of Christian faith. He saw the rise of Islam as an act of God to call Christians back to their true identity as Christians:

> Every pastor and preacher ought diligently to exhort his people to repentance and prayer. . . . This fight must be begun with repentance and we must reform our lives or we shall fight in vain. . . . Along with these must be cited the words and illustrations of Scripture in which God makes known how well pleased he is with true repentance or amendment made in faith and reliance on his word. . . . After people have thus been taught and exhorted to confess their sins and mend their ways, they should then be most diligently exhorted to prayer and shown that such prayer pleases God, that he has commanded it and promised to hear it, and that no one ought to think lightly of his

11. *LW* 46:184.

own praying or have doubts about it, but with firm faith be sure that it will be heard.[12]

In particular, Luther saw the rise of Islam as an incentive to rediscover a more disciplined form of Christian life. The Reformation can be seen in one sense as a renewal movement urging deeper Christian engagement with theology, Bible reading, prayer, and secular work as a profoundly Christian activity, done for the glory of God rather than for money or fame. All branches of the Reformation issued catechisms, aimed at instilling Christian doctrine in the lives of European believers.

The Reformation has often been criticized for undermining the institution of monastic life. However, another interpretation would be that it aimed not so much at eliminating monastic discipline as making such training possible for all Christians. Thomas Cranmer's Book of Common Prayer, with its recommendation that Christians should pray regularly, morning and evening, was in effect a form of the monastic pattern of devotion adapted for every Christian, whether in the home or the workplace, rather than purely for those who had entered the monastery.

Other factors could be cited in this story of the Reformation as a response to a range of social and economic problems facing Europe at the time. Yet at its heart was the doctrine of justification by faith, which, though more central to Luther's teaching than to that of any of the other reformers, still occupied pride of place as perhaps the main doctrine that united the various branches of the Reformation. This idea gave a new basis for self-worth and value in an age that left the individual exposed and uncertain. It made possible a new approach to social inequality and poverty, resolving the dilemma of its necessity within medieval schemes of salvation, and making possible a wholesale assault on poverty as a social disease. The doctrine led in an egalitarian direction, attractive to those who felt left behind in the social rat race of early-sixteenth-century Europe. It also advocated not force and violence but faith, repentance, and prayer in responding to the threat of a vigorous and potentially violent Islamic presence on Europe's edges.

The Reformation was, to be sure, a deeply flawed movement. Its polemics and aggression toward enemies, including adversaries within the different branches of the Reformation itself, helped lead to the breakup of a unified Western Christendom, which has split into ever increasing numbers of denominations. Such fragmentation has arguably

12. *LW* 46:170–72.

led to the hyperpluralism of the modern age, and perhaps even to the rise of acquisitive capitalism, as people gave up on theological debate, shrugging their shoulders to go shopping instead. These are arguments well made in Brad Gregory's recent book *The Unintended Reformation*.[13] Luther's writings on the Jews reflected medieval anti-Semitism and in fact were more severe than the views of most other medieval authors, so there is no room for a romanticized picture of the Reformation as a pure form of Christianity.

At its best, however, the Reformation was a movement centered on a simple idea, which offered a new vision of Europe based on a strong sense of self-worth and identity that turned people away from self-absorption toward a love for God and neighbor, gave a vision of social equality that reduced the gap between rich and poor, fostered a mentality that understood the needs and language of ordinary people, and offered a distinctively Christian vision of the world, robust enough to withstand some of the challenges that faced it from the outside.

These four factors are surely familiar to us. We, too, are living in one of the most individualistic and self-absorbed of human cultures, obsessed with self-expression and self-discovery. Charles Taylor, in his magisterial work *Sources of the Self*, traces the story of how the medieval world gave way to the modern, in which the entire cosmos has become disembedded from its source in the divine, society has become disembedded from its place in the cosmos, and individuals have become disembedded from the society in which they once found their place. The result is an extreme individualism, in which our identity is no longer given but must be constructed internally. The result of this change is a very competitive form of social life that requires us to establish our place in the world on the basis of our own achievements, talents, looks, or self-projection, leading to a great deal of anxiety as to whether we really are acceptable—not before the judgment of God but before the much harsher judgment of Tinder, Twitter, Facebook, or Instagram.

We, too, live in an age of great inequality between rich and poor, an inequality that has led to the migrant crisis, as those in impoverished parts of the world, often ravaged by warfare and conflict, seek a more prosperous future in the attractive cities of Western Europe.

In recent years we have also seen a revolt against the elites. Brexit and the election of Donald Trump in the United States have both been seen

---

13. Brad S. Gregory, *The Unintended Reformation: How a Religious Revolution Secularized Society* (Cambridge, MA: Belknap Press of Harvard University Press, 2012).

as revolts of the disfranchised against remote centers of power in Washington and Brussels that did not seem to relate in any organic or personal way to the needs of ordinary people, who often felt left behind in the prosperity that had come to some but not to all.

And of course, we also live in a time when Europe is uncertain about the presence of Islam in its midst. The increasingly visible presence of Muslims in Western societies has brought many benefits, yet the rise of European Islam also carries a dark side—the shadow of Islamic extremism and questions about the ongoing future character of Europe, raised by such authors as Douglas Murray[14] and Roger Scruton.[15]

Conclusions

At a time when Europe lacks vision, when the European Union has stalled and no longer inspires confidence and energy enough to provide unity for the people of that continent, a new vision is desperately needed. The Reformation is an example of a Christian movement that managed to inspire a new vision within Europe.

No one can turn back the clock to the medieval or postwar world (after 1945), but is it a coincidence that Europe seems to have lost its soul, or vision, not long after the EU made the historical and strategic mistake of erasing from its constitution any mention of Europe's Christian past? By taking leave of a huge source of past European vision, what was left was a project that somehow failed to inspire enthusiasm.

We need a vision that turns us away from ourselves, toward healing a world still full of poverty, violence, and migrants. Rather thin are the prospects of such a vision arising from a self-absorbed and acquisitive culture, with little common narrative, loosely held together by values such as tolerance and human rights.

The rise of the new atheism can be seen as an act of self-destruction. It has sought to undermine the Christian vision of life that held Europe together, but offered nothing to take its place. The question is whether the Christian churches can again recast such a vision, a vision that inspires allegiance, discipline, and focus for the next stage of Europe's life.

From the Reformation, we learn that such a renewal comes from a theological vision expressed in social form, in practical action that

---

14. Douglas Murray, *The Strange Death of Europe: Immigration, Identity, Islam* (London: Bloomsbury, 2017).

15. Roger Scruton, *Where We Are: The State of Britain Now* (London: Bloomsbury, 2017).

provides new perspectives and possibilities in some of the key issues that people face today. The task will require all the churches of Europe to work together with confidence, creativity, and compassion. It is a task too big for any one of our churches. We might say that the flaw in the Reformation, the reason it did not issue in the widespread cultural renewal hoped for, was its willingness to allow schism and division. It requires not more detailed historical theological analysis, nor endless papers written for internal church ordering, but the common voice of Eastern and Western churches, confessing Christ together, a renewal of faith and life so capturing our own imaginations that it has the capacity to capture the imagination of an entire generation.

Whether or not this vision catches fire and goes viral across Europe will depend on whether the church can be renewed in the life of the Spirit, recapture the heart of the gospel for today, express it in language that ordinary people can understand, and ensure that the gospel speaks again to our world, as it did in faltering, imperfect, yet powerful ways in the sixteenth century.

We might lament the effects of the sixteenth century in breaking up a unified Christendom in the West, but at the same time we might still remember the Reformation as an inspiration and challenge for the church today in offering a Christian vision of life that addresses urgent issues in the lives of ordinary people, with a dynamism that can show a new way forward for a continent that so badly needs a new vision to chart a path into the future.

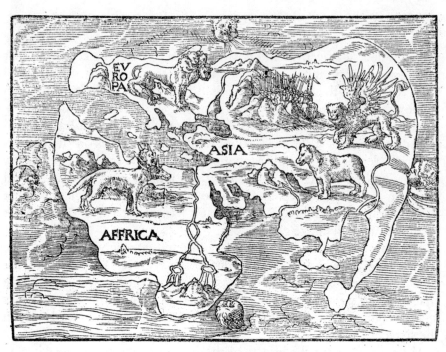

Vision of Four Beasts, in *Der Prophet Daniel Deudsch*,
by Martin Luther, Wittenberg, 1530

Chapter Ten

The Challenges of Sixteenth-Century Europe and Our Global Challenges Today

Margot Kässmann

With regard to the Reformation and Martin Luther, I am often asked: What would Luther say today? Mostly I answer: I do not know. And that is true. I have no idea, for instance, what he would say about fracking! We cannot transform Luther from the sixteenth century into the twenty-first. And yet we can trace some topics that were current during the Reformation and still have implications for global challenges today.

Nationalism

In 2008 the Evangelical Church in Germany (EKD) decided, in cooperation with public bodies and tourist associations, to launch a "Luther Decade," leading up to and preparing for the Reformation anniversary. At the opening of the decade, Bishop Wolfgang Huber, then head of the council of the EKD, stated in his inaugural speech, "As much as we value Luther's contribution to German culture, especially his impact on the formation of the German language, we have all the less reason to repeat the claims to superiority in which Martin Luther is associated with a supposed 'German identity.' For a long time the figure of Luther was used to mislead Germans both at home and abroad into confusing patriotism with nationalism." This was a key point for the 2017 celebrations, setting the tone with regard to a very critical topic.

We live in a globalized society. But that was already the case in the sixteenth century. Anyone who closely examines, for instance, the records of the Imperial Diet of Worms in 1521[1] will realize that Luther's appearance there, while important, was only one of the topics the Diet dealt with. Emperor Charles V was striving for a reform of the empire. Sultan Suleiman I had conquered Belgrade, and the supposed "Turkish threat" was high on the agenda. Securing sovereignty in the region of Spain was also an urgent matter, with an eye to the colonies. Movements for social revolution had arisen in the Kingdom of Valencia. Britain, France, and Italy were also on the scene. In the face of European expansion, particularly in the direction of Spanish and Portuguese colonies, Luther himself had a very restricted view of the world. In his biography of Luther, published in German in 2012, Heinz Schilling writes: "The world view of the Reformer remained a continental one to his death, and was rarely touched by the emerging new worlds."[2] And yet the Reformation was a European event that very soon took on international proportions.

In creating—in the real sense of the word!—the German language with his translation of the Bible, Luther became one of the founders of the German nation. Luther himself certainly did not think in those categories; it took another 250 years for the concept of nationalism to rise. But then Luther became a key figure for nationalism. In the nineteenth century, Leopold von Ranke regarded the Reformation as the "key event" for the German nation and Luther as its founder. The Reformation jubilee of 1817 was orchestrated as a religio-nationalist festival in memory of the Battle of the Nations near Leipzig in 1813, and Luther became a national German hero. In 1883, with the 400th anniversary of his birth, Luther was promoted to being the founding father of the German Empire, and in 1917, along with Hindenburg, he became the "savior" of the Germans in a time of great adversity. In 1933, the year the National Socialists seized power, Luther was surrounded on his 450th birthday with the aura of the God-sent great *Führer*, who was surpassed only by one greater Führer, Adolf Hitler. Then, on the 400th anniversary of his death, he was seen as the comforter of the German people—in 1946, when comfort was bitterly needed. In 1983, on his 500th birthday, a kind of competition over Luther's legacy arose between East and West: in the German Democratic Republic, Luther was no longer the servant of princes but the representative of early bourgeois revolution.

---

1. Fritz Reuter, ed., *Der Reichstag zu Worms von 1521: Reichspolitik und Luthersache im Auftrag der Stadt Worms zum 450-Jahrgedenken* (Worms: Stadtarchiv, 1971).

2. Heinz Schilling, *Martin Luther: Rebell in einer Zeit des Umbruchs* (Munich: C. H. Beck Verlag, 2012), 26.

The Reformation therefore has not only a relevance in the context of the church but also a public one, which relates to the state. Already in October 2011, the Bundestag, the German Parliament, discussed the 2017 Reformation Centenary. After a ninety-minute debate, all parties agreed that the Luther Decade and the Reformation Centenary 2017 would be an "event of world significance," with European and international effect. All deputies supported the motion, which set wide expectations: "The posting of the Theses on 31st October 1517 by Martin Luther is seen as the catalyst for the Reformation. It had a lasting impact on society and politics in the last five hundred years, not only in our country, but Europe-wide and worldwide."[3] Among other things, the Ministry of Foreign Affairs commissioned an exhibition that picked up this theme in Chicago and Seoul.

In 2012, before the EKD Synod, Chancellor Angela Merkel interpreted the 31st of October 1517 like this: "Luther's decision, to express his thoughts and doubts with words, to exhibit them publicly, had—as it emerged—expressed the sentiments of many people and gave them the strength to have more courage to express their unease and their unsettled and unresolved questions." Further, she remarked, "I say it quite openly—if one is still allowed to say it nowadays—this has a missionary component: I hope that something of the spirit of the Reformation will, once again, reach people who have perhaps never, or at least not for a long time, heard about this spirit."[4]

So then, what was this spirit of the Reformation? First of all, there were theological questions; Luther wanted to reform his church by referring back to the Bible. Only holy Scripture, only the Bible, faith alone, and Christ alone—concentration on the essentials—was his aim. Moreover, he overcame medieval fears of the agonies of hell in retribution for the sins of a lifetime, a thought that tortured him like everybody else. Nobody can buy themselves out of that: this is what he recognized. God is not a punishing, thundering God, but the God who turns toward you and promises you meaning.

But soon the Reformation also had a political dimension. Joachim Koehler, in his biography of Luther, sees this political dimension from the very beginning, with Frederick the Elector of Saxony using Luther

---

3. Deutscher Bundestag, 17. Wahlperiode, June 7, 2011, Drucksache 17/6465, p. 1 of http://dipbt.bundestag.de/dip21/btd/17/064/1706465.pdf.

4. Angela Merkel, "Greeting of the Chancellor to the Synod of the Evangelical Church in Germany," November 7, 2012, in Timmendorfer Strand.

for his own political purposes.[5] Luther, however, expected the princes
to deal with the abuses in the church if the pope would not address
them. In his 1520 letter *To the Christian Nobility of the German Nation*,
Luther details the scope of the need he sees for reform; for example,
he demands the abolition of celibacy and declares that the pope has
no authority over the emperor. Likewise, he asks the princes to establish schools for every child, no matter what their social background,
whether boy or girl. This last point is, I think, where a key to democracy lies. Luther got his courage to stand before the emperor and the
emissaries at the Diet of Worms from his reading of the Bible. He was
convinced: if the Bible did not refute him, then he had to act on grounds
of conscience. That was a risk. And an example. As a consequence, he
wished that all could read so that they could sharpen their conscience
by engaging with the Bible and finding an autonomous position. On
one hand, this is the origin of the idea of participation and justice in
education. On the other hand, it was the start of the path toward freedom of individual faith and conscience, even if it took a long time to
find its way into political reality—and in many countries around the
globe, this freedom still does not exist.

In all of this work, Martin Luther was an exceptionally gifted political tactician—and I do not mean this negatively. Again I refer to the
historian Heinz Schilling's observation: the fact that Luther did not see
the bishops in a leadership role in the church of the Reformation, but
rather held that the *princes* should fulfill these key functions, was "due to
[Luther's] insight into the realities of power."[6]

But this position made Luther enemies as well as friends. Thomas
Müntzer stands symbolically for the opposition. These two men struggled with each other fiercely. When Luther calls Müntzer the "Satan at
Allstedt," and Müntzer in turn refers to Luther's "soft life at Wittenberg," these are the friendlier descriptions. Certainly Müntzer expected
the imminent collapse of the existing world order with the eschaton. But
he also wanted justice in the here and now. During the Peasants' War, he
placed himself clearly on the side of the subjugated peasants and explicitly criticized those in authority. To validate a right to resistance against
the princes and authorities—even for Müntzer that was a long journey;

5. Joachim Koehler, *Luther! Biografie eines Befreiten* (Leipzig: Evangelische Verlagsanstalt,
2016).
6. H. Schilling, *Martin Luther*, 430.

yet at the end of that journey, he said that the princes should also be servants and relinquish power and privileges. After the devastating defeat of the peasants in the battle near Frankenhausen, Müntzer was tortured severely and soon afterward executed. Luther did not utter one word of compassion. Likewise, Calvin was silent in connection with the execution of Michael Servetus, who denied the Trinity. No, the Reformers did not tolerate difference in understanding.

The apostle Paul writes in the Letter to the Romans: "Let every person be subject to the governing authorities; for there is no authority except from God, and those authorities that exist have been instituted by God" (13:1). This verse stopped many Christians, men and women, from offering political resistance. In the book of Acts, however, we read, "We must obey God rather than any human authority" (5:29). This verse encouraged many Christians, men and women, to resist unjust circumstances.

To be sure, Paul did not write a fundamental treatise on the relationship of Christians to power or the limits of power. He did not discuss the questions of abuse of power and injustice tolerated or even encouraged by the state.[7] Rather, he resisted religious fervor that is so removed from this world as to be unconcerned with the church and the world and the need for some kind of ordering. It was against this detachment from the world that Paul argues for a recognition of state power, which serves to order life in peace and community.

Luther, following Paul, was convinced: There has to be a distinction between the secular and religious regimes. This view can be understood in many ways, but it seduced the Lutheran Church into remaining uncritical in the face of injustice. The so-called doctrine of the two kingdoms, or two regimes, appeared to quite a few Lutheran theologians and church leaders as justification not to name as absolute errors the crimes perpetrated between 1933 and 1945—and many remained silent even after 1945. Sometimes Protestantism has tied itself to a spirit of subservience, to an education into obedience to authority, in the guise of parents, teachers, ministers, or priests. Such an education certainly did not encourage a spirit of resistance.

Celebrating the Reformation in the twenty-first century therefore is quite a challenge with regard to the growing nationalism, indeed nativism, of our times. We live in a globalized world. And we have overcome nationalistic concepts of Christianity. Thus 2017 was not about a German

---

7. Walter Klaiber, *Der Römerbrief* (Neukirchen-Vluyn: Neukirchener Verlag, 2009), 223.

Luther commemoration but about an international challenge for the churches to ask: Where do we need reform and reformation today? In Germany, we started the discussion with a tour bus visiting sixty-seven cities and towns all over Europe and Germany, collecting theses about what reformation means to church and society in those places today. One aspect or insight—or maybe a problematical outcome or even fierce conflict—was highlighted, taken note of, and collected in each city. The various places revealed their own quite specific approach to the Reformation; Amsterdam differs from Rome, Dublin from Geneva.

Even more important in my view is that on May 20, 2017, we celebrated the opening of the World Exhibition of the Reformation in and around Wittenberg. There were contributions from culture and civil society, as well as from churches in other countries and continents. The town itself became an exhibition showground in the summer of 2017. We set aside sixteen weeks to discuss the relation between reformation and globalization, reformation and Europe, reformation and spirituality, and so on. For me, that was the key event in the entire year of celebration.

But globalization is also a matter of worldwide ecumenism, which has existed as a movement since 1910 and has been institutionalized since 1948 with the World Council of Churches, as well as having a voice through the Lutheran World Federation (LWF) and the World Communion of Reformed Churches (WCRC). We developed links between the Reformation celebration and churches in the wider world. We explored what contribution is offered by other Protestants. We examined what this anniversary means in Brazil—or in Tanzania and Ethiopia, where we find the fastest-growing Lutheran churches today. It is crystal clear: the Reformation anniversary in 2017 must be seen in a global perspective.

Ecumenism

The five hundredth anniversary of the Reformation was the first following a century of ecumenical movement. It therefore had to involve Roman Catholicism. The churches of the Reformation regard themselves—just as much as the Roman Catholic Church does—as the inheritors of the ancient church; that inheritance is our common history. Yet the Reformation era changed all. The Roman Catholic Church today is not the same as the church with which Luther and the other Reformers came into such deep conflict in the sixteenth century. For example, the Council of Trent (1545–63) said farewell to the practice of selling indulgences for money, and the Second Vatican Council (1962–65) introduced the saying of the Mass in the vernacular. Of course, many of the questions raised in the Reformation about the papacy, the veneration of the saints, and the ministerial office still remain. But Luther wanted to reform his own church, not split it. So, for Protestants to set themselves apart in commemorating the Reformation would not make any sense.

Luther's Ninety-five Theses probably would be accepted by many in the Roman Catholic Church today. One Catholic bishop has said that he shares Luther's criticism of the trade in indulgences in his day.[8] In Augsburg in 1999, the Roman Catholic Church and the Lutheran World Federation signed the Joint Declaration on the Doctrine of Justification. They asserted that the condemnations issued by the two churches in the sixteenth century do not apply to their teaching today. The signing of the Official Common Statement on the Joint Declaration in Augsburg on October 31, 1999, was an occasion for celebration. It did not mean—as was clear to all those who took part—that from now on the theoretical teachings of the different traditions would be based on exactly the same understanding. But the signing was welcomed as a step on a necessary path toward convergence. A breakthrough seemed close, meaning that this declaration would not eliminate our differences, but would hopefully lead to the possibility of being able to invite one another as guests to Communion. We can be grateful that it at least succeeded in finding common wording on a theological question that was once the cause of a break in unity.

In this respect, there is now a chance to give a clear ecumenical dimension to the Reformation anniversary. Whatever the differences and whatever the nature of our respective profiles, more binds us than separates us. Moreover, in a secularized society, the common witness of Christians is of great significance; the more strongly we speak out together, the more we will be heard. Thus on October 31, 2016, in Lund, where the Lutheran World Federation was founded, Pope Francis celebrated worship alongside the Palestinian bishop and president of the LWF Munib Younan, the LWF general secretary Martin Junge, from Latin America, and the (female!) archbishop of Sweden, Antje Jackélen. In Germany, a central ecumenical worship service under the theme "healing of memories" took place in Lent. Thus the tone for a Reformation jubilee sounded

8. Hans Jochen Jaschke, quoted in "Suffragan Bishop [of Hamburg] Criticises the Trade in Indulgences at the Time of Luther," *Protestant Press Service* (*Evangelischer Pressedienst Dokumentation* = *epd*), central edition, 212 (October 31, 2008): 11.

an ecumenical note, as the 2017 Reformation anniversary bore an ecumenical dimension.

Dialogue of Religions

The anniversary in 2017 was the first anniversary of the publication of the Ninety-Five Theses since the Holocaust. The failure of Christians with regard to the Jews in the National Socialist era has triggered a learning process. During the year called Reformation and Tolerance, we in Germany confronted Luther's anti-Judaism, especially in his *Concerning the Jews and Their Lies* of 1543. Some historians say we must even see him as an anti-Semite. *Simul iustus et peccator* ("at the same time righteous and a sinner")—that theological insight also has meaning for Luther himself. His hatred of Jews, especially in his old age, had its source in his anger that Jews would not read the Hebrew part of the Bible as pointing toward Jesus as the Messiah. That is an explanation but not an excuse. It was important, therefore, that before starting to celebrate the Reformation, our church confront this terrible heritage used by the Nazis to justify their murder of Jews.

The church calling itself Lutheran failed in protecting Jews. That is a terrible heritage to face. But there have been brave individuals. I mention Elisabeth Schmitz as a heroic representative of the church during the time of National Socialism; she was a teacher in Berlin who recognized very early where the evil spirit of National Socialism would lead. Already in 1935, three years before the Pogrom Night, or Kristallnacht, she wrote about the situation of children:

> Even a rudimentary human sensitivity will grant to children the entitlement of protection. But here? In the big cities Jewish children now go to Jewish schools, or their parents send them to Catholic schools in which according to general opinion they are much more protected than in Protestant ones. But what about non-Aryan Protestant children? And the Jewish children in small towns where there are no Jewish schools, and what about those in the countryside? In one small town the exercise books of Jewish children are again and again being torn up, their sandwiches taken from them and stamped into the dirt! It is Christian children who do that, and Christian parents, teachers, and pastors who allow it to happen! . . .[9]

9. Elisabeth Schmitz, quoted in the anonymously published *Wer war Elisabeth Schmitz? Über Ihre Denkschrift "Zur Lage der deutschen Nichtarier"* (San Francisco: Grin Publishing, 2015), 199.

Why do we have to hear again and again from non-Aryan Christians, that is, Christians with a Jewish background, that they feel abandoned by the church and the ecumenical networks? . . . Why is Pastor Bodelschwingh looking for Aryan medical interns when he advertises in medical journals? . . . Why is the church not doing anything? Why does it allow this abysmal injustice to happen?[10]

Whoever wanted to see could see, and whoever wanted to know could know. However, far too many looked the other way, most especially Protestants who, after the First World War and the abdication of the Kaiser, could not warm to the Weimar Republic.

Thanks be to God that there has been a learning process. After sixty years of Jewish-Christian dialogue, we can see that the Reformation church is capable of dialogue. In November 2015, our synod distanced itself from the writings of Luther on Jews. In November 2016 the synod declared that it would refrain from concepts of mission toward Jews. The Reformers themselves said that the church must always be reforming itself, and this is a decisive point that has proved true in the learning process.

Nevertheless, talking about global challenges today, we must recognize the growing anti-Semitism in our world today. Are we clear enough in challenging that? Furthermore, this word of caution also holds with respect to Muslims. Although Luther ranted against the Turks, today we live with Muslims in the same countries. We need dialogue, and it must be grounded in theology. This is a task, a challenge still to be answered. Only if we are in dialogue can we contribute to conflict resolution instead of pouring oil onto the fire of political and economic interests via religion.

The Reformation anniversary in 2017 must remind us of religious dialogue as a major concern for Protestantism.

Justice and Peace

We can also see a learning process in social movements and the dispute between Luther and Thomas Müntzer. The conflict between the command to be subject to authority and the command to obey God rather than human beings has been hotly debated ever since the Third Reich.

I recall brave people in the German Democratic Republic, East Germany. Christians like Christian Führer or Reinhard Höppner, who both

10. Ibid., 210.

died recently, opened the churches for people to express their political dissatisfaction. That was actually quite controversial inside the church. Do environmental questions about the chemical wastelands of Bitterfeld belong in the church? Is it wise to allow a singer/songwriter like Stephan Krawczyk, who is not even a Christian, to perform in the church? Is it right to debate the armament question in the Kreuzkirche in Dresden? Is that not far too political? Yet in the end, the cry "No Violence!" was carried out of the churches onto the streets in Leipzig, Dresden, and East Berlin. This fact contributed a lot to the first nonviolent revolution in Germany, which brought a dictatorship to its knees.

And today? I hear again and again that the church should concentrate on the "essentials," by which people mean a private niche of religious practice. Secular society wants to push religion back to the fringes of the discussion. But those who have in the back of their mind what the Sermon on the Mount describes as a countersociety, namely, a place where the merciful, the poor, and those who yearn for justice and peace are declared happy—those who understand the demand that we ought to be the salt of the earth and the light of the world—such people shape society in a different way: they apply special criteria to their actions, criteria proved reliable by a long tradition that guides them. For them, the priorities are not first and foremost security, growth, and majorities, but solidarity, an eye for the weak, the search for sustainable opportunities for the young.

What is the demand supposed to mean that Christian women and men, especially church officeholders, should remain behind church walls? Faith does not happen off-site. The way we live in everyday life—in family, in our neighborhood, at work, in society—is where our being a Christian is tested and proved. We feel challenged to open our mouth for those who are pushed to the margins, whose dignity is questioned; we feel challenged to work for justice, peace, and the integrity of creation. That is why the church cannot be a sphere segregated from everyday life: it is exactly in everyday life in all its dimensions, including the political one, where the so-called essentials manifest themselves. The essentials are the life the people lead and are accountable for through faith. For that life they gather strength by reading Scripture, attending worship, and praying; but this happens right in the midst of the world. I want to give two examples.

Migration was one consequence of the Reformation. People of different denominations left their countries to find freedom of religious practice, many of them emigrating to the Americas, later the United States.

Migration today is a global challenge, a worldwide phenomenon. Therefore we should keep one thing in balanced view: in Western Europe approximately 8 to 12 percent of the population are migrants; in some other countries they are 80 percent! This means that Europe takes in a minimum of the world's refugees. We should communicate this truth very clearly. Restrictive rejection of migrants is not an appropriate means for taking up this challenge as a society. More than 50 percent of funding from the European Union for migration management is spent on border controls, deportations, or the agency Frontex. I have visited parishes in Mexico, Guatemala, and El Salvador, where the Trump wall leads to fears. Refugees stay in those countries because they are losing hope about reaching the United States. These are issues we should talk about across the Atlantic Ocean!

Sometimes migration is an irritation, but always also a chance: a chance to discover the richness of cultures, to learn from one another, to celebrate life together, to enable encounter, to create spaces that make transnational life easier, not more difficult. A Kenyan woman said at a panel discussion in Berlin on the occasion of World Refugee Day, "You should understand that those who migrate are the creative ones, the ones with a desire for freedom, which they want to realize *together with you* when they come to Germany!"

The Bible is full of migration stories, beginning with the economic migrants, Abraham and Sarah, right up to the child of refugees with the name of Jesus, whose family flees with him to Egypt. Later on, the same Jesus will say that we meet *him* whenever we welcome strangers.

My second example of the church's need to live in the world concerns war and peace. The theological differences of the Reformation soon became caught up by political interests of the powers of the time. The seventeenth century brought thirty years of war that killed one-third of the population in parts of Europe. Only in 1648, finally, did a peace treaty attempt to open the way to tolerance. In preparing for 2017, we had a special year in 2014 under the heading "Reformation and Politics," to commemorate the hundredth anniversary of the start of the First World War and the seventy-fifth anniversary of the beginning of the Second World War. These anniversaries are reason enough to ask how the churches today should raise their voice. In 1914 and 1939, weapons were blessed and wars were sanctioned.

I am convinced that we can make a significant contribution toward peace first of all by discussing the production of weapons and export of armaments. Why does a country like Germany have to rise to third place in the league of armament-exporting countries? Yes, the economic factor always enters into the discussion, but we are talking about 0.2 percent of Germany's GDP. And yes, German weapons reputedly are technologically brilliant. But who wants to be admired the world over for that?

The weapons industry profits from all wars around the globe. The two large Christian churches in Germany have criticized this. I think this is their job. The Sermon on the Mount says, "Blessed are the peacemakers." The appeal—some say the threat—of U.S. Secretary of Defense James Mattis for all NATO states to reach a goal of 2 percent of state spending on defense has generated wide discussion in Germany. Today we spend 1.2 per cent, and the German citizens have no widespread willingness to increase that.

As these examples show, our church has a calling into the world. Our mission, of course, is first of all the proclamation of God's Word and pastoral care. But that cannot be separated from the reality of the world in which we live. This is especially true in Germany, where the churches are some of the largest employers, often in areas where people on the margins need care: in facilities for the elderly, in child care, in hospices, and in institutions for people with handicaps. Internally, the churches often struggle with the challenge of having to market themselves. But they also know what they are talking about. Theology never remains just a discipline in the humanities at the university—although certainly theology belongs there—but it also has to be translated into everyday life in the "real" world.

In that context, it is crucial not to duck away but to engage, to question, and to face controversial debates. Luther taught us to live out of a mind-set of the free conscience and to get involved in current issues. In a democratic and secular society, this is valid for the faithful of all denominations and religions as well as for religiously uncommitted people. If we dare to get involved in an open and respectful dispute, even controversy, about the right way forward, only then are we capable of facing the future and not languishing in everyday trivia. Personally, my faith encourages me again and again to think myself into things, to discuss them with others, to learn and also to argue. This I consider to be a legacy of the Reformation that I gladly take up together with others and continue, even in the face of the challenges of secularization. It is a legacy that has carried through in the work of latter-day martyrs like

Martin Luther King Jr., whose witness still has power today, including in Germany.

Women

The year 2017 marked the first anniversary of the Reformation on which the vast majority of the Protestant churches throughout the world—including 80 percent of the member churches of the LWF—have accepted women into the ordained ministry and even as bishops. For Martin Luther, it became more and more clear that baptism is the central event and sacrament of the Christian life. This is where God promises human beings divine grace, love, care, and a sense of the meaning of life. All the failures and aberrations of life cannot cancel that out. If we recall our baptism, we need no sacrament of repentance: we are redeemed, we have long been the children of God. "Baptizatus sum": I am baptized. Martin Luther reminded himself of this in his darkest hours and thereby found support and comfort.

And, declared Luther, everyone who has emerged from baptism is priest, bishop, and pope. From there, Luther also developed respect for women. They are baptized and therefore on an equal footing with men. That was an outrageous position to take in his time. Women were regarded as unclean when they were not virgins, and witch hunts were rampant (unfortunately Luther did not take a strong stand against them). Only after long debates did some concede that women have an immortal soul. In such an age, to say that women are baptized and thus equal before God was a theological breakthrough and, at the same time, a social revolution. This understanding of baptism gradually developed through the centuries into the conviction that women should be able to exercise any office in the church. For me, it is important to clarify these underlying theological grounds, especially when, in other churches, the ordination of women to the offices of minister and bishop is questioned.

In Luther's day, a celibate life was regarded as more valued before God—the direct way to heaven, as it were. For many Reformers, the step toward marriage was a signal that living in a family, with sexuality and children, is also a life blessed by God. The public marriage of previously celibate priests, monks, and nuns was a theological signal. Ute Gause, a professor of Reformation history, explains that it was a symbolic action intended "to make clear something elementary to the Reformation: the new faith's turning towards the world and the pleasures of the senses."[11] Yet in Germany, Protestants are actually considered less prone to sensory enjoyment than Roman Catholics or Orthodox Christians. But the Reformers wanted to make it quite clear that living out in the world is of no less value than life in the priesthood or the monastery. All are a matter of living our faith through the everyday things of the world.

This insight has had a lot of consequences. As one example, the first church regulations drawn up by the Reformers valued midwives as custodians of the church. A woman who had given birth was no longer regarded as unclean but should be cared for and looked after. Incidentally, Luther could be tremendously modern in this respect. There is the question whether grown men make themselves a laughingstock if they wash a baby's diapers. Here is a short extract from the original words of Luther:

> When a man goes ahead and washes diapers or performs some other mean task for his children, and someone ridicules him as an effeminate idiot, though that man is acting in . . . Christian faith, my dear fellow you tell me, which of the two is most keenly ridiculing the other? God, with all his angels and creatures, is smiling, not because the man is washing diapers, but because he is doing so in Christian faith. Those who sneer at him and see only the task but not the faith are ridiculing God with all his creatures, as the biggest fool on earth. Indeed, they are only ridiculing themselves; with all their cleverness they are nothing but the devil's fools.[12]

Silly nonsense spoken by other people does not matter. What matters is that I know who I am, that I live out my life before God and trust in God, and in doing so give an account of the hope that is in me. Furthermore, it is all part of God's creation that we should bring up children; it is part of the very existence of men and women. Said another way: "From the manner in which they both interact with each other in everyday tasks, this demonstrates if they truly believe what they confess."[13]

11. Ute Gause, "Durchsetzung neuer Männlichkeit = Ehe und Reformation," *Evangelisches Theologie* 73 (2013): 326, 337.

12. Martin Luther, *The Estate of Marriage* (1522), quoted and discussed by Gerta Scharffenorth and Klaus Thraede, "Luthers reformatorische Erkenntnisse als Basis für ein neues Verständnis von Mann und Frau," in *"Freunde in Christus Werden": Die Beziehung von Mann und Frau als Frage an Theologie und Kirche* (Gelnhausen: Burckhardthaus, 1977), 183–302, at 220.

13. See Margot Kässmann, ed., *Schlag nach bei Luther: Texte für den Alltag* (Frankfurt am Main: Hansisches Druck & Verlagshaus, 2012), 92.

The 2017 anniversary helps remind us that a distinguishing feature of the Protestant church is the theological conviction that women can be ministers and bishops. This conviction entails an obligation for churches today to stand up for women's rights in every country on earth, both in the developing world and, unfortunately, in the developed world.

Overcoming Divisions, Reaching Reconciliation

The Reformation anniversary in 2017 was the first since the Leuenberg Agreement of 1973—which acknowledged concord between Lutheran and Reformed churches in Europe—and similar agreements in the United States. The Reformation movement itself was subject to division, and Protestantism has experienced repeated splits, as most recently in the Lutheran churches in the United States over the question of homosexuality. During the last century, however, new perspectives have helped overcome division and move toward a reconciled community. Let me give two examples.

In Europe, the Leuenberg Agreement of 1973 sent a strong signal that such divisions could be overcome, and it showed a way to do this. Despite all their differences, Reformed, Lutheran, and United Churches are able, on the basis of the agreement, to recognize one another mutually as churches, along with their ministerial orders, and to celebrate Holy Communion together. Even though this fellowship of churches with different confessional backgrounds has been dismissed on a number of occasions as "minimalist ecumenism," and Cardinal Walter Kasper declared that the Roman Catholic and Orthodox churches could not follow the same model, it is a real-life example of how to overcome division. Differences do not necessarily have to divide. With respect to those who were persecuted as Anabaptists and Enthusiasts in the Reformation era, the 2010 LWF Assembly featured an act of repentance and plea for reconciliation with the Mennonites, their spiritual heirs. On top of that, Lutherans have full communion with Methodists, and Baptists participated in the Reformation jubilee.

Today the new challenge for finding common ground lies in the Pentecostal movement. When I asked a young pastor in Hong Kong what his denomination was, he remarked that his church was "post-confessional" and not interested in European differences of the sixteenth century. This is the great new division of our times: between traditional mainline churches and new, fast-growing Pentecostal churches all over the world.

What sort of dialogue is possible across this division? Can we find new concepts of unity and common witness?

Education

As he left the conceptions of the Middle Ages behind him, what really concerned Luther in lifting up the "freedom of a Christian" was for every woman and every man to be able to confess faith in the triune God and affirm their faith in Jesus Christ. For Luther, the precondition for a mature faith was the ability to read the Bible for oneself and not only to learn by heart the Small Catechism, the confession of faith for everyday use, but also to share it with others and thus be empowered to speak of one's faith. The basis for these preconditions was education for all, not just for the few who could afford it or who received it by entering a religious order.

The Bible presents justice as a behavior that God expects from human beings, and it defines justice first and foremost in terms of relationship. One consequence of studying the Bible is that justice can no longer be viewed as merely about distributing goods and money, but rather becomes a matter of enabling people to participate, to join in, to engage, and not to be excluded, whatever their level of capability or efficiency. For many, justice today has to do with economic resources. To be sure, money is important when its lack means one experiences the bitterness of exclusion from the community. But justice is also about empowering people so that they can contribute their own talents and gifts and be valued, even if their opportunities are limited. This empowerment also is connected to education, which is decisive when, for example, children from migrant families have fewer educational opportunities. How important is it that immigrant children learn the language of their new country before they start school? And how imperative is it to support schools that strengthen integration? These public institutions are where children spend every day; this is where investments should flow.

Equality and opportunity in education—Martin Luther was the first to make this a public issue and to declare himself a vehement supporter of it. He had theological grounds for this advocacy: for him, faith meant an educated faith, and thus a faith not based solely on convention or spiritual experience, but founded on an affirmation of the liberating message of the gospel. The conviction that faith must be educated is deeply a part of his own biography. Only through an intensive theological study of the

Bible, together with the writings of Augustine of Hippo, did he work out his liberating insight into the meaning of justification. For Luther, faith is always an autonomous faith: the individual Christian must answer to God for oneself and is loved by God as an individual. Although the church is the community of the baptized, it is not the mediator of salvation for the individual. Thus an educated and autonomous faith forms the essential theological motivation for Luther's vehement support for public education, available to every citizen, both male and female. An interesting but simple consequence of his theological approach was that he stood up for girls' education. In Germany, we have Luther to thank for the elementary school system as "schools for all."

All the Reformers underlined the importance of education: Philipp Melanchthon was a passionate teacher and in fact was dubbed the "teacher of the Germans" for his efforts to reform the school and university system. Both Lutherans and Reformed regard Martin Bucer as a doctor of the church. Ulrich Zwingli learned Greek to be able to read the original text of the New Testament edited by Erasmus of Rotterdam. He owned what for that time was the huge number of a hundred books, and in 1510 he founded a Latin grammar school in his parish house in Glarus. And then there was the Genevan Academy, founded by John Calvin, which took the Reformed education movement to many regions of Europe.

These were and still remain essential Reformation issues: being able to think, reflect, speculate, understand, and ask questions. Despite this Reformation emphasis on the freedom of the Christian that included freedom to think, religion has been imputed even today with an attitude of not asking questions—simply believing. Fundamentalism—whether Jewish, Christian, Islamic, or Hindu—does not like education and enlightenment. Every manifestation of fundamentalism sets itself against one of the core messages of the Reformation: think for yourself! You are liberated through God's promise of life. In your conscience you are subject to no one, and you are not dependent on dogmatic teaching, religious precepts, or authorities of the faith. So the global challenge of fundamentalism today must be countered by education.

Perhaps one of the most important contributions of the Reformation is its concern with educated faith, a faith that wants to understand, that is allowed to ask questions, even when relating to the book of the Christian faith, the Bible. Faith arises not out of obedience, convention, or spiritual experience, but rather out of a personal struggle.

Today we can say that study of the Bible also includes an awareness of the origins of the biblical books and the application of historical-critical exegesis. It remains a great challenge to make that point in dialogue with our brothers and sisters in faith in other churches of the world as well as in our own countries. The Reformation anniversary in 2017 offers a clear reminder: the churches of the Reformation are concerned with an educated faith, and this includes a historical-critical approach to the biblical texts.

Freedom

The 2017 Reformation anniversary was the first in which Germany, along with most nations of the world, recognized a clear separation between church and state and a clearly declared acceptance of constitutional law and human rights.

The further development of Luther's concept of freedom has led to many of the freedoms that democratic societies enjoy today. "Liberty, equality, fraternity," the slogan of the French Revolution, had its roots in Luther's *Freedom of a Christian*, even though the Enlightenment often pursued such freedom in the face of opposition from the church. The question today is whether Christian men and women are sufficiently aware of their heritage to advocate energetically for freedom—not only on their own behalf but also, and above all, for others. This advocacy is first and foremost about the freedom Christ gives us and, consequently, about freedom of conscience, freedom of religion, and freedom of opinion.

Today we can see that a central achievement of the Reformation was that it prepared the way for the Enlightenment, however much the churches resisted it. Thanks to the Reformation, faith and reason are able to coexist. Today we can say that it is good—for both sides—that a separation exists between religion and state. A kind of "theocracy" or indeed a "religious dictatorship" does not promote freedom. Thank God we live in a free society, in which men and women can be members of a religious community or not. This possibility fits with the *Freedom of a Christian*.

Luther's concept of freedom, however, is not individualistic. To be free also means to be everyone's servant! Therefore we must see the Reformation anniversary in 2017 as a reminder that the political dimension of the Reformation concept of freedom does not preach pure egomania but searches for new dimensions of global solidarity.

Justification

The 2017 Reformation anniversary occurred in an achievement-oriented society. Many people do not immediately understand Luther's question about a gracious God, but they do worry about whether their life has any purpose. They ask what will become of them if they cannot keep up because they do not have a job, do not earn enough, do not look good enough. The promise for life found by Luther—that God has long since endowed you with significance, regardless of what you can achieve for yourself—needs a new translation for our age. You are a person of high standing because God sees you as such. Your current account for life is in the black, and nothing you do, nothing you fail at, can bring it into the red as far as God is concerned. The inner freedom that such a fundamental conviction brings can be demonstrated today. The Reformation anniversary in 2017 thus helped clearly articulate the discrepancies in an achievement-oriented society that excludes the poor, the differently abled, the elderly.

Media

Certainly Martin Luther was a man of deep theological insight. But would he have been as successful as he was if he had not had the support of the media of his times? The critically important printing press was available to him. A censor could not just burn a book and delete ideas.

Luther's thoughts could be spread fast. It helped that he wrote in German, and succinctly! His scientific colleagues criticized his style: What good can that thinking be if it is not formulated in Latin and long sentences? And while important discussions before Luther's day took place in finely guarded circles, now writing in German and the founding of schools made it possible for ordinary people to take part in debates.

Luther was a best-selling author. Of all that was published in German in the sixteenth century, a third came from his pen. One of his biographers, Heinz Schilling, writes that the reformer had an "outstanding literary talent" and that "by the power of his language and the creative imagination of his pictures and argumentation, . . . Luther was fit to be the 'star' of the first media age."[14]

14. H. Schilling, *Martin Luther*, 620.

Luther's thoughts could no longer be suppressed simply by burning his books because he could spread them faster than the censors could agree on a ban. Book production went up, and single-page prints found a large audience. Soon opponents' pamphlets followed the "Lutheran propaganda." Since many people could not read, cartoons become popular, some of them malicious. A whole caricature battle developed, in which Luther was often portrayed as a hero—always with Cranach's portraits—while the "papists" were presented as coworkers of the devil, or sometimes Luther as the devil who destroyed the church.

The first highlight of these media conflicts occurred around the Diet of Worms, in 1521. Even though Luther's greatest creative phase began only in 1520, his three great works of that year—*Freedom of a Christian, The Babylonian Captivity of the Church, An Appeal to the Christian Nobility of the German Nation*—and above all his translation of the Bible reached gigantic editions. While the papal scholars were still struggling to elaborate a detailed refutation, Lutherans were blizzarded with pamphlets that showed Luther from their point of view: There stood the hero, and he did not recant. The picture of the brave Luther—asserting, "Here I stand. I can do none other. God help me. Amen"—was firmly established.

For me, this example can guide us in using the new media today confidently. Some of the caricatures produced in Luther's time were certainly not "politically correct" in our sense of the phrase. Likewise, some utterances in today's so-called social media are in no way fairly social. Protestants may indeed dispute the truth, and that is good. Never, however, are we allowed to reduce the dignity of persons: this applies to both Luther's time and our own. Churches have to stand up for the truth in an era of fake news.

We especially need the media in an age when secularization makes it more difficult to explain what faith means. Many people have turned away from the church; an immense loss of faith and indeed tradition is observed in the land of the Reformation. Many people no longer have any connection with religion. Luther was deeply concerned to enable people to talk about their faith for themselves.

One final thought: Once I was asked whether Martin Luther would use Twitter today like Donald Trump. My answer was yes, I am afraid he would. My hope, though, is that the Reformer would have undergone a learning process and guarded his sometimes violent language against people of other opinions.

Luther had many flaws, like all humans. But he was deeply rooted in his faith. It was this faith he wanted to realize in the world, and in attempting to do so he became a political person. According to Luther, the vocation of the Christian person is to be realized in the midst of life. In advocating this, he could be humorous, spirited, profound, and eminently practical. One piece of advice he offered to a speaker was "Tritt fest auf, tu's Maul auf, hör bald auf [present firmly, open your mouth, and keep it short]." I want to stick to that, and end.

Witness of John the Baptist, by Virgil Solis, in *Avßlegung der Epistelen vnd Euangelie[n]: Die nach brauch der Kirchen gelesen werden, durch den Advent, vnd dannenthin vom Christag biß auf den Sontag nach Epiphanie; Darin reichlich anzeygt vnd fürgebildet würt, was eim [sic] Christen menschen zuo*, by D. Martinus Luther, 1522

Postscript: The Need for "Reformed Repentance"

Wesley Granberg-Michaelson

The German National Tourist Board fell in love with Martin Luther in 2017. That year marked the 500th anniversary year of the Reformation, and a 36-page brochure outlined eight different routes you could take through Germany featuring "36 authentic Luther sites" across the country, with itineraries offering "surprises aplenty." They even produced a Luther Playmobil figure for ages 4 through 99.

The 500th anniversary year officially started in Lund, Sweden, on October 31, 2016, at an ecumenical worship service convened by the Lutheran World Federation and the Vatican, and attended by Pope Francis. Since then countless events, conferences, exhibitions, and anniversary observances were held not just in Germany, but also around the world, culminating on October 31, 2017, exactly 500 years after Luther's famous Ninety-Five Theses were nailed to the door of the castle church in Wittenberg.

But what exactly should we be doing on this 500th anniversary of the Reformation? Celebrate? Commemorate? Confess? Or even repent?

The impact of the Protestant Reformation, combined with the advent of the Gutenberg Bible and the dramatic increase in printed literature and literacy in Europe, produced revolutionary changes in religion and society. The German National Tourist Board exclaims that "trade, industry, art, architecture, medicine and technology flourished like never before." A glowing narrative of the Reformation's impact on the church and Western culture tends to dismiss any words of thoughtful critique.

It's indisputable that the inspired actions of Martin Luther and other reformers challenged the foundational authority of the established church with the power of God's Word, the efficacy of God's grace, and the direct access of believers to God's Truth, changing fundamentally the structure and governance of the church. Authority in the church had become hopelessly corrupted, epitomized by the sale of indulgences, but thoroughly compromised by avarice, greed, and prelacy, muting any resonant witness to the message and values of the gospel. Luther's protest saved the church from itself. As one who led a Protestant denomination with roots deeply embedded in this historical movement, I gratefully claim the Reformation's achievements.

But it also had unintended consequences that injured the church's life and witness, continuing to this day.

First, the Reformation established the precedent that a group of believers, convinced of God's revealed truth and its demands in specific circumstances, could break away from the authority of the church and even denounce it as heretical, establishing their own separate church structure. This practice has become so commonplace and so prolific that we barely give it a second theological or biblical thought. Looking at world Christianity's landscape, the reality is that what we confess as "the one holy catholic and apostolic Church" has, in fact, become endlessly and ceaselessly divided into separate denominations. Here's our present shameful and sinful state of affairs: today there are an estimated 43,800 denominations in the world, often living with sectarian distrust and judgment of one another. This staggering proliferation of divided institutionalized churches never could have been imagined in the first 1,500 years of Christian history. Despite the significant accomplishments of the ecumenical movement over the past sixty years, today we still assume an impunity for ongoing actions that ceaselessly sever the body of Christ and disobey the consistent, clear, repeated biblical commands to reconcile divisions and live together in unity. This is a legacy of the Reformation.

Second, as Richard Rohr once said to me, "The Reformation focused on the individual but missed the inner life." The individual's ability to know, think, and believe for oneself, rather than for the terms of faith to be dictated and mediated through the authority of the church, became primary. But as the Reformation spread especially into northern Europe and England, faith became codified in creeds and confessions requiring the intellectual consent of the individual believer.

At the same time in the turbulent sixteenth century, practices focused on reviving and deepening one's inner spiritual journey were growing in the Catholic Church, particularly seen in Spanish mystics like John of the Cross, Teresa of Avila, and Ignatius of Loyola. Ignatian spirituality in particular—with its practices of retreat, spiritual direction, detachment, examen of consciousness, finding God in all things, and union with Jesus—became a framework for deepening interior spirituality. But as this movement, and the emerging Jesuit order, became part of the Counter-Reformation, it all was rejected by the Protestant Reformers.

Certainly, other forms of piety emerged within the widening and splintering world of the Reformation. Historians argue that hymnody, for example, played a central role. Yet an emphasis on rational articulations of right doctrine often prevailed, even to this day, combined with a suspicion toward "Catholic" practices of spirituality, frequently alleged to be another form of works righteousness. It has taken the crossover success of the Catholic writers like Thomas Merton and Henri Nouwen to open the Protestant world to rich spiritual practices often ignored. It's only in the last thirty years that contemplative prayer, spiritual direction, detachment, intentional retreat, and the *examen* have emerged in the lexicon and experience of Protestants.

Third, the Reformation bred a mistrust of aesthetics. This is particularly true of those branches following John Calvin, and certainly Ulrich Zwingli. One sees it most in architecture and worship style. Reformed church buildings shunned art, rejecting the "idolatry" they saw practiced in the unreformed church. Walls were blank. The focus was on the pulpit, to hear the words of the Word. The emphasis, here again, was on right articulation of doctrine. "Smells and bells" were dismissively forgotten.

In some ways protecting the church from the influence of art and aesthetics derived from a strong division between the spiritual and the material worlds. The appendix to the Westminster Directory of Worship even declares, "No place is capable of holiness." This reflexive desire to keep matter and spirit detached from one another continues to infect much of Protestant thinking. The more recent movements toward liturgical renewal—including even sensory-saturated worship shaped by Hillsong, as well as the recovery of liturgical arts and dance within mainline and evangelical congregations—can be understood as finally rejecting the Reformation's war on aesthetics.

Fourth, the Reformation poisoned how we understand religious leadership. "Papists" became the derogatory term for those whom the Reformers opposed. Corrupt, craven, and desultory bishops, including the bishop of Rome, convinced many Reformers that no sole individual should be trusted with arbitrary religious authority. For most branches of the Reformation, this created forms of polity and governance that placed authority in councils, committees, synods, conferences, or other groups.

At their core, these methods of governing the church are based on the mistrust of any leadership vested in a person.

The wisdom of such a corrective is obvious. But it also has its deficiencies. I'm a Chicago Cubs fan. In 1961, instead of having a single manager with a coaching staff, the Cubs launched a "College of Coaches" to share responsibility. In 1962 the Cubs lost 103 games—a franchise record. Sociological wisdom shows that any group has some persons who function in a leadership capacity. When such leadership is not identified, there's no method of accountability, which frequently results in covert attempts to exercise influence and authority, resulting in dysfunction and chaos.

Similarly, the Reformation implanted a distrust of any personalized leadership within historic Protestantism. But even John Calvin was not against bishops in principle—he was simply opposed to the corrupt bishops he witnessed. The challenge five hundred years later, for Protestants and Catholics alike, is how to affirm the gift of leadership yet also hold it firmly accountable in the collegial governance of the church.

Martin Luther never intended to break completely from the established church; he desired its reform. But power was threatened, and positions became polarized. Recent decades of theological dialogue have minimized those differences, which some now call "misunderstandings." But they were costly. The antagonism generated by the Reformation and Counter-Reformation led to the Thirty Years' War a century later, killing 20 percent of the German population.

Nevertheless the Reformation began the process of separating the church from its wedding to the political authority and military power of the state, begun with Constantine. That challenging process continues today. In the aftermath of the five hundredth anniversary year, the whole church would be well advised to strengthen the best effects of the Reformation, but also repent from its worst results.

Bibliography

Adams, Nicholas. *Eclipse of Grace: Divine and Human Action in Hegel.* Oxford: Wiley-Blackwell, 2013.

———. "Scriptural Reasoning and Interfaith Hermeneutics." In *Interreligious Hermeneutics in Pluralistic Europe: Between Texts and People,* edited by David Cheetham, Ulrich Winkler, Oddbjørn Leirvik, and Judith Gruber, 59–78. Amsterdam: Rodopi, 2011.

Anttila, Miikka E. *Luther's Theology of Music: Spiritual Beauty and Pleasure.* Berlin: W. de Gruyter, 2013.

Arnold, Matthieu. "La notion d'*epieikeia* chez Martin Luther." *Revue d'histoire et de philosophie religieuses* 79, no. 2 (1999): 187–208.

Asamoah-Gyadu, J. Kwabena. "Did Jesus Wear Designer Robes?" In *The Global Conversation for November 2009,* posted October 27, 2009. www.christianitytoday.com/global conversation/november2009/.

Baird, Robert. *Religion in the United States of America.* Glasgow: Blackie & Son, 1844.

Barber, John. "Luther and Calvin on Music and Worship." *Reformed Perspective Magazine* 8, no. 26 (June 25 to July 1, 2006): 1–16.

Bartel, Dietrich. *Musica Poetica: Musical-Rhetorical Figures in German Baroque Music.* Lincoln: University of Nebraska Press, 1997.

Becker, Jürgen. *Ich bin so froh, dass ich nicht evangelisch bin.* Cologne: Record Co., 2006.

Bedford-Strohm, Heinrich. *Vorrang für die Armen: Auf dem Weg zu einer theologischen Theorie der Gerechtigkeit.* Gütersloh: Kaiser, 1993.

Begbie, Jeremy S. "Created Beauty: The Witness of J. S. Bach." In *Resonant Witness: Conversations between Music and Theology,* edited by Jeremy S. Begbie and Steven R. Guthrie, 83–108. Grand Rapids: Wm. B. Eerdmans Publishing Co., 2011.

———. *Music, Modernity, and God: Essays in Listening.* Oxford: Oxford University Press, 2013.

Bellah, Robert N., et al. *Habits of the Heart: Individualism and Commitment in American Life.* Berkeley: University of California Press, 1985.

Benedict, Philip. *Christ's Church Purely Reformed: A Social History of Calvinism.* New Haven, CT: Yale University Press, 2002.

Berman, Harold J. *Law and Revolution: The Formation of the Western Legal Tradition.* Cambridge, MA: Harvard University Press, 1983.

Beyer, Hermann W. *Luther und das Recht*. Repr. ed. Paderborn: Salzwasser-Verlag GmbH, 2013.

Beyer, Michael. "Wirtschaftsethik bei Martin Luther." In *Wirtschaft und Ethik in theologischer Perspektive*, edited by Udo Kern, 85–110. Münster: LIT, 2002.

Blackwell, Richard J. *Galileo, Bellarmine, and the Bible*. Notre Dame, IN: University of Notre Dame Press, 1991.

Bondolfi, Alberto. "Die Debatte um die Reform der Armenpflege im Europa des 16. Jahrhunderts." In *Die Entstehung einer sozialen Ordnung Europas*, edited by Theodore Strohm and Michael Klein, 1:105–45. 2 vols. Heidelberg: Universitätsverlag, 2004.

Bonhoeffer, Dietrich. *Dietrich Bonhoeffer Works*. 17 vols. Minneapolis: Fortress Press, 2001.

———. *Discipleship*. Translated by Barbara Green and Reinhard Krauss. Vol. 4 of *Dietrich Bonhoeffer Works*. Minneapolis: Fortress Press, 2001.

The Book of Concord: The Confessions of the Lutheran Church. bookofconcord.org/index.php.

Bourdieu, Pierre. *Distinction: A Social Critique of the Judgement of Taste*. Edited and translated by Richard Nice. Cambridge, MA: Harvard University Press, 1984.

Bower, Calvin M. "The Transmission of Ancient Music Theory into the Middle Ages." In *The Cambridge History of Western Music Theory*, edited by Thomas Christensen, 136–67. Cambridge: Cambridge University Press, 2002.

Bowman, Wayne D. *Philosophical Perspectives on Music*. New York: Oxford University Press, 1998.

Brakelmann, Günter, and Traugott Jähnichen. *Die protestantischen Wurzeln der Sozialen Marktwirtschaft*. Gütersloh: Gütersloher Verlagshaus, 1994.

Bray, Gerald Lewis, ed. *Documents of the English Reformation, 1526–1701*. Cambridge: James Clarke, 2004.

Brecht, Martin. *Martin Luther: The Preservation of the Church, 1532–1546*. Minneapolis: Fortress Press, 1993.

Breen, Timothy H., and Stephen Foster. "The Puritans' Greatest Achievement: A Study of Social Cohesion in Seventeenth-Century Massachusetts." *William and Mary Quarterly* 60 (January 1973): 5–22.

Brodie, Nicholas Dean. "A History of the English Parochial Poor Box c. 1547." In *Experiences of Charity*, edited by Anne M. Scott, 215–37. Farnham, Surrey, UK: Ashgate, 2015.

Brown, Christopher Boyd. "Devotional Life in Hymns, Liturgy, Music, and Prayer." In *Lutheran Ecclesiastical Culture, 1550–1675*, edited by Robert Kolb, 205–58. Leiden: Brill, 2008.

———. *Singing the Gospel: Lutheran Hymns and the Success of the Reformation*. Cambridge, MA: Harvard University Press, 2005.

Brown, Peter. *The Rise of Western Christendom: Triumph and Diversity, A.D. 200–1000*. 10th anniversary rev. ed. Chichester: Wiley-Blackwell, 2013.

Buck, Lawrence, and Jonathan Zophy, eds. *The Social History of the Reformation*. Columbus: Ohio State University Press, 1972.

Bugenhagen, Johannes. *Selected Writings*. Translated and edited by Kurt Hendel. 2 vols. Minneapolis: Fortress Press, 2015.

Bultmann, Rudolf. *Theology of the New Testament*. 2 vols. New York: Charles Scribner's Sons, 1951–95.

Butt, John. *Bach's Dialogue with Modernity: Perspectives on the Passions*. Cambridge: Cambridge University Press, 2010.

———. *Music Education and the Art of Performance in the German Baroque.* Cambridge: Cambridge University Press, 1994.

Calvin, John. *Calvin's Ecclesiastical Advice.* Translated by Mary Beaty and Benjamin W. Farley. Louisville, KY: Westminster/John Knox Press, 1991.

———. *Institutes of the Christian Religion.* Translated by John Allen. Philadelphia: Presbyterian Board of Christian Education, 1936.

———. *Institutes of the Christian Religion.* Translated by F. L. Battles. Edited by J. T. McNeil. 2 vols. Philadelphia: Westminster Press, 1960.

———. *Opera quae supersunt omnia.* In *Corpus Reformatorum,* edited by G. Bretschneider et al. 59 vols. Reprint, New York: Johnson Reprint Corporation, 1964.

Catechism of the Catholic Church. English ed. Liguori, MO: Liguori Publications, 1994.

Chang, Alvin. "Donald Trump's Poll Numbers Show a Big Divide between Christians and Churchgoing Christians." *Vox,* March 7, 2016. www.vox.com/policy-and-politics /2016/3/7/11174064/do-christians-really-favor-trump.

Chiffoleau, Jacques. *La comptabilité de l'au-delà. Les hommes, la mort et la religion dans la region d'Avignon à la fin du Moyen Age (vers 1320–vers 1480).* Rome: École Française de Rome, 1980.

Chillingworth, William. *The Religion of Protestants: A Safe Way to Salvation.* Oxford: Lichfield, 1638; Short Title Catalogue, 1167:13.

Clark, Kenneth, and Linda A. Stone-Ferrier. *An Introduction to Rembrandt.* Norwalk, CT: Easton Press, 1978.

Czaika, Otfried, and Heinrich Holze, eds. *Migration und Kulturtransfer im Ostseeraum während der Frühen Neuzeit.* Stockholm: Kungliga biblioteket, 2012.

Dabrock, Peter. *Befähigungsgerechtigkeit: Ein Grundkonzept konkreter Ethik in fundamental-theologischer Perspektive.* Gütersloh: Gütersloher Verlagshaus, 2012.

Dickens, Arthur G. *The English Reformation.* 2nd, repr. ed. London: Schocken Books, 2006.

Dreyfus, Laurence. *Bach and the Patterns of Invention.* Cambridge, MA: Harvard University Press, 2004.

Duchrow, Ulrich, Daniel Beros, Martin Hoffmann, and Hans G. Ulrich, eds. *Die Reformation radikalisieren / Radicalizing Reformation.* 5 vols. Berlin: LIT, 2015.

Durham, John I. *The Biblical Rembrandt: Human Painter in a Landscape of Faith.* Macon, GA: Mercer University Press, 2004.

Dyer, Joseph. "The Place of Musica in Medieval Classifications of Knowledge." *Journal of Musicology* 24, no. 1 (Winter 2007): 3–71.

Eby, Frederick. *Early Protestant Educators: The Educational Writings of Martin Luther, John Calvin, and Other Leaders of Protestant Thought.* Repr. ed. New York: AMS Press, 1971.

Ehler, Sidney Z., and John B. Morrall, eds. *Church and State through the Centuries: A Collection of Historic Documents with Commentaries.* Repr. ed. Getzville, NY: William S. Hein & Co., 2017.

Eire, Carlos M. N. *From Madrid to Purgatory: The Art and Craft of Dying in Sixteenth-Century Spain.* Cambridge: Cambridge University Press, 1995.

Eisenstadt, Shmuel N. "Some Observations on Structuralism in Sociology, with Special, and Paradoxical, Reference to Max Weber." In *Continuities in Structural Inquiry,* edited by Peter M. Blau and Robert K. Merton, 165–76. Beverly Hills, CA: Sage Publications, 1981.

Equiano, Olaudah. *The Interesting Narrative and Other Writings.* Edited by Vincent Caretta. 2nd ed. New York: Penguin, 2013.

Estep, William R. *The Anabaptist Story: An Introduction to Sixteenth-Century Anabaptism.* Grand Rapids: Wm. B. Eerdmans Publishing Co., 1996.

Evangelische Kirche in Deutschland. *Evangelische Kirche und freiheitliche Demokratie: Der Staat des Grundgesetzes als Angebot und Aufgabe; Eine Denkschrift der Evangelischen Kirche in Deutschland.* Gütersloh: Mohn, 1985.

Fabio, Udo Di. "Die Dialektik der Neuzeit im Geist der Reformation." In *Die Weltwirkung der Reformation: Wie der Protestantismus unsere Welt verändert hat,* edited by Udo Di Fabio and Johannes Schilling, 146-69. Munich: C. H. Beck, 2017.

Fabio, Udo Di and Johannes Schilling, eds. *Die Weltwirkung der Reformation: Wie der Protestantismus unsere Welt verändert hat.* Munich: C. H. Beck, 2017.

Ferguson, Niall. *Civilization: The West and the Rest.* New York: Penguin, 2011.

———. "Why America Outpaces Europe (Clue: The God Factor)." *New York Times.* June 8, 2003. www.nytimes.com/2003/06/08/weekinreview/the-world-why-america-out paces-europe-clue-the-god-factor.html.

———. "Wir löschen unseren Erfolg." *Die Zeit,* May 8, 2013. www.zeit.de/2013/20/der -niedergang-des-westens/komplettansicht.

Fernández-Armesto, Felipe, and Derek Wilson. *Reformations: A Radical Interpretation of Christianity and the World, 1500–2000.* New York: Scribner, 1997.

Finney, Paul Corby, ed. *Seeing beyond the Word: Visual Arts and the Calvinist Tradition.* Grand Rapids: Wm. B. Eerdmans Publishing Co., 1999.

Ford, David F. *Christian Wisdom: Desiring God and Learning in Love.* Cambridge: Cambridge University Press, 2007.

———. *The Future of Christian Theology.* Oxford: Wiley-Blackwell, 2011.

———. "Meeting Nicodemus: A Case Study in Daring Theological Interpretation." *Scottish Journal of Theology* 66, no. 1 (2013): 2–6.

———. "Reading Backwards, Reading Forwards, and Abiding: Reading John in the Spirit Now." *Journal of Theological Interpretation* 11, no. 1 (Spring 2017): 69–84.

———. "Scriptural Reasoning and the Legacy of Vatican II: Their Mutual Engagement and Significance." In *Interreligious Reading after Vatican II: Scriptural Reasoning, Comparative Theology and Receptive Ecumenism,* edited by David F. Ford and Frances Clemson, 93–119. Special Issue: *Modern Theology* 29, issue 4 (October 2013). Oxford: Wiley Blackwell, 2013.

Ford, David F., and Frances Clemson, eds. *Interreligious Reading after Vatican II: Scriptural Reasoning, Comparative Theology and Receptive Ecumenism.* Oxford: Wiley Blackwell, 2013.

Ford, David F., and Rachel Muers. *The Modern Theologians: An Introduction to Christian Theology since 1918.* Oxford: Blackwell, 2005.

Franklin, Benjamin. "Advice to a Young Tradesman." July 21, 1748. In *The American Instructor: or, Young Man's Best Companion,* edited by George Fisher, 375–77. 9th ed. Philadelphia: B. Franklin & D. Hall, 1748. founders.archives.gov/documents/Franklin/01 -03-02-0130.

———. *Poor Richard's Almanac: The Wit and Wisdom of Benjamin Franklin.* Lexington, KY: Seven Treasures Publications, 2008.

Freiburger Bonhoeffer-Kreis. *In der Stunde Null: Die Denkschrift des Freiburger "Bonhoeffer Kreises" Politische Gemeinschaftsordnung; Ein Versuch zur Selbstbesinnung des christlichen Gewissens in den politischen Nöten unserer Zeit.* Tübingen: Mohr, 1979.

Friedmann, Robert. *The Theology of Anabaptism.* 1973. Repr. ed., Scottdale, PA: Herald Press, 1998.

Garrison, Roman. *Redemptive Almsgiving in Early Christianity*. London: Bloomsbury Publishing, 1993.

Gause, Ute. "Durchsetzung neuer Männlichkeit = Ehe und Reformation." *Evangelische Theologie* 73 (2013): 326–38.

Geck, Martin. *Johann Sebastian Bach: Life and Work*. Translated by John Hargraves. New York: Harcourt, 2006.

Glass, William R. "Liberal Means to Conservative Ends: Bethany Presbyterian Church, John Wanamaker, and the Institutional Church Movement." *American Presbyterians* 68, no. 3 (1990): 181.

Goldschmidt, Nils. "Die Entstehung der Freiburger Kreise." *Historisch-Politische Mitteilungen* 4, no. 1 (1997): 1–17.

Goodman, Christopher. *How Superior Powers Ought to Be Obeyd*. 1558. Edited by Charles H. McIlwain. Facsimile ed., New York: Columbia University Press, 1931.

Greef, Wulfert de. *The Writings of John Calvin: An Introductory Guide*. Expanded ed. Louisville, KY: Westminster John Knox Press, 2008.

Gregory, Brad S. *The Unintended Reformation: How a Religious Revolution Secularized Society*. Cambridge, MA: Belknap Press of Harvard University Press, 2012.

Grindal, Gracia. "Luther and the Arts: A Study in Convention." *Word and World* 3 (1983): 373–81.

Groot, Jenny de. "Iranian Refugee's Paintings Displayed in British Columbia Church." *The Banner*, June 2017, 13.

Gunther, Karl. *Reformation Unbound: Protestant Visions of Reform in England, 1525–1590*. New York: Cambridge University Press, 2014.

Gupta, Arjun. *Lucas Cranach the Elder, Martin Luther, and the Art of the Reformation*. Calgary: Bayeux Arts, 2017.

Haigh, Christopher. *English Reformations: Religion, Society, and Politics under the Tudors*. Oxford: Clarendon Press, 1993.

Hamm, Berndt. "Den Himmel kaufen: Heilskommerzielle Perspektiven des 14. bis 16. Jahrhunderts." In *Himmel auf Erden / Heaven on Earth*, edited by Rudolf Suntrup and Jan R. Veenstra, 23–56. Frankfurt am Main: Peter Lang, 2009.

———. *The Early Luther: Stages in a Reformation Reorientation*. Translated by Martin Lohrmann. Grand Rapids: Wm. B. Eerdmans Publishing Co., 2014.

———. "Martin Luther's Revolutionary Theology of Pure Gift without Reciprocation." *Lutheran Quarterly* 29, no. 2 (2015): 125–61.

Hart, David Bentley. *The Beauty of the Infinite: The Aesthetics of Christian Truth*. Grand Rapids: Wm. B. Eerdmans Publishing Co., 2003.

Hart, Trevor A. "Protestantism and the Arts." In *The Blackwell Companion to Protestantism*, edited by Alister E. McGrath and Darren C. Marks, 268–86. Oxford: Blackwell, 2006.

Hartfelder, Karl. *Philipp Melanchthon als Praeceptor Germaniae*. Munich: Monumenta Germaniae Paedagogica, 1978.

Hays, Richard. *Echoes of Scripture in the Gospels*. Waco, TX: Baylor University Press, 2016.

Heckel, Johannes. *Lex Charitatis: A Juristic Disquisition on Law in the Theology of Martin Luther*. Translated by Gottfried G. Krodel. Grand Rapids: Wm. B. Eerdmans Publishing Co., 2010.

Heckel, Martin. *Martin Luthers Reformation und das Recht*. Tübingen: Mohr Siebeck, 2016.

Helmer, Paul. "The Catholic Luther and Worship Music." In *The Global Luther: A Theologian for Modern Times*, edited by Christine Helmer, 151–72. Minneapolis: Fortress Press, 2009.

Helmholz, Richard H. *Roman Canon Law in Reformation England*. Cambridge: Cambridge University Press, 1990.

Hendel, Kurt. "The Care of the Poor: An Evangelical Perspective." *Currents in Theology and Mission* 15 (1988): 526–32.

———. "Johannes Bugenhagen, Organizer of the Lutheran Reformation." *Lutheran Quarterly* 18, no. 1 (2004): 43–75.

———. "Paul and the Care of the Poor during the Sixteenth Century: A Case Study." In *A Companion to Paul in the Reformation*, edited by Ward Holder, 541–71. Leiden: Brill, 2009.

Herl, Joseph. *Worship Wars in Early Lutheranism*. Oxford: Oxford University Press, 2004.

Hershberger, Guy F., ed. *The Recovery of the Anabaptist Vision*. 1957. Repr. ed., Scottdale, PA: Herald Press, 2001.

Hicks, Andrew J. *Composing the World: Harmony in the Medieval Platonic Cosmos*. New York: Oxford University Press, 2017.

Hill, Christopher. *The English Bible and the Seventeenth-Century Revolution*. London: Allen Lane / Penguin, 1993.

Holthaus, Stephan. *Zwischen Gewissen und Gewinn: Die Wirtschafts- und Sozialordnung der "Freiburger Denkschrift" und die Anfänge der Sozialen Marktwirtschaft*. Berlin: LIT, 2015.

Hooker, Richard. *The Laws of Ecclesiastical Polity*. Edited by W. Speed Hill. Cambridge, MA: Harvard University Press, 1977.

Höpfl, Harro. *The Christian Polity of John Calvin*. Cambridge: Cambridge University Press, 1982.

Hopkins, Samuel, ed. *The Life and Character of Miss Susanna Anthony*. Worcester, MA: Hudson & Goodwin, 1799.

Horne, Brian. "A Civitas of Sound: On Luther and Music." *Theology* 88 (1985): 21–28.

Howe, Daniel W. *What Hath God Wrought: The Transformation of America, 1815–1848*. New York: Oxford University Press, 2009.

Irwin, Joyce L. *Neither Voice nor Heart Alone: German Lutheran Theology of Music in the Age of the Baroque*. New York: Peter Lang, 1993.

———. "'So Faith Comes from What Is Heard': The Relationship between Music and God's Word in the First Two Centuries of German Lutheranism." In *Resonant Witness: Essays in Theology and Music*, edited by Jeremy S. Begbie and Steven R. Guthrie, 65–82. Grand Rapids: Wm. B. Eerdmans Publishing Co., 2011.

Jähnichen, Traugott. "Das wirtschaftsethische Profil des sozialen Protestantismus: Zu den gesellschafts- und ordnungspolitischen Grundentscheidungen der Sozialen Marktwirtschaft." *Jahrbuch Sozialer Protestantismus* 4 (2010): 18–45.

Jenkins, Philip. *The New Faces of Christianity*. New York: Oxford University Press, 2006.

Joby, Christopher R. *Calvinism and the Arts: A Re-Assessment*. Leuven: Peeters, 2007.

Jüngel, Eberhard. *God as the Mystery of the World: On the Foundation of the Theology of the Crucified in the Dispute between Theism and Atheism*. Edinburgh: T&T Clark, 1983.

Jütte, Robert. "Die Sorge für Kranke und Gebrechliche in den Almosen- und Kastenordnungen des 16. Jahrhunderts." In *Medizin und Sozialwesen in Mitteldeutschland zur Reformationszeit*, edited by Stefan Oehmig, 9–21. Leipzig: Evangelische Verlagsanstalt, 2007.

Kässmann, Margot, ed. *Schlag nach bei Luther: Texte für den Alltag*. Frankfurt am Main: Hansisches Druck & Verlagshaus 2012.

Kaufmann, Thomas. "Die Reformation—ein historischer Überblick." In *Die Weltwirkung der Reformation: Wie der Protestantismus unsere Welt verändert hat*, edited by Udo Di Fabio and Johannes Schilling, 25–27. Munich: C. H. Beck, 2017.

Kim, Jim Yong. "Wir arbeiten weiter und beten für die Mädchen." Interview with Jim Yong Kim and Gerd Müller, by Manfred Schäfers. *Frankfurter Allgemeine Zeitung.* May 17, 2014, 21.

Kingdon, Robert M. "Calvin's Ideas about the Diaconate: Social or Theological in Origin?" In *Piety, Politics, and Ethics: Reformation Studies in Honor of George Wolfgang Forell,* edited by Carter Lindberg, 167–80. Kirksville, MO: Sixteenth Century Journal Publishers, 1984.

———. *Church and State in Reformation Europe.* London: Variorum Reprints, 1985.

———. "Social Welfare in Calvin's Geneva." *American Historical Review* 76, no. 1 (1971): 50–69.

Klaassen, Walter. *Anabaptism in Outline.* Scottdale, PA: Herald Press, 1981.

Klaiber, Walter. *Der Römerbrief.* Neukirchen-Vluyn: Neukirchener Verlag, 2009.

Koehler, Joachim. *Luther! Biografie eines Befreiten.* Leipzig: Evangelische Verlagsanstalt, 2016.

Kreighbaum, Andrew. "Falwell Higher Ed Task Force Won't Happen." *Inside Higher Ed,* June 9, 2017. www.insidehighered.com/news/2017/06/09/liberty-university-presi dent-wont-be-leading-task-force-higher-ed-regulation-after.

Kreiker, Sebastian. *Armut, Schule, Obrigkeit: Armenversorgung und Schulwesen in den evangelischen Kirchenordnungen des 16. Jahrhunderts.* Bielefeld: Verlag für Regionalgeschichte, 1997.

Küng, Hans. *Great Christian Thinkers.* New York: Continuum, 1995.

Labberton, Mark. "The Plain Sense? Scripture May Be Clear, But It's Not Easy." *Christian Century,* April 12, 2017, 31.

Lapp, Michael. "'Denn es ist geld ein ungewis, wanckelbar ding': Die Wirtschaftsethik Martin Luthers anhand seiner Schriften gegen den Wucher." *Luther: Zeitschrift der Luther-Gesellschaft* 83, no. 2 (2012): 91–107.

Langbein, John H. *Prosecuting Crime in the Renaissance: England, Germany, France.* Cambridge, MA: Harvard University Press, 1974.

Layman, Geoffrey. "Where Is Trump's Evangelical Base? Not in Church." *Washington Post,* March 29, 2016. www.washingtonpost.com/news/monkey-cage/wp/2016/03/29 /where-is-trumps-evangelical-base-not-in-church/?utm_term=.e6c40ce5ed49.

Leach, William. *Land of Desire: Merchants, Power, and the Rise of a New American Culture.* New York: Vintage, 1994.

Leaver, Robin A. *Luther's Liturgical Music: Principles and Implications.* Grand Rapids: Wm. B. Eerdmans Publishing Co., 2007.

LeCler, Joseph. *Toleration and the Reformation.* Translated by T. L. Westow. 4 vols. New York: Association Press, 1960.

Le Goff, Jacques. *Your Money or Your Life: Economy and Religion in the Middle Ages.* New York: Zone Books, 1988.

Leith, John. *John Calvin's Doctrine of the Christian Life.* Louisville, KY: Westminster/John Knox Press, 1989.

Lesnick, David. *Preaching in Medieval Florence: The Social World of Franciscan and Dominican Spirituality.* Athens: University of Georgia Press, 1989.

Liermann, Hans. "Protestant Endowment Law in the Franconian Church Ordinances of the Sixteenth Century." In Buck and Zophy, *Social History of the Reformation,* 340–54.

Lindbeck, George. "Progress in Textual Reasoning: From Vatican II to the Conference at Drew." In *Textual Reasonings: Jewish Philosophy and Text Study at the End of the Twentieth Century,* edited by Peter Ochs and Nancy Levene, 252–58. London: SCM, 2002.

Lindberg, Carter. *Beyond Charity: Reformation Initiatives for the Poor.* Minneapolis: Fortress Press, 1993.

———. *The European Reformations.* Cambridge, MA: Blackwell, 1996.

———. "Luther's Concept of Offering." *Dialog* 35, no. 4 (1996): 251–57.

———. "'There Should Be No Beggars among Christians': An Early Reformation Tract on Social Welfare by Andreas Karlstadt." In *Piety, Politics, and Ethics: Reformation Studies in Honor of George Wolfgang Forell,* edited by Carter Lindberg, 157–66. Kirksville, MO: Sixteenth Century Journal Publishers, 1984.

Lindberg, Carter, and Paul Wee, eds. *The Forgotten Luther: Reclaiming the Socio-Economic Dimension of the Reformation.* Minneapolis: Lutheran University Press, 2016.

Lis, Catherine, and Hugo Soly. *Poverty and Capitalism in Pre-Industrial Europe.* Atlantic Highlands, NJ: Humanities Press, 1979.

Little, Lester K. *Religious Poverty and the Profit Economy in Medieval Europe.* Ithaca, NY: Cornell University Press, 1976.

Loewe, J. Andreas (Melbourne College of Divinity). "'Musica est Optimum': Martin Luther's Theory of Music." *Music and Letters* 94, no. 4 (2013): 573–605. mcd.academia.edu /loewe/Papers/1074845/Musica_est_op:timum_Martin_Luthers_Theory_of_Music.

Lorentzen, Tim. *Johannes Bugenhagen als Reformator der öffentlichen Fürsorge.* Tübingen: Mohr, 2008.

———. "Theologie und Ökonomie in Bugenhagens Fürsorgekonzept." In *Der späte Bugenhagen,* edited by Irene Dingel and Stefan Rhein, 151–74. Leipzig: Evangelische Verlagsanstalt, 2011.

Luther, Martin, *D. Martin Luthers Werke: Briefwechsel.* 17 vols. Weimar: Böhlau, 1930–83.

———. *D. Martin Luthers Werke: Kritische Gesamtausgabe.* 78 vols. Weimar: Böhlau, 1883–1987.

———. *Luther's Works [LW].* Translated and edited by Jaroslav Pelikan, Helmut T. Lehmann, et al. 55 vols. Philadelphia: Fortress Press, 1955–68.

———. *Martin Luthers Werke: Kritische Gesamtausgabe* [WA = Weimarer Ausgabe]. 121 vols. Weimar: Hermann Böhlau / H. Böhlaus Nachfolger, 1883–2009.

MacCulloch, Diarmaid. *All Things Made New: The Reformation and Its Legacy.* Oxford: Oxford University Press, 2016.

Maddern, Philippa. "A Market for Charitable Performances? Bequests to the Poor and Their Recipients in Fifteenth-Century Norwich Wills." In *Experiences of Charity,* edited by Anne M. Scott, 79–103. Farnham, Surrey, UK: Ashgate, 2015.

Maissen, Thomas. *Geschichte der frühen Neuzeit.* Munich: C. H. Beck, 2013.

Mäkinen, Virpi, ed. *Lutheran Reformation and the Law.* Leiden: Brill, 2006.

Marshall, Robert L. *The Music of Johann Sebastian Bach: The Sources, the Style, the Significance.* New York: Schirmer, 1989.

Mattes, Mark C. *Martin Luther's Theology of Beauty: A Reappraisal.* Grand Rapids: Baker Academic, 2017.

McCurley, Foster R., ed. *Social Ministry in the Lutheran Tradition.* Minneapolis: Fortress Press, 2008.

McGrath, Alister. "Calvin and the Christian Calling." *First Things* 94 (1999): 31–35.

McKee, Elsie Anne. "The Character and Significance of John Calvin's Teaching on Social and Economic Issues." In *John Calvin Rediscovered: The Impact of His Social and Economic Thought,* edited by Edward Dommen and James Bratt, 3–24. Louisville, KY: Westminster John Knox Press, 2007.

————. *John Calvin on the Diaconate and Liturgical Almsgiving*. Geneva: Droz, 1984.

McKim, Donald Keith. *The Cambridge Companion to Martin Luther*. Cambridge: Cambridge University Press, 2003.

Meireis, Torsten. *Tätigkeit und Erfüllung: Protestantische Ethik im Umbruch der Arbeitsgesellschaft*. Tübingen: Mohr Siebeck, 2008.

————. "Was ist und worauf zielt sozialer Protestantismus." *Jahrbuch Sozialer Protestantismus* 4 (2010): 231–41.

Melanchthon, Philipp. *Melanchthon and Bucer*. Edited by Wilhelm Pauck. Library of Christian Classics 19. Philadelphia: Westminster Press, 1969.

————. *Melanchthon on Christian Doctrine: Loci Communes, 1555*. Translated and edited by Clyde L. Manschreck. Oxford: Oxford University Press, 1965.

————. *Philippi Melanthonis Opera quae supersunt omnia*. In *Corpus Reformatorum*, edited by G. Bretschneider et al. 28 vols. Braunschweig: C. A. Schwetschke, 1834–60.

Merkel, Angela. "Greeting of the Chancellor to the Synod of the Evangelical Church in Germany." November 7, 2012, in Timmendorfer Strand.

Mollat, Michel. *The Poor in the Middle Ages: An Essay in Social History*. Translated by Arthur Gold Hammer. New Haven, CT: Yale University Press, 1986.

Murray, Douglas. *The Strange Death of Europe: Immigration, Identity, Islam*. London: Bloomsbury, 2017.

Nelson, Benjamin. *The Idea of Usury: From Tribal Brotherhood to Universal Otherhood*. 2nd ed. Chicago: University of Chicago Press, 1969.

Nettl, Paul. *Luther and Music*. Translated by Frida Best and Ralph Wood. New York: Russell & Russell, 1967.

Neubauer, John. *The Emancipation of Music from Language: Departure from Mimesis in Eighteenth-Century Aesthetics*. New Haven, CT: Yale University Press, 1986.

Nissen, Johannes, and Sigfred Pedersen, eds. *New Readings in John*. London: T&T Clark International, 1999.

Noll, Mark A. *The Civil War as a Theological Crisis*. Chapel Hill: University of North Carolina Press, 2006.

————. *In the Beginning Was the Word: The Bible in American Public Life, 1492–1783*. New York: Oxford University Press, 2016.

Nussbaum, Martha. *Frontiers of Justice: Disability, Nationality, Species Membership*. Cambridge, MA: Harvard University Press, 2007.

Ochs, Peter, and William Stacy Johnson, eds. *Crisis, Call, and Leadership in the Abrahamic Traditions*. New York: Palgrave Macmillan, 2009.

Ochs, Peter, and Nancy Levene, eds. *Textual Reasonings: Jewish Philosophy and Text Study at the End of the Twentieth Century*. London: SCM, 2002.

O'Donovan, Joan Lockwood. *The Theology and Law of the English Reformation*. Grand Rapids: Wm. B. Eerdmans Publishing Co., 1991.

Oehmig, Stefan. "Der Wittenberger Gemeine Kasten in den ersten zweieinhalb Jahrzehnten seines Bestehens (1522/23 bis 1547)." *Jahrbuch für Geschichte des Feudalismus* 13 (1989): 141–45.

Oettinger, Rebecca Wagner. *Music as Propaganda in the German Reformation*. Aldershot: Ashgate, 2001.

Olson, Jeannine. *Calvin and Social Welfare: Deacons and the Bourse Française*. Selinsgrove, PA: Susquehanna University Press, 1989.

O'Siadhail, Micheal. *The Five Quintets*. Waco, TX: Baylor University Press, 2018.

Packer, J. I. "The Bible in Use." In *Your Word Is Truth*, edited by Charles Colson and Richard John Neuhaus, 59–78. Grand Rapids: Wm. B. Eerdmans Publishing Co., 2002.

Painter, F. V. N. *Luther on Education.* Repr. ed. Eugene, OR: Wipf & Stock, 2001.

Pawlas, Andreas. "Ist 'kaufhandel' immer 'Wucher'? Luther zu kaufmännischen Handel und Wucher als Beitrag zu einer evangelischen Wirtschaftsethik." *Kerygma und Dogma* 40 (1994): 282–304.

Pelikan, Jaroslav, and Valerie Hotchkiss, eds. *Creeds and Confessions of the Christian Tradition.* New Haven, CT: Yale University Press, 2003.

Peters, Albrecht. *Kommentar zu Luthers Katechismen.* Vol. 3, *Das Vaterunser.* Göttingen: Vandenhoeck & Ruprecht, 1992.

Pihlajamäki, Heikki. "Executor divinarum et suarum legum: Criminal Law and the Lutheran Reformation." In *Lutheran Reformation and the Law*, edited by Virpi Mäkinen, 171–204. Leiden: Brill, 2006.

Pollack, Detlef. "Protestantismus und Moderne. In *Die Weltwirkung der Reformation: Wie der Protestantismus unsere Welt verändert hat*, edited by Udo Di Fabio and Johannes Schilling, 81–118. Munich: C. H. Beck, 2017.

Porter, J. M., ed. *Luther—Selected Political Writings.* Philadelphia: Fortress Press, 1974.

Radkau, Joachim. "Leidenschaft im Eisschrank: Die lustvolle Qual Weberscher Wissenschaft; oder, Die Aktualität Max Webers." *Evangelischer Pressedienst Dokumentation* [*epd*] 35 (August 29, 2014): 23–28.

Raunio, Antti. "Luther's Social Theology in the Contemporary World." In *The Global Luther: A Theologian for Modern Times*, edited by Christine Helmer, 210–27. Minneapolis: Fortress Press, 2009.

Rawls, John. *A Theory of Justice.* Rev., 2nd ed. Cambridge, MA: Harvard University Press, 1999.

Reinhard, Wolfgang. "Die Bejahung des gewöhnlichen Lebens." In *Die kulturellen Werte Europas*, edited by Hans Joas and Klaus Wiegandt, 265–303. Frankfurt am Main: Fischer, 2005.

Reuter, Fritz, ed. *Der Reichstag zu Worms von 1521: Reichspolitik und Luthersache im Auftrag der Stadt Worms zum 450-Jahrgedenken.* Worms: Stadtarchiv, 1971.

Reuter, Hans-Richard. "Die Religion der Sozialen Marktwirtschaft: Zur ordoliberalen Weltanschauung bei Walter Eucken und Alexander Rüstow." *Jahrbuch Sozialer Protestantismus* 4 (2010): 46–76.

Rieth, Ricardo. "Luther on Greed." In *Harvesting Martin Luther's Reflections on Theology, Ethics, and the Church*, edited by Timothy J. Wengert, 152–68. Grand Rapids: Wm. B. Eerdmans Publishing Co., 2004.

Rivoire, Émile, and Victor van Berchem, eds. *Les sources du droit du canton de Genève.* 4 vols. Aarau: H. R. Sauerländer, 1927–35.

Rosenthal, Joel. *The Purchase of Paradise: Gift Giving and the Aristocracy, 1307–1485.* London: Routledge, 1972.

Rössner, Philipp. "Burying Money? Monetary Origins and Afterlives of Luther's Reformation." *History of Political Economy* 48, no. 2 (2016): 225–63.

Rupp, E. Gordon. *Studies in the Making of the English Protestant Tradition.* Cambridge: Cambridge University Press, 1966.

Salter, Frank R., ed. *Some Early Tracts on Poor Relief.* London: Methuen, 1926.

Sauer, James B. "Christian Faith, Economy, and Economics: What Do Christian Ethics Contribute to Understanding Economy?" *Faith & Economics* 42 (2003): 17–25.

———. *Faithful Ethics according to John Calvin: The Teachability of the Heart.* Lewiston, NY: Edwin Mellen Press, 1997.

Schalk, Carl. *Luther on Music: Paradigms of Praise.* St. Louis: Concordia Publishing House, 1988.

Scharffenorth, Gerta, and Klaus Thraede. "Luthers reformatorische Erkenntnisse als Basis für ein neues Verständnis von Mann und Frau." In *"Freunde in Christus Werden": Die Beziehung von Mann und Frau als Frage an Theologie und Kirche*, 183–302. Gelnhausen: Burckhardthaus, 1977.

Schilling, Heinz. *Martin Luther: Rebell in einer Zeit des Umbruchs.* Munich: C. H. Beck Verlag, 2012.

Schmidt, Samantha, and Amy B. Wang. "Jerry Falwell Jr. Keeps Defending Trump as Liberty University Grads Return Diplomas." *Washington Post*, August 21, 2017. www .washingtonpost.com/news/morning-mix/wp/2017/08/21/liberty-university-gradu ates-return-diplomas-because-of-support-for-trump-by-jerry-falwell-jr/?utm_term= .20a14e4a8b77.

Schmoeckel, Mathias. *Das Recht der Reformation.* Tübingen: Mohr Siebeck, 2014.

Schulze, Winfried. "Vom Gemeinnutz zum Eigennutz." *Historische Zeitschrift* 243 (1986): 591–626.

Schwarz, Hans. "Martin Luther and Music." *Lutheran Theological Journal* 39 (August–December 2005): 210–17.

Scruton, Roger. *Where We Are: The State of Britain Now.* London: Bloomsbury, 2017.

Seebass, Gottfried. "The Reformation in Nürnberg." In Buck and Zophy, *Social History of the Reformation*, 17–40.

Sehling, Emil, et al., eds. *Die evangelischen Kirchenordnungen des XVI. Jahrhunderts.* 24 vols. Leipzig: O. R. Reisland, 1902–13. New ed., Tübingen: Mohr, 1955–.

Seligman, Adam B. "Introduction." In *Religion and the Rise of Capitalism*, by R. H. Tawney, xi–xl. New Brunswick, NJ: Transaction Publishers, 1998.

Sen, Amartya. *Development as Freedom.* Oxford: Oxford University Press, 1999.

———. *The Idea of Justice.* Cambridge, MA: Harvard University Press, 2009.

Shapiro, T. Rees, et al., "Liberty University Students Protest Association with Trump." *Washington Post*, October 13, 2016. https://www.washingtonpost.com/news/grade -point/wp/2016/10/12/liberty-is-not-trump-u-students-protest-donald-trump/?utm _term=.4ef6b1e4d004.

Sica, Alan. *Max Weber and the New Century.* New Brunswick, NJ: Routledge, 2004.

Simon, Joan. *Education and Society in Tudor England.* Cambridge: Cambridge University Press, 1966.

Smith, Christian. *The Bible Made Impossible: Why Biblicism Is Not a Truly Evangelical Reading of Scripture.* Grand Rapids: Brazos, 2011.

Söding, Thomas. "Leuchtfeuer der Reformation—Luthers Bibelübersetzung." In *Die Weltwirkung der Reformation: Wie der Protestantismus unsere Welt verändert hat*, edited by Udo Di Fabio and Johannes Schilling, 73–80. Munich: C. H. Beck, 2017.

Spener, Philip Jakob. *Pia Desideria.* Translated by Theodore G. Tappert. Philadelphia: Fortress Press, 1964.

Spengler, Oswald. *The Decline of the West.* Translated by Charles F. Atkinson. New York: Oxford University Press, 1991.

Sprengler-Ruppenthal, Anneliese. "Zur Entstehungsgechichte der Reformatorischen Kirchen-und Armenordnung im 16. Jahrhundert: Eine Dokumentation." In Anneliese

Sprengler-Ruppenthal, *Kleine Essays und Nachträge zu den Kirchenordnungen des 16. Jahrhunderts*, 66–148. Hamburg: Selbstverl, 2011.

Stayer, James M. "Community of Goods." In *The Oxford Encyclopedia of the Reformation*, edited by Hans J. Hillerbrand, 1:389–92. 4 vols. New York: Oxford University Press, 1996.

Stegmann, Andreas. *Luthers Auffassung vom christlichen Leben*. Tübingen: Mohr Siebeck, 2014.

Steinmetz, David. *Reformers in the Wings*. 2nd ed. New York: Oxford University Press, 2001.

Stephenson, Carl, and Frederick G. Marcham. *Sources of English Constitutional History*. New York: Harper & Bros., 1937.

Strauss, Gerald. *Luther's House of Learning: Indoctrination of the Young in the German Reformation*. Baltimore: Johns Hopkins University Press, 1978.

Strohm, Christoph. *Calvinismus und Recht*. Tübingen: Mohr Siebeck, 2008.

Strohm, Theodore, and Michael Klein, eds. *Die Entstehung einer sozialen Ordnung Europas*. 2 vols. Heidelberg: Universitätsverlag, 2004.

Sugirtharajah, R. S. "Postcolonial Notes on the King James Bible." In *The King James Bible after 400 Years: Literary, Linguistic, and Cultural Influences*, edited by Hannibal Hamlin and Norman W. Jones, 146–63. New York: Cambridge University Press, 2010.

Tanner, Kathryn. "Christianity and the New Spirit of Capitalism: An Introduction." Videostream of the first of the 2016 Gifford Lectures, "Christianity and the New Spirit of Capitalism," at the University of Edinburgh. www.giffordlectures.org/lectures/christianity-and-new-spirit-capitalism.

———. "Inequality and Finance-Dominated Capitalism: Recommendations for Further Reading." *Anglican Theological Review* 98 (2016): 157–73.

Tatlow, Ruth. *Bach's Numbers: Compositional Proportion and Significance*. Cambridge: Cambridge University Press, 2015.

Tawney, Richard H. *The Acquisitive Society*. Repr. ed. Project Gutenberg, 2010. http://www.gutenberg.org/ebooks/33741?msg=welcome_stranger.

———. *Religion and the Rise of Capitalism*. Repr. ed. New Brunswick, NJ: Routledge, 1998.

Thomas, Downing A. *Music and the Origins of Language: Theories from the French Enlightenment*. Cambridge: Cambridge University Press, 1995.

Thomas, R. S. [Ronald Stuart]. *Collected Poems, 1945–1990*. London: Phoenix, 1995.

Thompson, W. D. J. Cargill. *The Political Thought of Martin Luther*. Edited by Philip Broadhead. Totawa, NJ: Barnes & Noble, 1984.

Tocqueville, Alexis de. *Democracy in America*. Edited by Eduardo Nolla. Translated by James T. Schleifer. 4 vols. Indianapolis: Liberty Fund, 2010.

Tomlin, Graham. *Bound to Be Free: The Paradox of Freedom*. London, Bloomsbury, 2017.

———. *Luther's Gospel: Reimagining the World*. London: T&T Clark, 2017.

Torrance, Thomas F. *Divine and Contingent Order*. Oxford: Oxford University Press, 1981.

Troeltsch, Ernst. *The Social Teaching of the Christian Churches*. 2 vols. Louisville, KY: Westminster/John Knox Press, 1992.

Tuininga, Matthew J. *Calvin's Political Theology and the Public Engagement of the Church*. Cambridge: Cambridge University Press, 2017.

United States Catholic Bishops Conference. *Economic Justice for All: Pastoral Letter on Catholic Social Teaching and the U.S. Economy*. Washington, DC: National Conference of Catholic Bishops, 1986. http://www.usccb.org/upload/economic_justice_for_all.pdf.

Valeri, Mark. "Religion, Discipline, and the Economy in Calvin's Geneva." *Sixteenth Century Journal* 28, no. 1 (1997): 123–42.

Varwig, Bettina. "One More Time: J. S. Bach and Seventeenth-Century Traditions of Rhetoric." *Eighteenth-Century Music* 5, no. 2 (2008): 191.

Veit, Patrice. *Das Kirchenlied in der Reformation Martin Luthers: Eine thematische und semantische Untersuchung.* Stuttgart: Franz Steiner Verlag, 1986.

Venard, Marc, et al. *Le temps des confession (1530–1620/30). Histoire du Christianisme des orignes à nos jours,* vol. 8. Paris: Desclée, 1992.

Waller, Giles. "Tragic Drama, Tragic Theory, and Martin Luther's *Theologia Crucis.*" PhD diss., Cambridge University, 2017.

Walsham, Alexandra. "Reformation Legacies." In *The Oxford Illustrated History of the Reformation,* edited by Peter Marshall, 227–68. Oxford: Oxford University Press, 2015.

Walton, Jonathan L. *Watch This! The Ethics and Aesthetics of Black Televangelism.* New York: New York University Press, 2009.

Wandel, Lee Palmer. *Always among Us: Images of the Poor in Zwingli's Zurich.* Cambridge: Cambridge University Press, 1990.

———. *Voracious Idols and Violent Hands: Iconoclasm in Zurich, Strasbourg and Basel.* Cambridge: Cambridge University Press, 1995.

Weber, Max. *Asketischer Protestantismus und Kapitalismus: Schriften und Reden, 1904–1911.* Edited by Wolfgang Schluchter and Ursula Bube. Tübingen: Mohr Siebeck, 2014.

———. *Die protestantische Ethik und der Geist des Kapitalismus: Die protestantischen Sekten und der Geist des Kapitalismus; Schriften 1904–1920.* Edited by Wolfgang Schluchter and Ursula Bube. Tübingen: Mohr Siebeck, 2016.

———. *The Protestant Ethic and the Spirit of Capitalism: And Other Writings.* Edited by Peter Baehr and Gordon C. Wells. New York: Penguin Books, 2002.

Welker, Michael. *God the Revealed: Christology.* Grand Rapids: Wm. B. Eerdmans Publishing Co., 2013.

Welker, Michael, Michael Beintker, and Albert de Lange [WBL], eds. *Europa Reformata: European Reformation Cities and Their Reformers.* Leipzig: Evangelische Verlagsanstalt, 2016.

———. *Europa Reformata: Europäische Reformationsstädte und ihre Reformatoren.* Leipzig: Evangelische Verlagsanstalt, 2016. 2nd ed., 2017.

Wer war Elisabeth Schmitz? Über Ihre Denkschrift "Zur Lage der deutschen Nichtarier." San Francisco, CA: Grin Publishing, 2015.

Wesley, John. *The Works of John Wesley.* Edited by W. Reginald Ward and Richard P. Heitzenrater. 26 vols. Nashville: Abingdon, 1988.

Westhelle, Vítor. "Communication and the Transgression of Language in Martin Luther." In *The Pastoral Luther: Essays on Martin Luther's Practical Theology,* edited by Timothy J. Wengert, 59–84. Grand Rapids: Wm. B. Eerdmans Publishing Co., 2009.

"Why Evangelicals Love Donald Trump: The Secret Lies in the Prosperity Gospel." *The Economist,* May 18, 2017. www.economist.com/news/united-states/21722172-secret -lies-prosperity-gospel-why-evangelicals-love-donald-trump.

Williams, George Huntston. *The Radical Reformation.* 3rd rev. ed. Kirksville, MO: Truman State University Press, 2000.

———, ed. *Spiritual and Anabaptist Writers.* Philadelphia: Westminster Press, 1957.

Williams, Peter F. *Bach: The Goldberg Variations.* Cambridge: Cambridge University Press, 2001.

Wimbush, Vincent. *White Men's Magic: Scripturalization as Slavery*. New York: Oxford University Press, 2012.

Witte, John, Jr. "An Evangelical Commonwealth: Johannes Eisermann on Law and the Common Good." In *Caritas et Reformatio: Essays on Church and Society in Honor of Carter Lindberg*, edited by David M. Whitford, 73–87. St. Louis: Concordia Publishing House, 2002.

———. *From Sacrament to Contract: Marriage, Religion, and Law in the Western Tradition*. 2nd ed. Louisville, KY: Westminster John Knox Press, 2012.

———. *Law and Protestantism: The Legal Teachings of the Lutheran Reformation*. Cambridge: Cambridge University Press, 2002.

———. *The Reformation of Rights: Law, Religion, and Human Rights in Early Modern Calvinism*. Cambridge: Cambridge University Press, 2007.

Witte, John, Jr., and Joel A. Nichols. *Religion and the American Constitutional Experiment*. 4th ed. Oxford: Oxford University Press, 2016.

Witte, John, Jr., and Robert M. Kingdon. *Sex, Marriage, and Family in John Calvin's Geneva*. 2 vols. Grand Rapids: Wm. B. Eerdmans Publishing Co., 2006–18.

Wolf, Kenneth B. *The Poverty of Riches: St Francis of Assisi Reconsidered*. Oxford: Oxford University Press, 2003.

Wolff, Christoph. *Johann Sebastian Bach: The Learned Musician*. New York: W. W. Norton & Co., 2000.

Wright, William J. *Capitalism, the State, and the Lutheran Reformation: Sixteenth-Century Hesse*. Athens: Ohio University Press, 1988.

———. "Reformation Contributions to the Development of Welfare Policy in Hesse." *Journal of Modern History* 49, no. 2 (1977): D1145–79.

Young, Spencer E. "More Blessed to Give *and* Receive: Charitable Giving in Thirteenth- and Early Fourteenth-Century *Exempla*." In *Experiences of Charity*, edited by Anne M. Scott, 63–78. Farnham, Surrey, UK: Ashgate, 2015.

Zahl, Simeon. *Pneumatology and Theology of the Cross in the Preaching of Christoph Friedrich Blumhardt: The Holy Spirit between Wittenberg and Azusa Street*. London: T&T Clark, 2010.

———. "What Has the 'Lutheran' Paul to Do with John? Passive Righteousness and Abiding in the Vine." In *The Vocation of Theology Today: A Festschrift for David Ford*, edited by Tom Greggs, Rachel Muers, and Simeon Zahl, 61–76. Eugene, OR: Cascade Books, 2013.

Zenck, Martin. "Reinterpreting Bach in the Nineteenth and Twentieth Centuries." In *The Cambridge Companion to Bach*, edited by John Butt, 226–50. Cambridge: Cambridge University Press, 1997.

Zhisheng, Gao. "Struggle against the Gods." *First Things*, no. 272 (April 2017): 21–25.

Index

Joint Lutheran-Roman Catholic Declaration on Justification (1999), 59, 215
joy, 24, 68, 71, 77
jubilee, Reformation, 210, 215, 223
Judaism, 48, 58–64, 216–17, 225
  Jewish-Christian dialogue, 217
  Luther's anti-Judaism, 216
  Luther's writings on, 205
  Roman Catholics and Jews, 59–62
  See also anti-Semitism
judgment, divine, 57n20, 110, 143, 195, 203, 205
Junge, Martin, 215
Jüngel, Eberhard, 47–48, 54–55, 67
jurisdiction, 10, 13, 100, 106–9, 117, 119, 121, 123, 125–27, 153
jurists, 10–11, 34, 97–98, 111, 113–14, 120, 146
justice, 147–48, 174–76
  the Bible's presentation of, 224
  civil, 147
  contributive, 174–76
  distributive, 175
  in education, 212
  enabling, 175
  equity and, 143
  freedom and, 174
  participatory, 175
  peace and, 217–21
  See also injustice; social justice; two-kingdoms doctrine
justification, 5, 20, 55, 77, 122, 132, 167–70, 215, 227
  through faith alone, x, 18, 51, 134, 195, 197, 211
  Joint Lutheran-Roman Catholic Declaration on Justification (1999), 59
  Luther and/Luther's doctrine of, 25, 156, 167–70, 195, 197, 199, 203–4, 225, 227
  meaning of, 225
  paradigm shift in, 143
  Paul's formulation of, 167
  and poverty, 143
  Protestant doctrine of, 134, 167–70, 195, 197, 199, 203–4
  sola scriptura and, 25, 31, 36–37

Kálmáncsehi Sánta, Márton, 98
Kant, Immanuel, 30
Karlstadt, Andreas Bodenstein von, 101, 144n17
Károli, Gáspár, 90
Kasper, Walter Cardinal, 223
Kässmann, Margot, xviii, 19, 209–29
kerygma of the gospel, 77
Kierkegaard, Søren, 48, 54, 67
Kim, Jim Yong, 162
King, Martin Luther, Jr., 221
kingdoms, two. *See* two-kingdoms doctrine
King James Bible, 31, 117, 201
kings, 23, 107, 119, 122, 171
  prophet, priest, and king, x, 122
  See also monarchy; *individual kings*
Kirchenordnungen (church ordinances), 106. *See also* ordinances
knowledge
  knowing God, 50, 100
  practical, 176
  printing as democratizing, 18, 200
  and status, 185
  See also education; truth
Knox, John, 19, 122, 149
Koehler, Joachim, 211
Korea, 37, 162
Krawczyk, Stephan, 218

Labberton, Mark, 27
labor
  asceticism and, 183–84
  cheap, 142
  digitization of, 175
  valuing of, 167, 174
  as vocation, 185
  Weber on, 161
  See also work; work ethic; works, good; *specific topics, e.g.,* globalization
laity, 39–40, 44, 95, 117–18, 133, 140, 148, 165–66, 199–200
  importance of, 101
  Luther as writing tracts in German for, 150
  See also priesthood of all believers

righteousness, 25, 125, 142, 195–96
  gift of, 7, 76, 195
  internal/external, 195
  Luther's exegetical discovery, 142
  passive, 66–69
  works righteousness, 101, 135, 233
  See also simul justus et peccator; two-
    kingdoms doctrine
rights
  and duties, 114, 129
  "unalienable," 122
  women's, 223
  See also civil rights; human rights
rituals, 40, 183. *See also* sacraments
Robinson, Marilynne, 43
Rohr, Richard, 232
Roman Catholicism. *See* Catholic Chris-
    tianity/Roman Catholicism
Roman Empire. *See* Holy Roman
    Empire
Roman law, 107, 109, 120
Romans, Paul's Letter to, 26, 213
Roosevelt, Theodore, 188
Rousseau, Jean-Jacques, 30
Ruokanen, Miikka, 62–65, 67

Sabbath, 37, 111–12, 120–21, 123
Sachins, Claude de, 172
sacraments, 107–8, 112–15, 117, 126–27,
    133, 135, 183
  as marks of grace, 129
  seven, 113–14
  See also baptism; Eucharist
saints, 100, 108, 110, 215. *See also simul
    justus et peccator*
Salem witch trials, 35
salvation, 141–43
  bonuses (Weber), 166–67
  born again, 24, 44
  certainty of, 170
  Christian freedom and, 168
  election and, 166
  as God's free gift, 142–43
  Heilsprämie (salvation premium), 165
  poverty and, 141
  "salvation aristocracy," 166
  the Weber thesis, 161–67, 182–88

See also election; faith: faith alone;
    grace, divine: grace alone; indul-
    gences; justification; Jesus Christ:
    Christ alone; predestination
sanctification, 188
  of poverty, 140, 143
sanctity, 122
sanctuary, 7, 13, 108, 112, 129
Sattler, Michael, 25
Saunders, Richard (Benjamin Franklin),
    186
Saxony, Frederick the Elector of, 200,
    211–12
Scandinavia, 105–7, 110–11, 127, 192. *See
    also specific countries*
Schilling, Heinz, 227
schism, 33, 58, 207. *See also* division;
    heresy
Schleitheim Confession (1527), 105, 155
Schmitz, Elisabeth, 216–17
scholasticism/scholastic theology, 28,
    141
Schulordnungen (school ordinances), 132
Schuman, Robert, 191
Schwabach, Germany, 145
Schwäbisch Hall, 91, 97–98
Schwenckfeld, Caspar von, 101, 114,
    155
science, 100, 154
Scotland, 10, 33–34, 105, 132
  Calvinism in, 132
  Presbyterians, 33–34, 123
  See also Edinburgh; Knox, John
Scriptural Reasoning, 5–6, 60–65
Scripture
  "external clarity" *(claritas externa)* of,
    63n28
  normative role of, 73, 87
  and tradition, 28, 36–37
  truth of, 29, 63n28
  witness of, 100
  See also Bible; gospel; New Testament;
    Old Testament; *sola scriptura*
Scruton, Roger, 206
Search for a Usable Future , The (Marty),
    20
Second Vatican Council. *See* Vatican II

CPSIA information can be obtained
at www.ICGtesting.com
Printed in the USA
FSHW01n1840160918
52120FS